Photoshop®
Web Graphics
f/x & Design

Laurie Ulrich

President and CEO
Roland Elgey

Publisher
Al Valvano

Associate Publisher
Katherine R. Hartlove

Acquisitions Editor
Beth Kohler

Product Marketing Manager
Patricia Davenport

Project Editor
Marcus Huff

Technical Reviewer
Eric Infanti

Production Coordinator
Meg E. Turecek

Cover Designer
Carla Schuder

CD-ROM Developer
Michelle McConnell

Photoshop® Web Graphics f/x and Design

The Coriolis Group, LLC
14455 N. Hayden Road
Suite 220
Scottsdale, Arizona 85260

(480)483-0192
FAX (480)483-0193
www.coriolis.com

Library of Congress Cataloging-In-Publication Data
Ulrich, Laurie Ann.
    Photoshop Web graphics f/x & design / by Laurie Ulrich.
        p.   cm
    Includes index.
    ISBN 1-58880-199-3
    1. Computer graphics. 2. Adobe Photoshop. 3. Web sites--Design.   I. Title:
Photoshop Web graphics f/x and design.   II. Title.

T385 .U47   2001
005.7'2--dc21   2001047683
                                                                          CIP

A Note from Coriolis

Thank you for choosing this book from The Coriolis Group. Our graphics team strives to meet the needs of creative professionals such as yourself with our three distinctive series: *Visual Insight*, *f/x & Design*, and *In Depth*. We'd love to hear how we're doing in our quest to provide you with information on the latest and most innovative technologies in graphic design, 3D animation, and Web design. Do our books teach you what you want to know? Are the examples illustrative enough? Are there other topics you'd like to see us address?

Please contact us at the address below with your thoughts on this or any of our other books. Should you have any technical questions or concerns about this book, you can contact the Coriolis support team at **techsupport@coriolis.com**; be sure to include this book's title and ISBN, as well as your name, email address, or phone number.

Thank you for your interest in Coriolis books. We look forward to hearing from you.

Coriolis Creative Professionals Press
The Coriolis Group
14455 N. Hayden Road, Suite 220
Scottsdale, AZ 85260

Email: **cpp@coriolis.com**

Phone: (480) 483-0192
Toll free: (800) 410-0192

Visit our Web site at **creative.coriolis.com** *to find the latest information about our current and upcoming graphics books.*

Other Titles for the Creative Professional

Flash™ *5 Visual Insight*
By Sherry London, Dan London

Adobe® *LiveMotion*™ *Visual Insight*
By Molly Joss

Photoshop® *6 In Depth*
By David Xenakis, Benjamin Levisay

Flash™ *5 f/x & Design*
By Bill Sanders

Flash™ *ActionScript f/x & Design*
By Bill Sanders

GoLive™ *5 f/x & Design*
By Richard Schrand

Adobe® *LiveMotion*™ *f/x & Design*
By Daniel Gray

Dreamweaver® *4 f/x & Design*
By Laurie Ulrich

Digital Audio
By Russ Haines

I dedicate this book to my mom, Ann Miller Talbot. She taught me to read, to draw, to write, to sing, to believe in amazing things, and to unleash my imagination. She continues to teach me about not giving up, that it's never too late to pursue your dreams, and how to grow a beautiful garden.
—Laurie Ulrich

About the Author

An artist through heredity and education, a teacher by nature, and a writer since she was old enough to pick up a crayon, **Laurie Ulrich** is a Web designer, graphic artist, computer trainer, and the author and co-author of more than 15 books on computer software, including the recently published *Dreamweaver 4 f/x & Design* and *The Web Design Virtual Classroom*. She has written hundreds of computer training manuals for universities and corporate training centers, and in the last decade, Laurie has trained more than 10,000 people to make more creative and effective use of their computers. In the early 1990s, after spending way too many years working for other people (including jobs managing computer training centers and running computer systems), Laurie started her own firm, Limehat & Company, Inc., putting her experience, ideas, and contacts to good use. Her firm provides consulting, training, Web design, and Web hosting, focusing on the special needs of growing companies and non-profit organizations.

When not writing about or teaching people to use computers, Laurie can be found supporting a variety of animal rights organizations—through protests, writing educational articles, and contributing to various Internet sources for animal rights information. She also enjoys her family, gardening, antiques, old houses, and adding to her collection of books. You can find out more about Laurie and her interests, skills, and experience at **www.planetlaurie.com**, and she welcomes your email at laurie@planetlaurie.com.

Acknowledgments

I'd like to thank Marcus Huff for all his hard work and guidance throughout this project. He was consistently helpful, thorough, encouraging, and patient, and he always had the information I needed, when I needed it. I must also thank Alisha Blomker for the opportunity to write this book and for her dedication to its success. I extend my deepest appreciation to Eric Infanti, Liz Welch, Meg Turecek, and Beth Kohler. Without a great team, you don't get a great book, no matter what it's about or who's writing it—I think we had a great team.

Thanks must also go to my agent, Margot. As always, she provides unflagging support as well as great advice, and she listens to me rant when I need to.

—*Laurie Ulrich*

Contents at a Glance

Table of Contents

Introduction

Photoshop has long been the software of choice for print work—graphic artists and photographers swear by its powerful features and comprehensive set of tools for creating and manipulating images. When it comes to designing for the Web, Photoshop remains the software of choice, despite a handful of worthy competitors. Why? Because the same tools that give you a seemingly unlimited ability to build and edit images of all kinds are very easily applied and adapted to Web-bound graphics.

My Goal in Writing This Book

This book does not pretend to cover everything Photoshop does—you could probably guess that when you saw that it wasn't as thick as the New York City phone book. Rather, it is intended to cover the aspects of Photoshop that Web designers and graphic artists designing Web content need and will use. My goal in writing this book is to create a reference for people who need to use Photoshop now—this minute—to create and edit graphics that will be used in Web pages. A book that does this and that also gives people design ideas and tips for creating great-looking artwork is needed, and I hope that I've accomplished this for my readers. I also hope that the fact I use Photoshop every day to design Web-page prototypes, create logos and line art, retouch photos, and draw original works of art will give you the incentive to buy—and, more important, use—this book. I'm a fan of Photoshop; I use it to earn a living, and I teach people to use it in a classroom setting. If I've achieved my goal, after reading this book you'll be a fan and an efficient, creative Photoshop user as well!

Who Will Enjoy This Book

I wrote this book with several different Photoshop users in mind. You'll probably find yourself somewhere in this list:

- If you currently use Photoshop for print work, you'll enjoy this book because it will show you new ways to use Photoshop and to adapt its tools to meet the needs of Web browser software.

- If you currently design Web pages and are using Photoshop to create and edit graphics, you'll enjoy this book because it contains tips and tricks for getting the job done faster.

- If you're new to Photoshop and are trying to figure it out on your own, you'll enjoy this book because it will shorten your learning curve considerably. Reading this book is as close as you can come to attending one of my classes without driving to Philadelphia and paying a few hundred dollars.

- If you're a fan of another graphics and illustration program and find that many of the Web designers and graphic artists with whom you work are asking for your files in Photoshop format, you'll enjoy this book because it will enable you to use the application that more Web and graphic designers use. Sometimes it's good to go against the tide, but when it comes to tools—for any job—it pays to watch both your coworkers and the competition to see which ones they're using.

How This Book Is Organized

This book consists of 15 chapters, plus a Color Studio.

From a guided tour of the Photoshop interface, concentrating on Web-related tools, to coverage of matching print colors and Web colors, the first section of the book helps you get started with Photoshop and figure out where everything is and what it does. As you move through the next section, you'll be creating original artwork for specific Web tasks—Web text to convey information in fonts and styles not supported by the small group of fonts browsers like, navigation buttons, tracing images, and page prototypes. You'll also learn to retouch photographs and tinker with existing images to make them pop on a Web page. The final section of the book deals with Photoshop and its companion products—ImageReady and LiveMotion, as well as competitors' products, such as Macromedia Flash. You'll learn to build animations and mouse-over effects, and to use your Photoshop creations in movies.

The Chapters

Each of the chapters focuses on a specific Web design task and/or Photoshop feature. In one of the following 15 chapters, you can find just about anything you'll need to know to generate Web-friendly graphics:

- *Chapter 1: Understanding Web Graphic Requirements*—This chapter will acquaint you with the special needs for graphics and color as imposed by Web browsers. You'll learn about the different Web-safe formats and how Photoshop supports their creation. In addition, the saving and preservation of Photoshop-format files for future use will be covered, including preservation of layers.

- *Chapter 2: The Photoshop Interface*—In this chapter, you'll be given a tour of the tools used for creating Web-safe graphics—the menu commands that allow the user to control the size and pixel depth of images, the toolbox, and the palettes. This chapter will be of particular interest to readers who are not familiar with Photoshop for use in print media—the many Web designers who are working with Photoshop for the first time.

- *Chapter 3: Creating Original Artwork for the Web*—This chapter will prepare you to create original images—using the drawing and fill tools to create graphics for the Web. The process of saving images as GIF, JPG and PNG files, and the tools for controlling image size and quality, will be covered in detail.

- *Chapter 4: Retouching Images for Use on the Web*—In this chapter, the use of images created outside of Photoshop will be covered—editing clip-art images and working with images created in Illustrator and other vector-image creation tools. Tools for retouching photographs (whether scanned or captured with a digital camera) will be covered.

- *Chapter 5: Matching Print Colors and Style to Web Pages*—This chapter discusses the specifics of Web-safe color—matching print colors (process and Pantone colors, for example) to Web-safe equivalents. You'll also find tips for re-creating the look and feel of existing printed marketing material in a Web page.

- *Chapter 6: Designing Graphic Text for the Web*—Avoiding the limitations of Web-safe fonts sends many Web designers to Photoshop for the creation of graphic text. This chapter will cover Photoshop's type tools in detail, focusing on building and formatting text and turning it into visually pleasing, legible graphic elements for the Web.

- *Chapter 7: Creating Web Navigation Tools*—In this chapter, you'll learn to build buttons and navigation bars, utilizing Photoshop's tools for building shapes and applying fills and effects that create a 3-D look, giving depth to Web content. The importance of achieving navigational consistency will also be covered, and the need to create navigational tools that are easily integrated into the Web page will be stressed.

- *Chapter 8: Creating Backgrounds and Tracing Images*—WYSIWYG Web design software offers the ability to place a tracing image behind the page content to assist the designer in placement of objects, the structuring of tables and frames, and the positioning and sizing of layers. Background images are also key to the overall look of a Web page. Photoshop's use in creating these key elements will be covered in this chapter, as well as coverage of how these elements are actually put to use in applications such as Macromedia Dreamweaver and GoLive.

- *Chapter 9: Building Page Prototypes with Photoshop*—When auditioning for a potential client or attempting to communicate a design idea for a new project, a Web designer needs a quick but powerful tool for creating a sample page. Using Photoshop to develop a prototype will be covered in this chapter, along with tips for designing a layout that's actually achievable in an HTML or WYSIWYG design environment.

- *Chapter 10: Touring the ImageReady Interface*—This chapter will focus on the animation tools of Image Ready, part of the Adobe suite of graphics tools. You'll also discover when and where to use animations, and how they can be effective tools on a Web page if used properly.

- *Chapter 11: Working with Animations and Rollovers*—Once you know what animation capabilities Photoshop affords them, this chapter shows you how to create an animation—setting up frames and using the "tween" command to create the animated effect—and how to control the speed and quality of the animation.

- *Chapter 12: Slicing Images for Dynamic Effects*—This chapter shows you which kind of images can be sliced and how to slice them. The use of sliced images in tables and the benefits of slicing will be discussed and demonstrated.

- *Chapter 13: Sending Photoshop Images to LiveMotion*—Adobe's answer to Macromedia Flash is LiveMotion. In this chapter, you'll take a tour of the LiveMotion interface and find out how Photoshop images become part of a LiveMotion movie bound for the Web.

- *Chapter 14: Using Photoshop Images with Macromedia Flash*—Until and unless LiveMotion takes a big percentage of the market, Flash will remain the major application for creating Web movies. This chapter shows you the Flash interface and demonstrates the insertion of a Photoshop image into a Flash movie.

- *Chapter 15: WYSIWYG Web Design with Photoshop*—Most readers of this book use programs like Dreamweaver to create Web pages. Using Photoshop-created images in designs will be covered in this chapter, including the mapping of hot spots on larger images, the use of Fireworks (part of the Macromedia Dreamweaver Studio package, and therefore on many designers' desktops) to edit Photoshop images, and the use of Photoshop to edit images created in Fireworks.

The Color Studio

The Color Studio is a series of glossy, colorful pages that show you what's possible with Photoshop—the intention is to inspire you to dig deeper and be more creative with Photoshop, to help you see what some of the black-and-white examples throughout the book look like in color, and to give you ideas for your own designs.

Completing the Chapter Projects

Most of the chapters in this book have at least one project in them. The projects are designed to give you the chance to use the features discussed in the chapters, acquiring hands-on experience with new tools and skills. In addition, it is my hope that the projects will serve to give you ideas for better and faster ways to get things done. I'm not a big fan of wasted or redundant effort, and as I've honed my own Photoshop skills, I've done so by figuring out the quickest way to accomplish my design goals while still generating visually appealing, effective artwork for the Web. Through the projects, it is my goal to pass these techniques along to you.

Of course, you don't need to use the projects to derive benefit from this book, but they'll help. If you want to complete any of the projects, you may need the CD-ROM found in the back of this book—I've put all the files that you'll need to perform the projects' steps on the CD-ROM, in a logical folder structure—the folders on the CD-ROM are named to match the chapter and project to which their contents apply. For example, if you need a file for the first project in Chapter 3, look on the companion CD-ROM in the Chapter 3 directory.

Copy the CD to your C Drive

If you find it to be time-consuming to insert the CD and open files that way each time you want to work on a project, you can copy the CD's folders to your local drive, or copy individual files from the CD to your hard drive into any folder hierarchy you prefer. If you copy the folders, you'll be re-creating the same construct that the project instructions refer to—if you copy the files to your own folders, realize that you might have trouble figuring out which image goes with which project. In either case, best of luck, and feel free to contact me via email if you have any questions as you read the book and/or work through the projects. I can be reached at laurie@planetlaurie.com.

Chapter 1

Understanding Web Graphic Requirements

Photoshop's default PSD format is fine for print work, but if you offer such a thing to a Web browser, the response will be one of those rather unpleasant-looking icons that represent a missing graphic. Web browsers (the two main ones, Microsoft Internet Explorer and Netscape Navigator) will display only certain graphic file types, and Photoshop gives you all the tools you need to build and save them in a Web-safe format.

Working with Web-Safe File Formats

Graphic files come in two flavors—vector and bitmap. Vector images are complex yet small files in which images are seen as a collection of lines and curves, represented by mathematical instructions. These images, created by products such as Adobe Illustrator, QuarkXpress, and CorelDRAW, are not Web-friendly. This is because the Web browser software that people use to view Web pages (software like Internet Explorer and Netscape Navigator) is not able to display the vector images. These Web browsers are not set up to interpret the file information or to "do the math." It's not that their developers weren't smart enough or that the software is backward in any way—it's just that the need to have a Web page look the same on every computer through which it's viewed is paramount. By creating a simple standard for how images should be stored (in other words, in which file formats), you reduce the variables, making it possible for a wide spectrum of computers—new and old, powerful and not-so-powerful—to display Web content in the same way.

So why are bitmap images the answer to the need for a "simple standard"? Web browsers more easily display bitmap images because the files are stored as a collection of values, one for each pixel of the image. The color of each pixel is stored as part of the bitmap file, and the browser converts that information to the image you see before you on the screen. Because each pixel's information is part of the file, bitmap images tend to be much larger than their vector counterparts. The dimensions (pixel width and height) of the image will affect its size if the file is in a bitmap format, but the same image in the same visual size in a vector format might be quite small.

Another difference between vector and bitmap images is the type of images to which they're best suited. Vector formats are best for line art—typographic images and simple drawings, as shown in Figure 1.1. Bitmaps, on the other hand, are great for photographs and other images with many colors and tones—subtle effects such as drop shadows and embossed edges. Figure 1.2 shows an image that could bring a lot of depth and texture to a Web page.

Figure 1.1

(Left) Simple, flat graphics are well suited to the vector file format.

Figure 1.2

(Right) A complex image with a lot of color information requires a bitmap format.

Identifying Web-Safe Formats

The three accepted Web-safe file formats for graphics are GIF, JPG, and PNG, the latter being the most recent addition to the list. GIF stands for graphics interchange format, JPG stands for Joint Photographic Experts Group (the "E" is dropped from the extension), and PNG stands for Portable Network Graphics. The first two (GIF and JPG) have long been accepted formats for the Web, and PNG was added recently when the World Wide Web Consortium (W3C) officially endorsed it. When W3C endorsed it, the browser manufacturers began integrating into their latest browser versions tools for dealing with the PNG format.

Choosing the Right Format for Your Image

With three formats available to you, which one should you use? If you're not sure which version of the two main browsers your typical Web site visitor will be using, steer clear of PNG, because it's a newly accepted format—versions prior to 5.0 of both Netscape Navigator and Internet Explorer might not show the image at all, or will show it in a degraded form—with odd color shifts and jagged edges. That leaves JPG and GIF as the two formats you can reliably use and not have to worry that visitors won't be able to see them properly or at all. But which one should you use? It depends on the image:

- GIF is the best format for line art—typographic images, clip art, simple drawings. GIF images have a limited color range (256 colors or less), making them less appropriate for displaying complex, color-rich images such as photographs. GIF image backgrounds can be made transparent so that the image consists only of the shapes and lines within it—no white or other-colored background surrounding them, as shown in Figure 1.3. If it's essential that the image not be in a box, you might want to use the GIF format in spite of the fact that the image might not lend itself to the GIF format's strengths.

Saying It Right

The pronunciation of the various Web-safe formats is often a bone of contention—some people pronounce GIF with a hard G, as in "golf," and others with a soft G, as in "gentle." JPG format should be pronounced like a word, "Jaypeg," although a few people will sound out each letter, as in "Jay Pea Gee." When it comes to the PNG format, some people sound out each letter ("Pea En Gee"), and others say "PING," although that has other computer-related meanings. It's up to you, but be prepared for someone to say, "Huh?" if you pronounce one of the format names in an unfamiliar way.

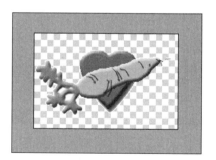

Figure 1.3

GIF is a great format for simple images, and you can remove the background by making the GIF transparent.

- JPG is better for photographs and complex images that have a lot of colors and tones. JPGs support millions of colors, so the image's actual colors, pixel by pixel, can be represented accurately. When in doubt as to whether your image is complex or not, go with JPG—better to be safe than sorry.

You've probably heard the term "animated GIF" used to describe the buttons, icons, and logos that move on a Web page. Not to be confused with movies, such as those created in Macromedia Flash or Adobe LiveMotion, animated

GIFs are simply a series of GIF images that are displayed one after the other, in place. The switching from image A to image B to image C and so on continues indefinitely (known as *looping*) by default, or you can set it to occur just once. Adobe Photoshop's ImageReady tools are used for creating animated GIFs, and you'll read about them in Chapter 10. JPG images cannot be turned into animated images, although they can be used in a movie created with Flash or LiveMotion.

Something that you can set both GIF and JPG files to do is appear gradually on the Web page. At first the image will look choppy and blurry, and then it will clear up as the entire image is transferred to the visitor's computer. When you're working with GIF files, the term for this is "interlaced," and for JPGs, the term is "progressive." Figure 1.4 shows a progressive JPG file in its early stages as a Web page composes on-screen.

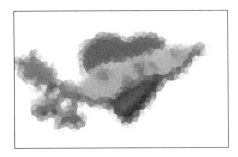

Transparent Backgrounds

If you need the aforementioned transparent background for the image but you absolutely need JPG format's ability to store a lot of color information, make the background color of the image match the color on which the image will be placed. If, for example, you need to place an image inside a table cell with a light blue background, apply that color to the background layer of the Photoshop image so that when the image is placed in the cell, it looks as though its own background is clear, allowing the cell's background color to be seen. It's all an illusion, of course.

Figure 1.4
Progressive or interlaced graphics look terrible at first, but at least the site visitor knows something is coming.

JPG and Older Browsers

Older browsers don't support progressive JPGs, so if most of your visitors are using old (pre-5.0) versions of Internet Explorer or Netscape, they won't see the image until it's completely transferred to their computer. They will see it eventually, though—so don't hesitate to use this feature, because it's helpful to the people who are using post-5.0 browsers, a population that grows every day.

If your image is large in terms of file size, it's a good idea to invoke the interlaced or progressive feature so that visitors don't see a blank spot until the image is completely transferred—as you probably know, large files (more than 35KB) tend to load very slowly for people on a dial-up connection to the Internet. Using interlaced or progressive images is especially important if you want viewers to wait for the image to compose completely so that they can click links in the image or follow instructions that are typed or drawn as part of the image. If the image doesn't appear at all until the file is completely transferred, visitors might assume something's missing and click on another already-visible link or leave the page entirely.

Using Color on the Web

For an entirely visual medium, the Web has a limited capacity for color. Web browsers impose that limitation, like the limited list of acceptable graphics file formats. Browser software is designed to work within the confines of the least color-capable computer, on any platform (Windows-based PCs or Macs) and therefore won't display more than 216 colors—the Web-safe palette, as shown in Figure 1.5.

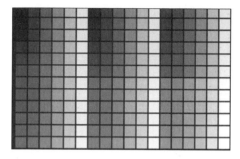

Figure 1.5
Also known as the "browser-safe" palette, these 216 colors are the only ones you should use in graphics bound for the Web.

The colors of the Web-safe palette each have their own number, such as FFFFFF for pure white, and CC0066 for deep, dark pink. The colors are made up of different levels of red, green, and blue, also known as RGB levels. FFFFFF is 255 Red, 255 Green, and 255 Blue. CC0066 is 204 Red, 000 (no) Green, and 102 Blue. By adjusting the RGB levels, you get different colors, so if you add green to CC0066, you get a different shade, probably closer to an orange. So how does the Web browser turn that mathematical data into color on the screen? Web browsers see the color number in the HTML document that makes up a Web page and display that color if the color is to be applied to a page background or to text typed onto the page directly. When it comes to colors in a graphics file, the browser interprets the color information (RGB levels) stored about each pixel in the file and displays the color using the 216-color palette.

Viewing the Web Palette

As you know, Photoshop was originally designed to be a tool for creating printed graphics—for retouching photographs and creating original artwork that would end up on paper. With the overwhelming success of the Web and the plethora of people designing for it, Photoshop responded by offering a Web-safe-only palette so that you know you're choosing colors that will translate well when viewed online. There's no sense using colors that will be changed when the photograph or drawing is viewed on the Web—you want to start out knowing that the color you're looking at as you design or retouch the graphic is the same color site visitors will see on their computer, no matter how old their computer or how limited their video capabilities.

To view the Photoshop Web-safe palette, simply click the Color Picker for either foreground or background color (see Figure 1.6) and in the resulting Color Picker dialog box, click the Only Web Colors checkbox, as shown in Figure 1.7. Using this dialog box, you can mix your own colors by entering RGB levels, by entering a color number, or by clicking on colors in the palette if you're searching by eye for just the right color. You'll find out more about creating colors, and about matching print colors to Web-safe colors, in Chapter 5.

Black and White

In art school, they tell you that white is the presence of all color and black is the absence of all color. That seems impossible to most people, because black seems like the color you'd get if you mixed all the other colors together—surely if you mix every color there is, you wouldn't get white, right? Wrong. The RGB levels of white and black really prove that white is all colors and black is no color. When you view the RGB levels, you'll see that White is 255 Red, 255 Green, and 255 Blue—as much of all three color levels as is possible. Black, on the other hand, is 0 Red, 0 Green, and 0 Blue—no color at all.

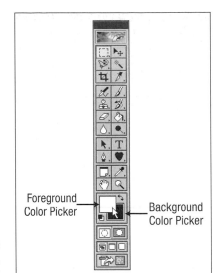

Foreground
Color Picker

Background
Color Picker

Figure 1.6
The Color Picker is aptly named—
you use it to pick a color!

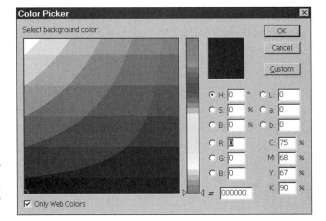

Figure 1.7
Click anywhere on the vertical
spectrum to see the Web-safe
colors in that shade.

Working Toward the Web in Photoshop

When you create a new graphic in Photoshop, the Save command will create a PSD file, which is Photoshop's native format. If you used the Web-safe palette of colors as you worked, you know that the image you're creating or editing is going to look just fine when viewed on the Web. Of course, you can't put a PSD file into a Web page, so you need to save it in a Web-safe format. Photoshop makes that possible with the Save For Web command on its File menu. The full use of this command is covered more thoroughly in Chapter 3, but for our purposes here, think of it as a conversion—the PSD file is saved in a Web-safe format, storing color information in either a GIF or a JPG file, with each pixel's color identified numerically. Figure 1.8 shows both the original PSD version of a graphic and the optimized (prepared for the Web) version in the Save For Web dialog box.

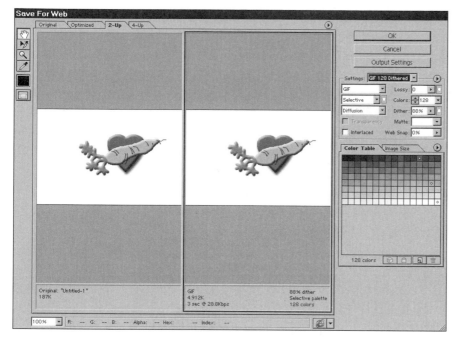

Figure 1.8
The image looks the same, but the file size is smaller and the color information is stored for each pixel. The range of colors appears in the Color Table.

Maintaining Your Photoshop Roots

It's a good idea to keep both the Web-safe version and the Photoshop PSD file for all Web-bound graphics you create or edit, if only so you can go back to the Photoshop PSD version and tinker with all of the aspects of the image. When you work in the PSD format, you have multiple layers in your image, keeping, for example, the text separate from the background, which is separate from any shapes or lines you've drawn (see a Photoshop image and the Layers palette in Figure 1.9).

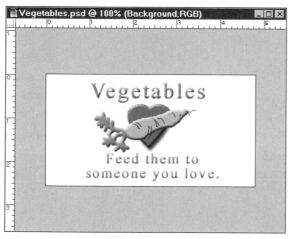
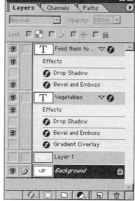

Figure 1.9
Photoshop images are made up of several layers, and the layers give you the power to edit parts of the image without affecting others.

Once the file is saved in a Web-safe format, the image is flattened into a single layer, and any ability to edit the parts is lost. By saving both the PSD and the Web-safe formats of the same image, you can upload the image you have now

Archiving PSD Files

When you upload images to the Web, don't upload the PSD files—they're bigger than their GIF and JPG counterparts, and you don't need them on your Web server. Do save them to your local hard drive or some easily accessed portable media, such as a zip disk, so you can get at them when you need to revamp an existing Web image.

to the Web and know that if you need to make changes, you can use the PSD file as the basis for those changes, resave the file in GIF or JPG format, and upload a subsequent version of the file later. This technique is also great for making several Web graphics that are similar to each other—create one, save it for the Web, and then go back and change or add something—text or a color—and save it again, this time with a new name, in a Web-safe format. One base PSD file can then be used to create many GIF or JPG files, saving you the work involved in creating the elements common to all of the images.

Moving On

In the next chapter, you'll take a tour of Photoshop's interface, concentrating on the features that lend themselves to building Web-safe graphics. You'll learn about menu commands, toolbar buttons, and how to use all of the drawing, fill, line, and selection tools that you'll be using throughout the rest of the book to create and edit drawings, photographs, and typographic images.

Chapter 2

The Photoshop Interface

Like following directions or using a map, if you're familiar with the terrain, it's much easier to find your way from point A to point B. Use this chapter to familiarize yourself with Photoshop's workspace and tools, making your use of the software an easier trip.

An Overview

The Photoshop workspace is made up of two main windows:

- The application window, which houses the menus, options bar, and toolbox, and which also provides a space where the rest of the workspace windows can be opened, moved, and resized

- The file window, which contains an image

Figure 2.1 shows the Photoshop workspace, as it appears when you open the application without opening a graphics file at the same time.

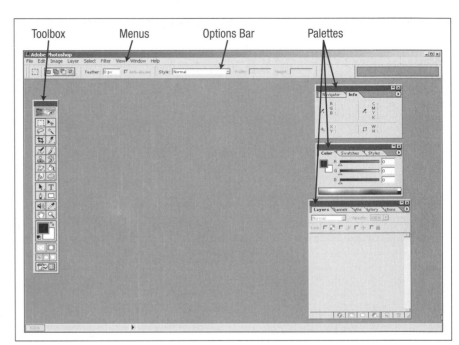

Figure 2.1
The Photoshop interface starts with the basic tools.

More Than Meets the Eye

When it comes to toolbar buttons, if you see a small triangle in the lower-left corner of the button, it means that there are variables for that button. For example, if you click and hold the mouse for a second on the Gradient Fill button, it offers two fill buttons—the Gradient Fill and the Paint Bucket (which applies a solid color fill). The key is to hold your mouse on the button until the options are displayed—a quick click will merely invoke the button as is and won't show you the alternatives.

After you open an existing file or start a new one, the file window is added to the workspace, as shown in Figure 2.2. To open a new file, choose File|Open, or choose File|Open Recent to reopen a file you've worked on recently. If you're starting a new file, choose File|New.

All of the windows within the workspace can be moved around to suit your needs. For example, you can move the palettes to the left side of the window, or you can move the toolbar anywhere on the screen. You can resize any window by pointing to its edge and dragging when your mouse pointer turns into a two-headed arrow. To move a window—a file window, a palette, the toolbar—grab the title bar with your mouse and drag the window to any spot on the workspace that works for you.

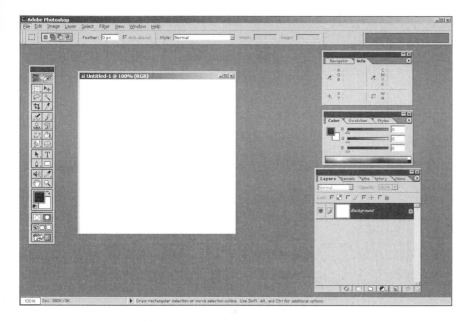

Figure 2.2
A new file window has no content but already has a background layer, seen in the Layers palette.

Working with the Menus and Options Bar

Photoshop menus are like just about any application's menus—the commands are listed down the left side of the menu, and any keyboard shortcuts are listed on the right. If a triangle appears to the right of a command (see Figure 2.3), you know that a submenu will appear if you make that selection. If an ellipsis (…) follows a command, a dialog box will open when you choose that command from the menu.

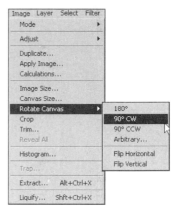

Figure 2.3
The menus tell you how to issue keyboard commands and give you advance notice about submenus and dialog boxes.

The menus are fairly logical in terms of their names and the group of commands each one offers. The File menu, for example, offers commands that pertain to your file as a whole—opening new files, saving open files, printing the active file, and so on. The Edit, Image, and Layer menus might be confusing, however; commands such as Transform and Free Transform are on the Edit menu, yet you might think of them as Image commands or Layer commands because they affect the appearance and content of the image in general and are applied to specific layers. Other than that, though, you shouldn't have any trouble remembering which commands are on which menus.

The options bar appears directly below the menus, and it changes depending on which tool or element of your image is active in the open file. For example, if you click the Text tool, the options bar displays tools for formatting text, as shown in Figure 2.4. If you prefer to work with floating toolbars, you can detach the options bar by dragging it down from its current perch and releasing it on the main workspace. The downside to this is that the bar will probably overlap a portion of your image, but if you work with images maximized, removing it from the strip below the menus gives you a larger space for the image window.

Figure 2.4

The options bar is context-sensitive and offers only the appropriate tools for whatever you're doing.

Another feature of the options bar is the Palettes button that appears with various sets of tools. When you click this button, Photoshop opens a palette box that displays an expanded set of context-sensitive tools, as shown in Figure 2.5. The complete set of character- and paragraph-formatting tools repeat some of the options bar's offerings, as well as offering many additional features.

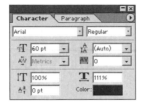

Figure 2.5

Display context-sensitive palettes by clicking the Palettes button.

Help Is Just a Hover Away

To identify the tools on the options bar, hover your mouse over a tool and wait a second for the ToolTip to appear.

Working with the Toolbox

Appearing by default on the left side of your screen, the toolbox offers 22 different tools for drawing and editing your images, along with the Color Picker and tools for changing the display in which you see your image. The toolbox is floating, and you can move it to any spot on the workspace. To close the toolbox, double-click the blue bar across its top. If you right-click or double-click the Photoshop logo picture below the blue bar, a window pops up, providing links to support, registration tools, and other services through the Adobe Web site. Figure 2.6 shows the toolbox, with its main sections identified.

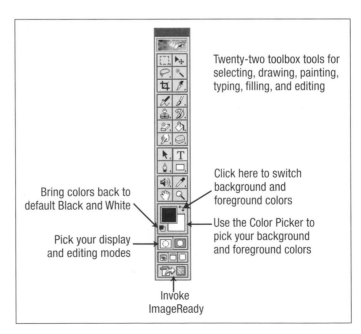

Figure 2.6

The Photoshop toolbox gives you just about everything you need to draw, type, and retouch any image.

Note that some of the toolbox buttons have triangles in their lower-right corners. These triangles indicate that the button can be changed to one of two or more different buttons. For example, if you click the triangle on the Gradient tool, you can switch to the Paint Bucket instead. Some of the tools have several options, as shown in Figure 2.7. For example, you can choose from four different marquee tools rather than being stuck with the default rectangular marquee.

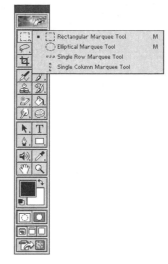

Mastering the Selection and Move Tools

The first four tools on the toolbox allow you to select and move parts of the active image. These tools include the marquee tools (with four marquee shapes available), the Move tool, the Lasso tool (with three options), and the Magic Wand. The selection tools (Marquee, Lasso, and Wand) allow you to select parts of the image for editing, moving, copying or cutting (using the Edit|Copy or Edit|Cut command), and deleting. The Move tool allows you to move the selected content or the active layer.

Figure 2.7
Click the button's triangle to view options for that button.

Selecting with the Marquee Tools

The marquee tools allow you to select sections of the active layer or map out an area that will become a new layer. To use the marquee tools, first select the marquee shape you want to use (the default shape the first time you open Photoshop is the rectangle, but thereafter, the last one you used will be the default). Then, click and drag across the surface of your image.

Once the marquee shape is drawn, you can fill, cut, copy, move, or delete the section marked off by the marquee. Because the marquee serves as a mask, you can also draw or paint on the section, covering everything but what's within the confines of the marquee itself. Figure 2.8 shows the Paintbrush tool being used to apply a color to a marquee-selected area of an image.

Of course, you want to pay attention to which layer is active before you use the marquee tools. If you use the tools to select an area on the image and then press Delete or use the fill tools, you may find that you've removed or filled in an area you didn't want to touch. If this happens, use Edit|Undo to reverse the action.

Using the Lasso Tools

The Lasso tool comes in three "flavors"—the standard Lasso, with which you can draw a closed shape around a portion of your image; the Magnetic Lasso, which adheres to the edges of areas within your image; and the Polygonal Lasso, which selects freeform areas but with straight sides, as shown in Figure 2.9.

You'll notice that when you select the lasso or marquee tools, the options bar offers a series of tools, as shown in Figure 2.10.

Quick and Easy Layer Selection

To select the entire contents of a layer, right-click that portion of the image on-screen and choose the layer by name from the resulting shortcut menu. This saves you from going to the Layers palette (discussed later in this chapter) to select the layer you want to deal with.

Deselecting an Area

To deselect an area, press Ctrl+D.

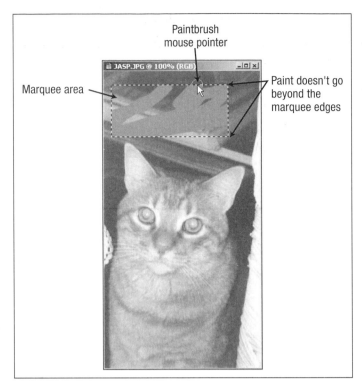

Figure 2.8
Before painting a wall, you tape off sections; similarly, the marquee tools mask off parts of your image to control the effects of painting, erasing, or solid/gradient fills.

Figure 2.9
(Right) If you need to select a geometric shape (here, a stack of books), use the Polygonal Lasso tool.

Figure 2.10
(Below) The Lasso tool's options bar.

From left to right, the options bar tools are as follows:

- *New Selection*—This tool deselects anything currently selected and leaves only your newly mapped area selected.

- *Add To Selection*—If an area is already selected, turning this option on before selecting a new area will leave both the old and new areas selected.

- *Subtract From Selection*—Did you select more than you wanted the first time? Need to hollow out an area and select the area around something? Turn this option on and make a selection within or overlapping an existing selection area, and the new selection will be deleted, or *subtracted*. Figure 2.11 shows a doughnut-shaped ring selection that was created by selecting a large oval and then subtracting a smaller oval from inside it.

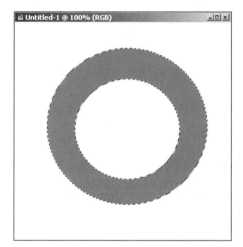

Figure 2.11
Cut away from an existing selection with the Subtract From Selection option.

- *Intersect With Selection*—This option allows you to create a single selection from two selections. As shown in Figure 2.12, with this option on, you can marquee or lasso an area, and then marquee or lasso an area that overlaps the first one. Only the intersection remains selected after you release the mouse on your second selection.

- *Feather*—This option (set to 0 pixels by default) allows you to create a soft, diffused edge to the selection when the selected content is moved or deleted. As shown in Figure 2.13, with the Feather set to 10 pixels, a 10-pixel-wide fuzzy edge appears within the empty section created when the Delete key is pressed to remove content.

- *Anti-aliased*—Anti-aliasing (checked by default) smoothes the edge of the selected area so that if you cut, move, or delete the selected area, the remaining edges are not choppy.

Top of selected area was created with an elliptical marquee

The rectangular marquee was included, creating this odd shape from the intersection of both selections

Figure 2.12
Select the common elements within two selection areas with the Intersect With Selection option.

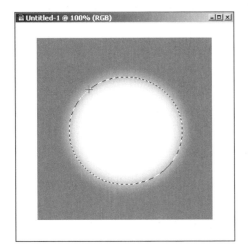

Figure 2.13
By using the Feather option, you create the appearance of something being softly smoothed away rather than cut out of your image.

When the marquee tool (any of the shapes) is in use, three additional options appear, as shown in Figure 2.14:

- *Style*—This option, which is set to Normal by default, gives you two additional options: Constrained Aspect Ratio or Fixed Size. If you choose either of these two options, the Width and Height options become available.

- *Width and Height*—If you're working in Constrained Aspect Ratio mode, this option is a number (1 by default) representing the proportion of the selection that is represented by the Width setting. For example, if you want to select a perfect square shape, set both Width and Height to the same number. If, on the other hand, you want a box that's twice as tall as it is wide, set Width to 2 and Height to 1. If you're using the Fixed Size option for Style, the numbers entered in the Width and Height boxes represent actual pixel dimensions for the selected area.

Selecting with the Magic Wand

The Magic Wand selects all content based on the color of the pixel you click after invoking the tool. This makes it possible to recolor, move, or delete everything in a particular area that's currently filled or drawn with the same color. You can set the tolerance level for the selection, raising or lowering the color selection standards that the Wand uses in selecting colored areas.

Figure 2.14
The marquee options bar allows you to control the way selections are made and how they affect the image.

When the Magic Wand is selected, the options bar offers four tools (in addition to the New, Add, Subtract, and Intersection buttons), as shown in Figure 2.15:

Figure 2.15
The options bar gives you more control over the Magic Wand.

- *Tolerance*—This setting raises or lowers the threshold for color recognition. By default, it's set to 32. The lower the number you enter, the fewer pixels will be selected by the Magic Wand, because only areas colored very similarly (if not identically) to the sampled pixel will be within the tolerance level. If you want to select a lot of the image, increase the Tolerance setting.

- *Anti-aliased*—This option, which is enabled by default, ensures that the edges of the selected area(s) are smooth should the content be moved, cut, or deleted. The smoothing effect will also apply to painting or color fills applied to the selected area.

- *Contiguous*—This option means that the Magic Wand will select only pixels that are touching pixels that fit the tolerance level. For example, if you click the Magic Wand on a cell that's dark blue, only blue pixels that are touching that pixel and that meet the tolerance level will be selected. If, say, a strip of white pixels falls between the sampled blue pixel and some other blue pixels on the other side of your image, the blue pixels on the other side of the white strip won't be selected.

- *Use All Layers*—Off by default, this option allows your Magic Wand selection to transcend layers. By default, if you click on a pixel on Layer 1, only other pixels on that same layer that meet your wand tolerance will be selected. If you turn this option on, any pixels on any layers that meet your tolerance settings will be selected.

Shift Into a Higher Gear

You can extend the Magic Wand's reach to other pixels by pressing and holding the Shift key and clicking other areas of the image. Based on your Tolerance, Contiguous, and Use All Layers settings, you'll pick up other pixels and groups, thereby increasing the selection.

Moving Selected Content

Once you've selected content on one layer, you can use the Move tool to reposition the selection. Simply click the Move tool, and then drag the selection to a desired location. The options bar offers alignment and distribution tools (see Figure 2.16) that allow you to relocate the selected content with respect to another selected area or another layer's content, or to align the nonselected areas of the image with the selection should there be only one layer and no other selections made.

Figure 2.16

Use the Align and Distribute buttons on the options bar to move a selection relative to other layers, selections, or nonselected areas of the image.

You're Transformation Bound

The Show Bounding Box option is off by default, but if you turn it on, Transform handles (for dragging to resize a selected area) appear on the perimeter of the selection. The handles look like small boxes on the corners and sides of the selection. Point to any of the handles, and when your mouse pointer turns into a two-headed arrow, drag outward to increase the size of the selected area or drag inward to decrease it. Remember, you're resizing the selected portion of the image, not the selected area.

Figure 2.17

(Left) Zoom in on part of your image to increase the accuracy of your mouse movements when drawing and selecting.

Figure 2.18

(Right) Zoom out by right-clicking with the Zoom tool.

Zooming In and Out

To get a better look at any part of your image, use the Zoom tool (see Figure 2.17). It's a good idea to zoom in closer to anything you're selecting with the Lasso tool so that you can be much more exact in your mouse movements. Zooming in also enhances your use of the Magic Wand, because if you zoom in close enough, you can see the individual pixels and easily click on the one you want. To use the Zoom tool, click once on the tool to turn it on, and then move your mouse onto the image—you'll notice that it becomes a magnifying glass with a plus sign in it. Click on the specific area of the image that you want to magnify, and continue to click that spot until you've zoomed in close enough for your purposes. If you get too close, right-click with the magnifying mouse pointer and choose Zoom Out from the shortcut menu, as shown in Figure 2.18.

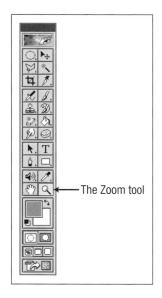

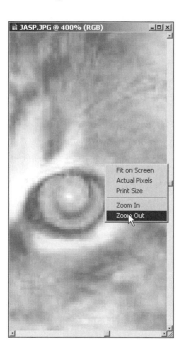

The Zoom tool

Panning with the Hand Tool

If you've zoomed in on your image and now you can't see the whole thing within the file window, you can use the Hand tool to move the image around within the available space. Simply click on the Hand tool and go out onto the image and drag—pulling the image up, down, left, or right, until the portion you want to see at the present magnification is visible within the window. Figure 2.19 shows panning in progress.

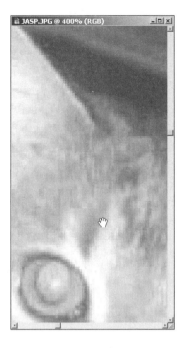

Figure 2.19
In too close and too far to the right? Drag the image back to the left with the Hand tool.

Setting Foreground and Background Colors

The group of four coloring tools shown in Figure 2.20 allows you to set the fill color (Foreground color) and outline color (Background color) for your shapes, layers, and lines. You can also return to the default Black and White, and swap the current Foreground and Background colors. If you click either the Foreground or Background Color tool, the Color Picker dialog box opens.

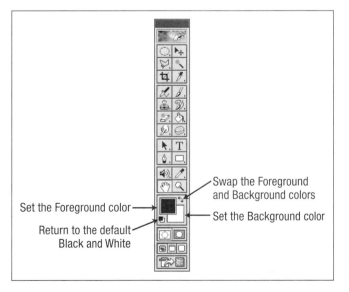

Set the Foreground color ——
Return to the default Black and White
Swap the Foreground and Background colors
Set the Background color

Figure 2.20
Set your fill and outline colors.

Selecting and Sampling with the Eye Dropper

If your image contains a color that you want to use again, you can sip it up with the Eye Dropper tool (see Figure 2.21), making it the new Foreground color. If you simply want to check the statistics on some of the colors in your image—viewing their RGB and CMYK levels, for example—you can use the Color Sampler, shown in Figure 2.22. You can sample up to four different colors. Each sampled pixel will be marked with a number that you can click on to review the color statistics for that spot on the image.

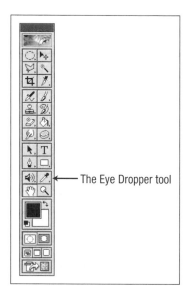

The Eye Dropper tool

Figure 2.21
The Eye Dropper allows you to select a color that's already in use and use it again.

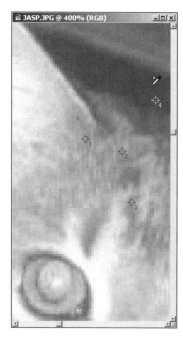

Figure 2.22
Sample colors in your image without selecting them as the new Foreground color.

Working with Photoshop's Drawing Tools

Photoshop offers three tools that "draw," if you define drawing as applying color with your mouse as though you had a pen or pencil in your hand. You can use the Airbrush tool to draw a diffused, soft line; you can use the Paintbrush tool to create strokes of varying thickness and consistencies; or you can use the Pencil tool to create solid strokes. The options bar (as shown in Figure 2.23) offers brush/pencil options, opacity settings, and a variety of modes for each tool, enabling you to mimic anything from a sharp, fine pencil point to the artistic look of watercolor painting.

Painting and Drawing Lines

Applying strokes to your image is as easy as dragging your mouse—simply click where the stroke should begin, and drag until the stroke is completed. If you're painting to fill in a space, it's a good idea to mask the area first with a marquee or lasso shape so that you don't have to worry about painting on something you didn't mean to paint. A steady mouse hand is helpful but not essential, because you can Undo your stroke if you make a mistake.

Zooming in on the target area is another good idea—the closer you are to the image, the more slowly and precisely you can draw. Dragging just a tiny bit with your mouse at a high magnification can result in a long painted or drawn line on your image at its actual size. To zoom in, try these techniques:

- Ctrl++ (Ctrl with the plus sign) zooms in closer each time you press the +.

- Ctrl+- (Ctrl with the dash) zooms out farther away each time you press the -.

- Choose View|Zoom In or View|Zoom Out.

- Click the Zoom tool and click on the area on which you want to zoom.

If you use the keyboard or View menu commands, you might have to move the image around to view the portion on which you want to draw or paint. To do that, click on the Hand tool and pull the image with short mouse drags, tugging it up, down, left, or right until the desired portion of the image is in view.

Using Paintbrushes and Pencils

The Paintbrush tool appears by default, but if you click the button's triangle, you can switch to the Pencil tool instead. Depending on which tool is selected, the options bar displays tools for customizing the way the tool creates lines and strokes. As shown in Figures 2.24 (the Paintbrush options) and 2.25 (the Pencil options), you can adjust everything from the size of the brush or pencil point to the intensity of the color applied.

Figure 2.23

Click on a drawing tool and use the options bar to customize your drawing effects.

Paint in Small Strokes

Draw or paint in small stages so that you don't lose everything you've done if you have to Undo to remove an error. If you draw something in one long, wandering drag with your mouse, when you inevitably veer off course and create an unwanted stroke, you'll end up wiping out all of your work when you issue the Undo command. It's better to draw little bits at a time and know that only the mistake (assuming it's your last action) will be undone.

Paint the Background Over the Foreground

The Auto Erase option applies the Background color to pixels currently colored with the Foreground color, and it paints the Foreground color over any other colors in your path as you draw.

Back in Time with the History Brush

The History Brush has two variations—the History Brush and the Art History Brush. The History Brush allows you to paint over an area, restoring it to its previous state. The Art History brush does the same thing—it simply does it with stylized strokes.

Figure 2.24

Click the Wet Edges option to create a watery effect.

Figure 2.25

The Brush options for the Pencil tool include solid and patterned effects only.

Working with the Airbrush

By default, the Airbrush creates a diffused, fuzzy line with soft edges, intended to look like the paint applied by an actual airbrush. The options bar, shown in Figure 2.26, gives you the following controls:

- *Brush*—Pick the size of the Airbrush nozzle, or specify how wide a stroke will be created by the brush. You can choose from plain round and patterned options in the palette.

- *Mode*—Some of the Mode options have no effect when you apply them to the Airbrush, but you can lighten or darken, remove colors, or adjust saturation and luminosity. It's a good idea to take the time to tinker with some of the Mode options so you know what's available and have seen firsthand what effect they have on an image.

- *Pressure*—This option (set to 100% by default) allows you to change the intensity of the Airbrush flow. By reducing this setting, you reduce the effect of any Mode option you choose, which can give you subtle yet effective results.

Figure 2.26

Choose the Airbrush and then customize its effects with the options bar.

Drawing with the Pen Tools

The Pen tool has five variations: the Pen, the Freeform Pen, Add Anchor, Delete Anchor, and Convert Point. Each one has its own version of the options bar. The Pen tool is used for drawing shapes; it creates a series of connecting curves. As shown in Figure 2.27, to use the Pen tool, click and drag to draw a line, and then click to draw the next segment. Using the nodes that appear on each curve, you can adjust the direction and shape of the curve.

The Pen tool's options, shown in Figure 2.28, include the following:

- The role the new shape will serve—a shape layer that becomes part of the image, or a work path that helps you draw new content on the active layer

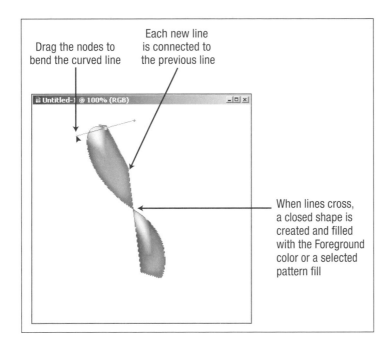

Figure 2.27
Create a figure 8 with just a couple of lines and some dragging with your mouse.

Figure 2.28
Before you draw your shape, set up the way it will work and look.

- The Layer Style palette (which lets you choose a pattern fill)

- The Mode option

- The Opacity level

If you want to have the shape fill with the current Foreground color, choose None from the Layer Style palette. (None looks like a box with a red diagonal line through it.)

The Freeform Pen works very similarly, except that you can drag the pen as though you were writing or drawing on paper. Each line drawn has nodes on each curve, but the nodes are not active until you finish drawing the shape and go back and click on a line, as shown in Figure 2.29.

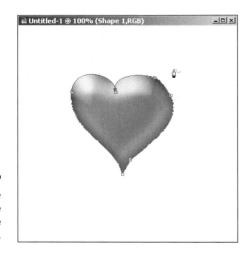

Figure 2.29
Freeform shapes are drawn more
quickly because you make the
adjustments after drawing the
basic shape.

Drawn to the Magnetic Pen

The Freeform Pen has a Magnetic option, which makes it easy to draw a shape that adheres to existing image content. If, for example, you want to create a shape that's the same shape as something in your image—a person, a building, a flower—turn on the Magnetic option and draw along the edges of the object you want to mimic. The shape will fill and obscure the object, but you can move the new shape layer so that it's behind the layer containing the object and serves as a backdrop instead.

The Add and Delete Anchor Point tools allow you to increase the number of bends and intersections in the shape (Add Anchor Point) or remove them to create more streamlined shapes (Delete Anchor Point). To use these tools, simply click along a side of the shape that currently has no anchor point to add one, or click on an existing point to delete it.

You can use the Convert Point tool to convert a smooth point to a corner point, or a corner point to a smooth point. To convert an existing point, just click on it with the Convert Point tool and it changes to the alternate point type. After converting a point, you can grab the nodes attached to that point and adjust them, changing the curve of the line and thus changing that portion of the overall shape. Figure 2.30 shows a point that's now a corner point; what was previously a gently rounded side on the shape is now a sharp point.

Figure 2.30
Add some angles to your shape
by converting smooth points to
corner points.

Drawing Shapes

New to Photoshop 6.0 is the ability to draw shapes. In previous versions, you had to use the marquee and lasso tools to select an area within a layer and then apply color to that area to create the illusion of a drawn shape. Now, you can draw actual shapes, each on its own layer, and apply fills, outlines, and filters to them.

By default, the Rectangle tool is the displayed Shape tool. You can click the button's triangle, however, and switch to any one of the following buttons:

- Rounded Rectangle
- Ellipse
- Polygon
- Line
- Custom Shape

Once you've chosen the shape you want to draw, observe the options bar (see Figure 2.31) for any options you want to set before drawing the image. Your main choice with regard to Web graphics is whether or not the new shape should be part of the active layer or become a new layer unto itself. This is important from a Web graphics perspective because having separate layers for distinct parts of your image makes it easier to tweak existing images by moving, resizing, and recoloring specific parts of the image quickly. If key elements of the image aren't on separate layers within the Photoshop (PSD) version of the file, those quick tweaks aren't possible.

> ### Drawing Lines
>
> If you opt to draw a line with the Shape tool, the options bar offers a Weight button. Here, you enter the pixel depth of the line you're about to draw. The default is 1 px (one pixel), and that results in a very fine line. The color of the line will be dictated by your current Background color, so use the Color Picker to choose a new Background color before drawing your line.

Figure 2.31

The options bar allows you to control how your new shape will affect the image.

To draw a shape, be it on its own new layer or on the existing active layer, simply click a Shape tool (Rectangle, Rounded Rectangle, Ellipse, Polygon, Line, or Custom Shape), and then click and drag on the surface of your image to draw the shape. It's not essential that you position the shape exactly because you can always reposition it. You can also resize it easily, as long as it's on its own layer.

When you're drawing a custom shape, you'll want to pick which shape you want to draw—the options bar offers a new button as soon as you pick the Custom Shape tool. As shown in Figure 2.32, simply click the drop arrow on the Custom Shape Picker and choose to draw a heart, a checkmark, a star, a moon, a footprint—any one of 14 different shapes. After selecting one, just click and drag on the image to draw the shape.

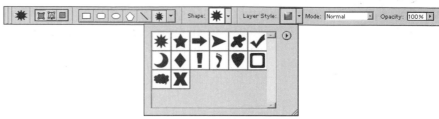

Figure 2.32
The Custom Shape Picker offers
14 different shapes that you can
draw on a new layer or add to
the active layer.

Using the Shading and Fill Tools

Shapes, areas you've selected with the marquee or lasso tools—these can all be filled with solid color or a gradient fill. You can also fill them with artistic patterns and special effects. Figure 2.33 shows three shapes: one with a solid color fill, one with a gradient fill, and one with the Bubbles pattern fill.

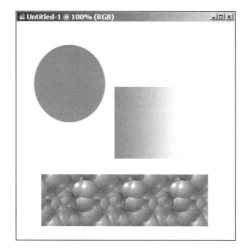

Figure 2.33
Photoshop offers Web-safe
colors, gradient effects, and
artistic fills to jazz up your shapes
and selected areas.

Applying Solid Color Fills

To fill a selected area or shape with color, use the Color Picker. Click once on the Foreground color or Background color to open the Color Picker dialog box (see Figure 2.34). With the Only Web Colors checkbox selected, choose a color.

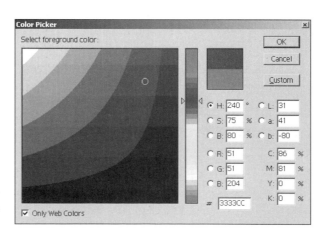

Figure 2.34
The Color Picker offers
Web-safe colors.

Once you picked a color, you can use the Paint Bucket tool to apply that color to a selected area. To apply color to a shape on its own layer, go to the Layers palette and double-click the Layer Thumbnail (see Figure 2.35) to open the Color Picker. As soon as you pick a color by clicking on it, that color is applied to the active shape layer.

Figure 2.35
The Layer Thumbnail opens the Color Picker for a shape on its own layer.

Using the Gradient Fill

The Gradient Fill tool (the alternative to the Paint Bucket tool) can be applied to areas selected with the marquee or lasso tools, or even to areas selected with the Magic Wand. To apply a gradient, click on the tool and use the options bar (shown in Figure 2.36) to choose the type of gradient (Linear, Radial, Angle, Reflective, or Diamond) and to select from a variety of colorful preset gradient effects.

Figure 2.36
Choose the type of gradient you want to apply, or work with preset effects from one of eight different groups.

Once your gradient options are set, with your mouse point to the left, right, or middle of the selected area and drag across the shape. Drag from left to right to apply the gradient from Foreground color to Background color, or from right to left to reverse that effect. If you drag from the middle out, you will start the Foreground color in the middle of the selection and fade to the Background color on the side where you stop dragging. Figure 2.37 shows a Radial gradient applied from the center out.

Working with Artistic Pattern Fills

Pattern fills can be applied to selected areas and to drawn shapes. With an area selected (with the marquee, lasso, or Magic Wand tools), click the Paint Bucket tool to change the options bar. Click the Fill drop-down list (see Figure 2.38) and choose Pattern (the default is Foreground, which results in a solid color fill).

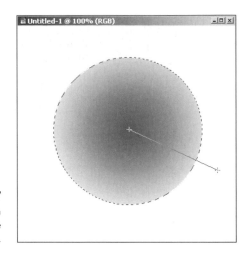

Figure 2.37

The starting point and direction you drag dictates the appearance of your gradient fill.

Figure 2.38

Choose Pattern to activate the Pattern tool on the options bar.

As soon as Pattern is selected as the Fill type, the Pattern drop-down list becomes available. Click the drop arrow on that tool to display a group of 12 different artistic patterns. Your choices include such interesting effects as Tie Dye, Nebula, and Satin. Figure 2.39 shows the palette of patterns and the Tie Dye pattern applied to a shape in the image.

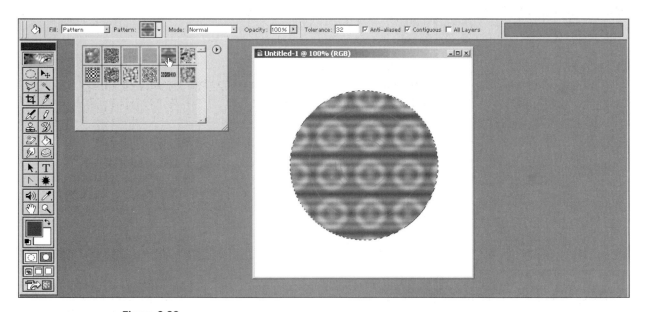

Figure 2.39

Apply an artistic pattern to your shape.

To apply a pattern to a shape layer, you need to double-click the layer on the Layers palette. As soon as you double-click it, the Layer Style dialog box opens. Here, you can enable the Pattern Overlay option (see Figure 2.40), which will apply the pattern fill that's currently selected on the options bar.

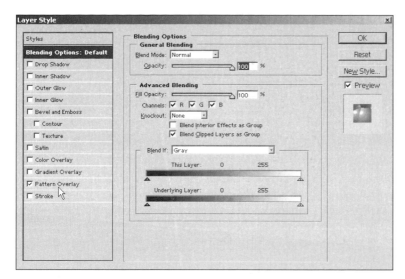

Figure 2.40
A few extra steps are involved in applying patterns to shapes.

Once you've applied a pattern to a shape layer, you can change to a different pattern by clicking the Effects arrow on the shape layer and then double-clicking the Pattern Overlay effect that appears. This reopens the Layer Style dialog box, and you can click the Pattern palette to choose a different pattern for the selected shape layer, as shown in Figure 2.41.

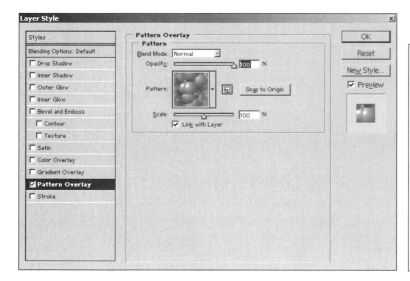

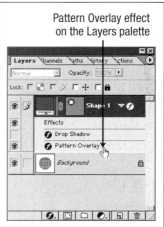

Pattern Overlay effect on the Layers palette

Typing and Formatting with the Text Tools

One of the most important things to remember about text on the Web is that you have to work with a small set of fonts (Times New Roman, Arial, and Verdana are the safest) so that you know all of your visitors will have the font you're using. If the font you use isn't on the viewers' computers, their browsers will substitute a font they do have. This can be a problem if the substitution

Figure 2.41
Change your mind about the pattern for a shape layer? Use the Layer Style dialog box to pick a new one.

Figure 2.42
Avoid unwanted font substitutions by using only Times New Roman or Arial for the text you type directly onto the Web page.

isn't compatible with the other fonts on the page, creating an unappealing effect from a design perspective. Figure 2.42 shows the fonts that are listed by default in Dreamweaver. This list shows you the safe fonts to use, and it also shows you which substitutions will be made. If the visitor doesn't have Verdana, Arial or Helvetica will be displayed instead, depending on which one is loaded on that visitor's computer.

Of course, this applies only to the text you type directly on the page, not to the artistic text you create in Photoshop. Figure 2.43 shows a list of words and phrases, each serving as a link to other pages within a Web site. Rather than typing these words and phrases directly on the page and having to use a standard font like Times New Roman or Arial, the designer created text images in Photoshop. The browser sees each word or phrase as a picture, so no font conflicts exist and no substitutions are required.

Figure 2.43
Want to use a special font? Create a graphic in Photoshop and Web browsers will see it as an image, not as text.

Creating a Type Layer

To add text to your image, simply click the Type tool, and then click on the image to indicate where the text should begin. Unlike with previous versions of Photoshop, in version 6.0 you type the text directly on the image and formatting tools appear on the options bar, rather than in a separate dialog box. Figure 2.44 shows text being typed in an image.

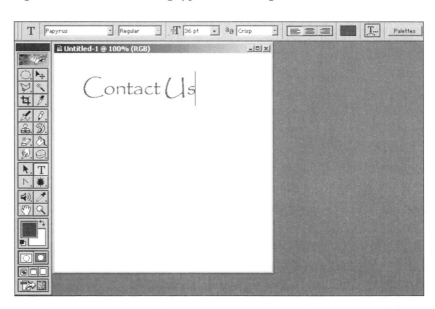

Figure 2.44
Type your text and format it using the options bar.

Choosing Fonts, Sizes, and Colors

It's a good idea to set your fonts, sizes, and colors before you type your text. Just click the Type tool to display the type-related tools on the options bar, and then make your choices. Figure 2.45 shows the options bar with a list of fonts displayed. Unfortunately, Photoshop 6.0 still doesn't show the list of fonts graphically—you won't see what a particular font looks like until you apply it to selected text.

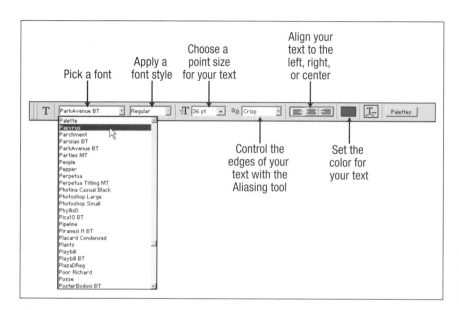

Figure 2.45

Choose your font, size, and color for the text you're about to type or for selected existing text.

After making your selections, type your text. You can still reformat it later by dragging through it with your mouse. If your text layer is no longer active, click the layer on the Layers palette to activate it, and then click the Type tool. With the Type tool active, you can drag through some or all of the text on the active layer.

To apply a font size to selected text (or before typing new text), click the Set The Font Size option's drop arrow. A series of sizes (in points, not pixels) appears, ranging from 6 to 72. You can type other numbers in the box if the size you want isn't in the list. This is especially handy if you want really big text and 72 points isn't big enough.

Color is applied by clicking the Set The Text Color box. This opens the Color Picker, and as soon as you click on a color in that dialog box, the color is applied to the selected text. If you haven't typed any text yet, the color is set as the default for the text you will type.

Changing Fonts

The font style drop-down list is set to Regular by default, but you can change it to Italic, Bold, or Bold Italic. If this button isn't available, that's because the font you've selected cannot be visually altered.

Understanding the Retouching Tools

Existing images—photographs, drawings, clip-art files—they can all be changed and improved through Photoshop to meet the needs of a particular Web page design. Perhaps you're designing a company Web site and want a group photo

---

Displaying the Character and Paragraph Palettes

You can display the Character and Paragraph palettes by clicking the Palettes button on the options bar. In addition to containing many of the tools already on the options bar, these palettes offer other tools. The Character palette has tools for adjusting tracking, leading, kerning, and text shape, and on the Paragraph palette, you can set indents. You display the palettes in order to access these extra tools and to make a movable, conveniently sized group of features available on-screen even when the Type tool isn't active. Changes made through the palettes apply to the active layer's text (all of it) even if another tool is selected at the time.

---

on one of the Web pages. Imagine that the group photo contains someone who is no longer with the company—what do you do? Reshoot the photo? No, simply edit out the person who shouldn't be in the picture. Have a piece of clip art that has too much green in it or that's filled with primary colors and you need softer pastel shades? Open the file in Photoshop and marquee the areas that need color changes, and then apply new fills. You can remove wrinkles from someone's shirt, plant grass over mud puddles, remove a trash can from a storefront, change the color of someone's eyes, erase creases and cracks on old photos, or clean up the appearance of graphics text. Anything is possible with Photoshop's retouching tools.

Working with the Clone and Pattern Stamp Tools

The stamp tools allow you to take something from one part of your image and reproduce it on another spot in the same image. You can use the Clone Stamp tool to cover something in an image by stamping the fill from one area onto the undesired content (stamp green grass from one area over an unwanted mud puddle, for example). You can use the Pattern Stamp tool to fill an area with one of Photoshop's preset pattern fills.

The options bar, as shown in Figure 2.46, offers tools for choosing the brush size of the stamp, a Mode option for choosing from a variety of effects (such as Soft Light or Luminosity), and an Opacity option, which enables you to create a "see-through" effect for whatever you stamp.

Figure 2.46

Before stamping, set your options for how the stamp will work and how the stamped content will appear.

The Clone Stamp tool is an essential tool for photo retouching. As shown in Figure 2.47, content you don't want in the image can be "stamped out," or covered by stamping content from elsewhere in the image. To use the Clone Stamp tool, press the Alt key on your keyboard and click on the portion of the image that you want to stamp onto another spot on the image. Then, release the Alt key and click to stamp the selected content.

When pressing the Alt key to select the area to use for stamping, you can set a distance between the area to be copied and the target area. For example, as shown in Figure 2.48, the cat's fur that's being stamped over the fabric tie is about an eighth of an inch from the tie. That means that as I continue to click

Figure 2.47
Want to get rid of that fabric tie draped over the cat and replace it with fur? Use the Clone Stamp tool.

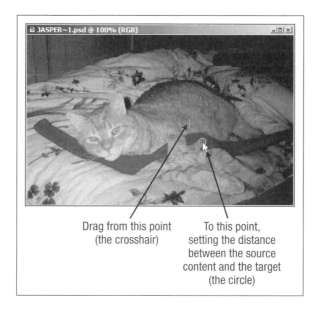

Drag from this point
(the crosshair)

To this point,
setting the distance
between the source
content and the target
(the circle)

Figure 2.48
Press the Alt key and drag to set the distance between sampled content and the target location for the stamp.

around on the tie, I'm grabbing whatever is an eighth of an inch from my current click location. This prevents the same exact spot of fur from being stamped repeatedly, which wouldn't look natural. The downside? If I click on a spot where an eighth of an inch away isn't on fur, I'll stamp something else—perhaps the comforter pattern—onto the cat, which isn't desirable. You can resample the stamp area as needed to prevent this.

The Pattern Stamp tool allows you to stamp a pattern on top of the image. As soon as you choose the Pattern Stamp tool, the options bar offers a variety of tools, including a Pattern drop-down list, from which you can select the pattern to be stamped. Figure 2.49 shows the palette of patterns.

Using Smudge, Blur, and Sharpen

This set of three tools is available by clicking the triangle on the Smudge tool—the button that's displayed by default. Each of these tools can play an important role in cleaning and improving the appearance of photographs and other artwork; smoothing away unwanted marks; reducing a choppy, pixilated look; or increasing the clarity of some or all of an image.

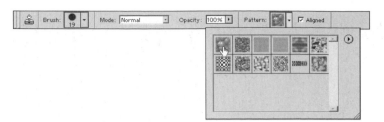

Figure 2.49

In addition to choosing a brush size and opacity setting, pick a pattern to stamp onto your image.

When you choose any one of these tools, the options bar offers tools for customizing how the tool will work—the size of the brush, the mode, and the amount of pressure applied as the tool is used. Further, you can enable the Use All Layers option, which allows you to apply the effects of the selected tool to all the layers at once, rather than affecting only one selected layer. One variation of the options bar appears when you turn on the Smudge tool. The Finger Painting checkbox allows you to apply the selected Foreground color (as shown on and selected through the Color Picker) at the same time that the smudge is applied. Figure 2.50 shows a smudge done with Finger Painting on (on the left side of the image) and one without (on the right).

Figure 2.50

Smudge your image to smooth the edges of two adjoining shapes or to blend away a blemish.

The Blur and Sharpen tools don't move the content of the image the way the Smudge tool does—rather, they adjust the quality or the image. The Blur tool does just what you'd expect it to: It reduces the sharpness of portions of the image as you drag your mouse. Conversely, the Sharpen tool heightens the difference between adjoining shapes or colors, and it brings out the detail in parts of the image that might not be clear enough. Figure 2.51 shows an image with everything but the face blurred and with the face sharpened to stand out.

Adjusting Image Quality with Dodge, Burn, and Sponge

The Dodge and Burn tools are used to lighten and darken areas of your image, respectively. The options bar (see Figure 2.52) for each tool enables you to choose a brush size, the range of colors and tones that should be affected by the tool (Shadows, Midtones, or Highlights), and the degree of exposure, which is set to 50% by default.

Figure 2.51

Like the effect of petroleum jelly on a camera lens, the Blur tool reduces sharp lines and crevices. Its companion, the Sharpen tool, heightens detail and brings out every pixel.

Figure 2.52

Control the lightening and darkening effects of the Dodge and Burn tools.

How will these options affect the way the tools work? If you dodge (lighten) an image and your range is set to Shadows, only the very darkest colors will be lightened, while choosing Highlights will brighten the bright/light points in the image. Midtones will adjust everything equally. By changing the exposure, you're adjusting the degree of lightening that is applied—the higher the exposure, the brighter everything becomes, potentially resulting in what looks like a picture taken with too bright a flash, as shown in Figure 2.53.

Figure 2.53

Use the Dodge tool to lighten and brighten your image.

Figure 2.54
Sun got in their eyes?
Burn away the bright spots
that reduce detail.

The Burn tool does the opposite—it darkens Shadows or Midtones, or it can be used to dull the effect of existing bright or light areas. As shown in Figure 2.54, you can deepen shadows and bring back detail lost to overexposure by burning certain areas of a photograph.

The Sponge tool can be used to increase or decrease color intensity. When you choose this tool, the options bar offers a Mode option rather than the Range option provided for Dodge and Burn. As shown in Figure 2.55, the Sponge Mode options are Desaturate and Saturate, the former reducing color intensity and the latter increasing it. When would you use such a tool for Web graphics? If you have a photograph with very bright colors and you want to use it on a page that's rather subtly colored, use the Sponge to reduce the saturation of color in key areas. Conversely, if you have an old, faded photograph that needs to look new and its colors more juicy and alive, use the Sponge in Saturate mode to bring those colors back to life.

Understanding Your Eraser Options

The Eraser comes in three flavors—a Background Eraser, which erases only the Background layer, leaving the other layers intact; a Magic Eraser, which erases only one color at a time, much like the Magic Wand selects only certain color pixels; and the standard Eraser, which erases everything in its path as you drag your mouse on the active layer.

The options bar for each version of the Eraser varies to give you tools for controlling the way the selected eraser works—for example, as shown in Figure 2.56, the Background Eraser's options include Brush Size, Limits, Tolerance, and Sampling. You've seen Brush Size and Tolerance before, and there are no

Figure 2.55
Use the Sponge to absorb color or wring it out to add color intensity.

surprises here. What's unique about the Background Eraser is the ability to control which background pixels are erased—by choosing Contiguous, you confine the erasure to pixels that are touching. If you choose Discontiguous from the Limits menu, you expand the eraser's capability to erase pixels whether they're touching previously erased pixels or not. Find Edges, the last of the three Limits options, allows you to maintain object edges where a high contrast exists between areas of color.

Figure 2.56
The Background Eraser's options help you control a very powerful tool.

The Sampling menu offers three choices as well: Continuous, which erases all pixels on the background, leaving a transparent background behind; Once, which allows you to choose a sample pixel and then erase only those that closely match it (set Tolerance to 1% to erase only one color); and Background Swatch, which makes it possible to pick a Background color (with the Color Picker) and erase only pixels that match it exactly.

The Magic Eraser assumes that you want to erase only one color and/or colors that are a close match. Use the Alt key to click on a pixel that will serve as the sample, and then click or drag around the image to erase the pixels that come within the tolerance level you've set on the options bar. Enable the Anti-aliased option if you want a soft edge on the erased areas. You can also use the Contiguous option (see the options bar in Figure 2.57) if you want to restrict the erasure to pixels that are touching.

Defend the Foreground

If you want to preserve any pixels that are currently colored in the selected Foreground color, turn on the Protect Foreground Color box and choose Once from the Sampling menu. Use the Alt key as you click on the color you want to protect.

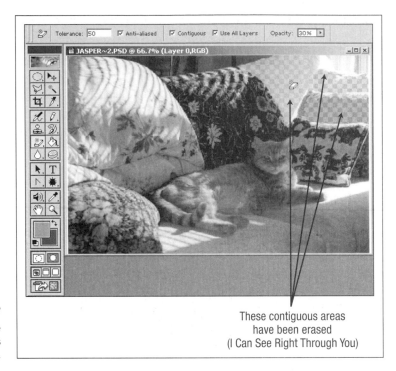

These contiguous areas
have been erased
(I Can See Right Through You)

Figure 2.57
The Magic Eraser works like
the Magic Wand, but it erases
rather than selects.

By default, the Magic Eraser's Opacity is set to 100%, which means that whatever is erased is completely erased. If you reduce the opacity, however, you can leave a percentage of the content behind—sort of a ghost of the colors that met your Tolerance setting and selected pixel color.

Cropping an Image

The Crop tool gives you the ability to select and preserve an area of the image while the rest is removed—reducing an image to a desired portion of its current content, getting rid of unwanted edges (imagine a scanned photo with the photo's matting still included in the image), or simply reducing the overall size of the image by removing peripheral content. Of course, you can also crop an image by using the Marquee tool to select a portion of it and then using the Image|Crop command. That approach is certainly quick and easy, and it has pretty much the same result.

Using the Crop tool, however, makes the Crop options bar available. The options bar lets you control the size of the cropped area (if using your mouse doesn't allow you to be exact enough) and adjust the resolution of whatever part of your image is left after cropping. Figure 2.58 shows the Crop tool's options bar, the version that appears before the tool has been used. Note that after you've used the Crop tool to select an area to be cropped, you have to issue the Image|Crop command to perform the actual crop.

Figure 2.58
When you click on the Crop tool,
these options appear; they
change as soon as you select an
area for cropping.

Once you've used the Crop tool—dragging a rectangular shape on the image—the Crop tool's options change, as shown in Figure 2.59. Now, the options bar pertains to how the cropping will be executed, and it also provides tools for simplifying the cropping process. The Shield Cropped Area command darkens the area to be cropped, helping you to see the effect of your intended cropping. If you adjust the Opacity setting, you can completely hide the cropped area (100%) or darken it more or less than the default by raising or lowering the percentage. You can use the Color option to apply a specific colorcast to the cropped area.

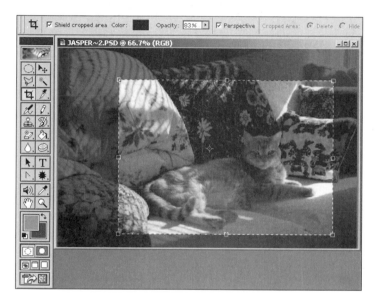

Figure 2.59
Use the Opacity tool to adjust how the cropped areas look before you actually crop them—hiding them completely might help you envision the results of your crop.

In terms of controlling how the crop is executed, you can use the Cropped Area: Delete or Hide options to literally delete the cropped areas, or simply hide them so that they remain part of the file. These options aren't available if your image has only one layer.

If you'd rather crop a nonrectangular shape—say a triangle shape is more what you're looking for, or perhaps a diamond—turn on the Perspective option. With this option enabled, you can use the handles that appear when you select the area to remain after cropping to change the shape of the cropped area. Drag the corner handles as shown in Figure 2.60.

Using the Slicing Tools
Slicing is done to reduce the upload time of large images. If you slice large images into smaller sections, the overall image takes less time to load through a Web browser. You arrange the slices in table cells or frames on the Web page, and the browser puts the single image together from all the slices based on your arrangement. Figure 2.61 shows an image divided into several slices.

Let's Start That All Over Again

If you haven't cropped yet and want to start over, press the Esc (Escape) key. The Crop tool remains active, but any selection you've made, including any changes to its shape or dimensions, is removed.

Figure 2.60

Drag in toward the center of the selected area to create a concave line, and drag out to create a convex one.

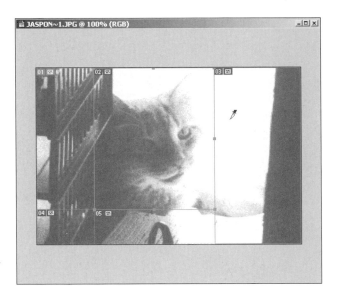

Figure 2.61

Serving a large image is easier if you slice it first.

Slicing can be done through the Slice menu found in the ImageReady application (discussed in detail in Chapter 10) or through the use of Photoshop's Slice tool. The Slice tool comes in two forms: Slice and Slice Select. The former is used for creating the slices and the latter for selecting existing slices.

When you're using the Slice tool, the options bar offers tools for creating the slices: a Style option, for choosing from a list that includes Normal; Constrained Aspect Ratio; and Fixed Size (see Figure 2.62). "Normal" simply means that you can use the Slice tool to draw any size slice you want, slicing the image into as many boxes as you see fit. If you opt for Constrained Aspect Ratio, all of the slices you create will follow the default Width and Height, which are set to 1. You can change this, of course, and set a new constrained ratio. For example, if you want slices that are twice as wide as they are tall, set Width to 2 and leave Height set to 1.

Figure 2.62
For precision in slicing, control the proportions or choose a fixed slice size.

If you choose Fixed Size, the Width and Height boxes change to accept pixel dimensions. After setting a size, all you have to do is click anywhere on the image and drag your mouse, and a slice the size that you've specified will be created automatically. The slice will follow your mouse, and as soon as you release the mouse button, the slice is positioned.

If you switch to the Slice Select tool, you can assign names and link information to specific slices on the image. Switch to the tool and click on a particular slice, and then click the Slice Options button on the options bar and enter information in the Slice Options dialog box, as shown in Figure 2.63. You can enter a Web address (URL) that the slice should point to; create an Alt Tag, which is the text that appears in a Screen Tip when visitors move their mouse over the slice; and give your slice a name to help identify it later when you're setting up slices in a Web page.

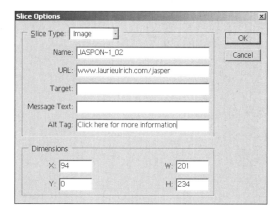

Figure 2.63
Set up your selected Slice options.

After you create your slices, save the file. You can open the sliced image in ImageReady, at which point the individual slices can be saved for use on the Web. You'll learn about slicing an image in Chapter 13, and the specifics of using ImageReady are discussed in Chapter 10.

Inserting Comments with the Notes Tool

With more and more Photoshop users working as part of a team to develop graphics for the Web, the need has arisen for people to comment on and ask questions about an image and pass those notes on to other members of the team. The Notes tool (see Figure 2.64) allows you to draw comment boxes on the image, type inside them, and then move them around as needed. The notes only appear when clicked on—after you've typed them and click away, the note disappears, leaving only a tiny see-through icon to indicate that a note exists.

Any Way You Slice It

You can also access the Slice Options dialog box for any slice by right-clicking the slice and choosing Edit Slice Options from the resulting shortcut menu.

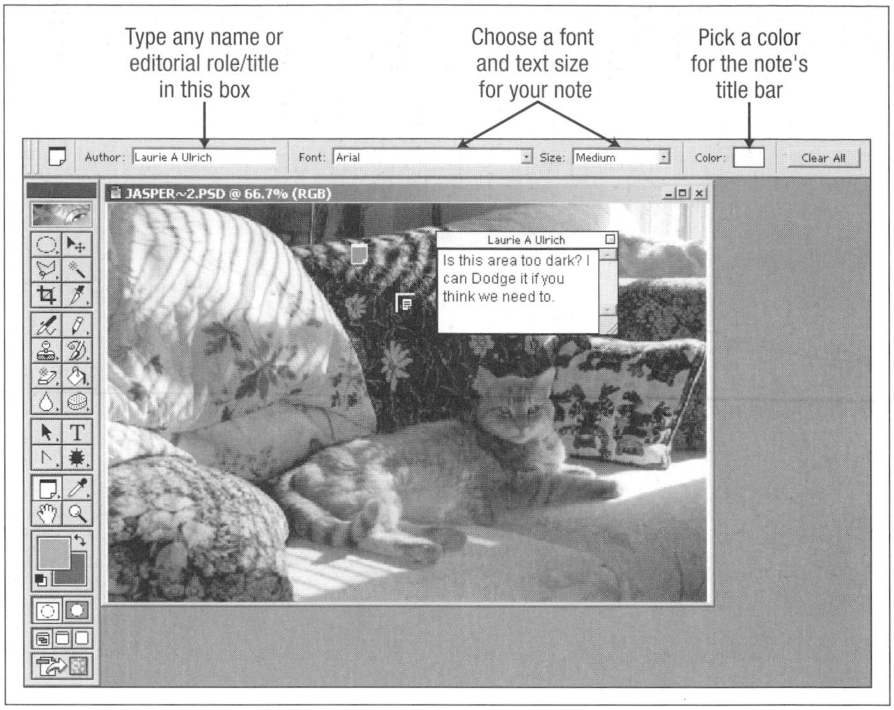

Type any name or editorial role/title in this box

Choose a font and text size for your note

Pick a color for the note's title bar

Figure 2.64

Click the Notes tool and draw a box to house your comments, questions, and suggestions for the rest of your design team.

Make Yourself Heard

You can add audio annotations to your image by clicking the Audio Annotation tool. After you click the tool, click on your image to indicate the spot that's to be annotated. A dialog box appears, asking you to click Start to begin recording your annotation. Of course, your computer has to be equipped with a sound card, speakers, and a microphone in order for this feature to work. If you'll be sending the image to others for review, they need sound capability, too, in order to hear your audio annotations.

If you want to move a note, click on its icon, and when the Note box opens, use the Move tool to drag it to another location on the image. You can also delete notes by right-clicking the note or its icon and choosing Delete Note from the shortcut menu.

Working with Views and Modes

Adobe realizes that different people work in different ways. Some people like to have all the tools, menus, and bars on screen at all times so they have instant access to whatever they might need, and they like to tinker with the size of their file window. Others like to have as much space for their image as possible, and consider any tool they're not using right now to be clutter. Whether you're at one end of that spectrum or the other (or somewhere in between), Photoshop has a view that you'll like working in. Further, Photoshop offers two work modes: one for editing, and one for masking parts of the image in preparation for work. You'll find that although you probably use one much more often than the other, you'll be glad the alternate is there.

Viewing Your Image Full Screen

As far as the Photoshop workspace is concerned, you have three options:

- *Standard Screen Mode*—This is the default, with menus, the toolbox, the options bar, and default palettes on screen.

- *Full Screen*—Maximizes the file window at its current zoom setting and turns the space behind the file window black (see Figure 2.65). The menu and title bars are also removed.

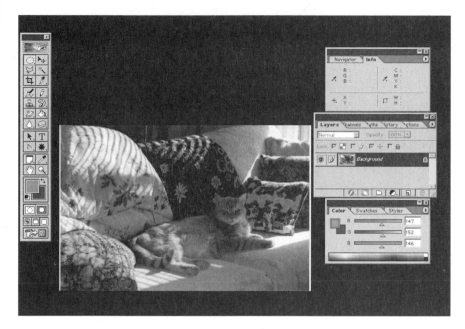

Figure 2.65
A black background gives you maximum contrast with your image, and no workspace is wasted on the menu or title bars in Full Screen view.

- *Full Screen With Menu Bar*—This is the same as Full Screen view, but the background becomes gray and the menu bar is restored, just as the name implies.

Understanding Mask Modes

Photoshop gives you two modes to work in: Standard and Quick Mask (see Figure 2.66). These modes enable you to either directly edit your work or mask off areas so that the next work you perform won't affect certain areas of the image. By default, you're in Standard mode when you open the application, and in this mode you'll do most of your work—drawing shapes and lines, typing text, and using the retouching tools to edit your image content. When you switch to Quick Mask mode, any tool you use—the Paintbrush, the Type tool, the Smudge tool—creates a mask on the surface of the image (see Figure 2.67). A mask protects the image from other actions so that when you switch back to Standard mode to edit the image, the mask created by your actions in Quick Mask mode will prevent your edits from affecting the masked areas.

Working with the Palettes

Photoshop offers 12 different palettes to help you create and edit your images. To save space within the application window, these 12 palettes are broken into four floating palette windows, grouped as follows:

- *The Navigator Palette*—Helps you control your view of the image—drag the triangle to the left to zoom out, or to the right to zoom in. (Figure 2.68)

- *The Info Palette*—You can view the color levels and other image statistics within your file in the palette. (Figure 2.69)

Ready, Set, Jump to ImageReady!

The last button on the toolbox opens ImageReady in a separate application window. You can leave Photoshop running and hop back and forth between the applications by clicking the taskbar buttons for each application. Or you can use the Alt+Esc keyboard shortcut to toggle between them. If you have programs in addition to Photoshop and ImageReady open, you can also use Alt + Tab to display a list of the applications you're running and by tapping the Tab key (with the Alt key still pressed), move through the list to select the application you want.

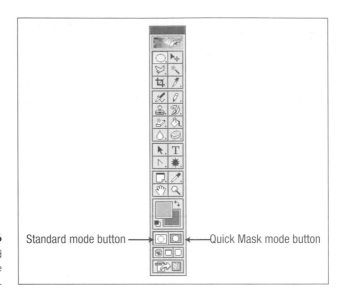

Figure 2.66

Switch between the Standard and Quick Mask modes at the click of a button.

Standard mode button ⟶　⟵ Quick Mask mode button

Figure 2.67

Shown as a semitransparent gray here, a painted mask appears in orange on your image, protecting the areas over which you paint, draw, type, or smudge.

The Polygon Lasso was used to select the area

The Paint Bucket was used to fill the selection

Figure 2.68
(Left) The Navigator palette.

Figure 2.69
(Right) The Info palette.

- *The Color Palette*—You can adjust RGB levels to set a new Foreground color on the Color palette. (Figure 2.70)

- *The Swatches Palette*— Allows you to pick from a variety of Web-safe colors to work with. (Figure 2.71)

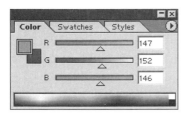

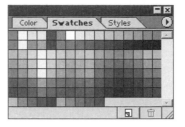

Figure 2.70
(Left) The Color palette.

Figure 2.71
(Right) The Swatches palette.

- *The Styles Palette*—Utilizes preset styles that can be applied to an image with the Paint Bucket tool. (Figure 2.72)

- *The Layers Palette*—Allows the user to view, hide, rearrange, copy, or delete image layers. (Figure 2.73)

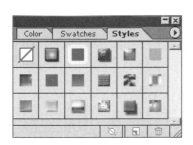

Figure 2.72
(Left) Choose a preset Style for your fills—the one you pick is applied as soon as you use the Paint Bucket.

Figure 2.73
(Right) The Layers palette gives the user the ability to make a multi-layered document.

- *The Channels Palette*—Gives the user the ability to turn the color channels in an image on or off to assist in editing the image. (Figure 2.74)

- *The Paths Palette*—Identifies the outlines of shapes created in the document. (Figure 2.75)

Figure 2.74
(Left) The Channels palette.

Figure 2.75
(Right) Users can view the paths they've created in the Paths palette.

- *The History Palette*—Displays the previous actions, with the ability to edit or undo, on the current document. (Figure 2.76)

- *The Actions Palette*—Actions are a series of automated tasks that apply special effects. They can be viewed here. (Figure 2.77)

- *The Character Palette*—Gives the user the ability to change the appearance of text, letter by letter. (Figure 2.78)

- *The Paragraph Palette*— Changes paragraph alignments and indents in the document. (Figure 2.79)

Figure 2.76

(Left) Go back in time to view and/or undo a series of actions with the History palette.

Figure 2.77

(Right) View the actions associated with an image with the Actions palette.

Figure 2.78

(Left) The Character palette.

Figure 2.79

(Right) The Paragraph palette.

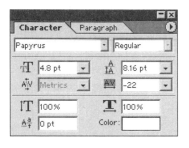

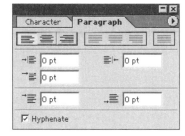

To display any palette, choose it from the Window menu. If it's not showing now, it will appear by name, preceded by the word "Show" in the menu. If one of the other palettes from the desired palette's group is displayed, you can simply click the tab of the palette you want to see.

Most palettes can be resized. Just move your mouse to one of the outermost edges of the palette, and if your mouse pointer turns to a two-headed arrow, you can resize the palette by dragging outward to make it bigger or inward to make it smaller. If you use a corner, you can adjust the width and height simultaneously. To move a palette, grab its title bar and drag it to a new location with your mouse.

Customizing the Photoshop Interface

Found in the Edit menu, the Preferences command offers 10 different options for customizing the way Photoshop looks and works. Most of the option headings in the Preferences submenu are rather self-explanatory. You can adjust everything from the way things are measured (inches, pixels, centimeters) to how transparent backgrounds are displayed. For Web work, you don't need to tinker with too many of them, although making sure that your transparency settings are correct is important. As shown in Figure 2.80, make sure your Transparency Grid Size is set to Small, Medium, or Large (as opposed to None) and that the color of the grid is Light. If you have your Transparency Grid set to None, you'll see a white background even if there is no background, and that can be very confusing. By setting the color to Light, you don't cause yourself undue confusion between the grid and any patterns or shapes in your image.

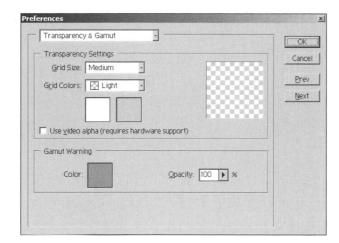

Figure 2.80
Check your Transparency settings to make sure they're set up for designing Web graphics.

Of course, you also want to be working in pixels when it comes to measuring things for the Web. You can reset all measurements to pixels by choosing Edit|Preferences|Units And Rulers. If one of the other Preferences dialog boxes is already open, simply choose Units And Rulers from the drop-down list at the top of the dialog box. Figure 2.81 shows the Units And Rulers options. Note that the Column measurements cannot be set to pixels—the only options are inches, points, picas, or centimeters.

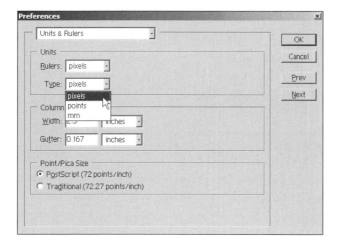

Figure 2.81
Make sure you're measuring in pixels, the unit of measure most appropriate for Web design.

When it comes to color, be sure that you've told Photoshop you're designing graphics for the Web. Choose Edit|Color Settings, and in the resulting Color Settings dialog box (see Figure 2.82), choose Web Graphics Defaults. You can mouse over all of the various options in the dialog box and read the descriptions for them at the bottom of the dialog box. By changing to Web Graphics Defaults, you're electing to use the settings that will help you design images that will display reliably on the greatest number of computers within your intended audience.

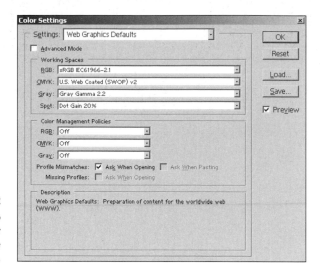

Figure 2.82

Prepare your Photoshop application for Web design by adjusting the settings in the Color Settings dialog box.

Moving On

In this chapter, you were introduced to the Photoshop workspace and tools. You can now identify all the menus, toolbar buttons, and context-sensitive controls that appear as you work. You've learned how the drawing tools work, and you should be familiar with the tools used to apply fills and outlines. You'll now be able to recognize the text-formatting tools that appear on-screen as soon as you begin creating a text layer. In addition, you'll know how to display Photoshop's palettes and how to work within them. In the next chapter, you'll put all of this knowledge to use and create original artwork.

Chapter 3

Creating Original Artwork for the Web

As people flock to the Web to stake out their acre of cyberspace, the need to make your acre unique becomes more important than ever. If you need a graphic for your site and you want it to stand out, my advice to you is to design your own, and Photoshop makes it a painless process.

Starting a New Image

The File|New command opens the New dialog box, where you can set the size of your new image and determine the color of the background. As shown in Figure 3.1, you can have a White, Background color, or Transparent background. If you choose the Background Color option, the color currently selected for the Background color on the toolbox will be applied to the image background.

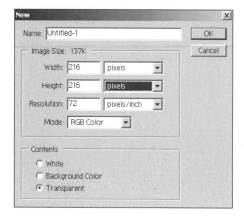

Figure 3.1
Choose the width, height, and background color for your new image.

You should also set the resolution for your image. Aim high, but not too high. Before saving your image for the Web, it's a good idea to reduce its resolution to 72 pixels per inch (ppi); however, if you start out with at least 100 ppi, you have more detail to work with as you manipulate your image. Many manipulations take place at the pixel level, such as using the Eye Dropper to select a color or using the Magic Wand to select like pixels. Starting out with a setting higher than 300 ppi will create huge PSD files. Depending on the size of the image, it might not fit on a disk or be easily transmitted via email (many Internet service providers restrict email attachments to 2MB or less). A huge file can become a liability if you're working with others on the image or if you want a simple backup procedure for individual image files.

After you've set the size, mode, resolution, and background of your new image, click OK to create it. As shown in Figure 3.2, a new image window opens, sized to match the exact dimensions of the new image. You can resize the window by dragging its edges (your mouse pointer will turn into a two-headed arrow), or you can use the Maximize button in the upper-right corner to make the image window the full size of the application window.

Using Photoshop's Creative Tools

There's a difference between creating a new image and editing an existing one, especially if you didn't create the existing image in the first place. If the file isn't a Photoshop file, you will have limited ability to easily edit it, because it won't have editable layers. If you don't have access to the original photograph or

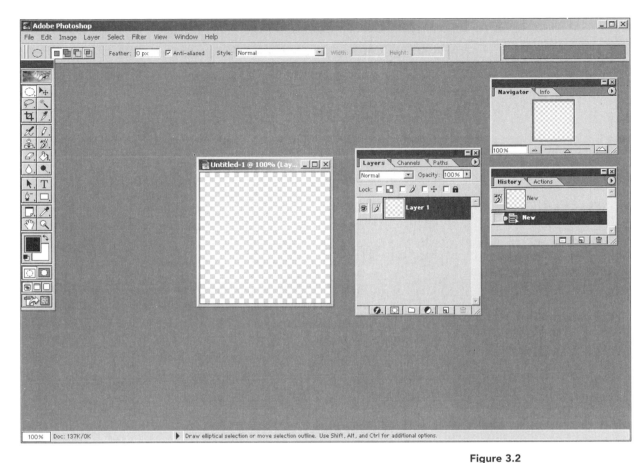

Figure 3.2
A blank slate, awaiting your
creativity.

drawing that was scanned, you're stuck with whatever the original creator did with that hard-copy artwork. Creating artwork from scratch, however, means that you have layers (which you can preserve by keeping a Photoshop version of the file even after you've saved it for the Web), and you probably have all the contributing content should you need to rescan or tinker with files that were used whole or in part to make your image. Figure 3.3 shows a Photoshop image with each of its components on a separate layer.

Although all of Photoshop's tools can be used for either creating or editing, in this chapter we're concerned with building new images from scratch. Using all the drawing tools in the Photoshop toolbox, you can create anything from a logo to a complex image that will serve as multiple graphics links to pages within your site. You can incorporate existing graphics content, such as photographs or pieces of existing clip art, but in the end the creation is your own because you turn it into something unique and effective with the help of Photoshop.

Drawing Shapes

Prior to Photoshop 6.0, the only way to draw a geometric shape was to use the marquee tools. Now, in this latest version, you can draw virtually any geometric shape, and some interesting freeform shapes as well—such as hearts, footprints, moons, and stars—and create a new layer at the same time. For

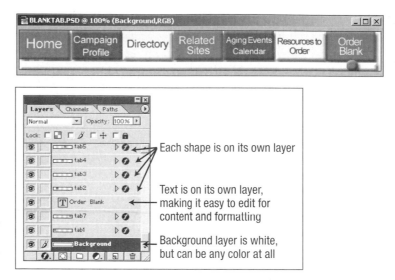

Figure 3.3

What appears to be a simple image (shapes and text, artfully arranged) can be easily edited because each part resides on its own layer.

people accustomed to using the marquee tools for shape creation, this seems like added, unnecessary complexity, because the shape layer requires special handling. The ability to draw shapes quickly and easily, however, more than makes up for these potential drawbacks.

Creating a Shape Layer

To create a shape layer, simply click on the Shape tool, and using the options bar (see Figure 3.4), choose the shape you want to draw. If you want to draw a rectangle, ellipse, or simple polygon, choose one of them from the tool button itself—just hold the button down and pick the shape you'd like to draw.

Other choices to make before you draw your shape include whether the shape will reside on a new shape layer, whether it will serve as a work path, or whether it will simply be a filled region on the currently active layer. The options bar offers these three choices, as Figure 3.5 shows. If you're not sure which one to use, think about how the shape will be utilized within the image. If you want to be able to format the image without using the marquee, lasso, or Magic Wand tools to select it later, put it on its own layer. If you want to draw a shape on the active layer or a layer of your own creation that might or might not contain other elements, choose to make the new shape a simple filled region.

As you draw the shape you've elected to create, remember to drag diagonally. The distance and angle from your starting point dictate the size and proportions of the shape. As shown in Figure 3.6, if you hold the Shift key as you drag, the shape will have equal width and height. Be sure to release the mouse before you release the Shift key, though, or the proportions dictated by the angle of your dragging will take over and the equal proportions will be lost.

When it comes to shapes in Web graphics, you can use them with text (covered in detail in Chapters 6 and 7), placing them behind a text layer (see Figure 3.7), or you can place them alongside other page elements. Better than simply applying a Background color to a table cell, using a shape creates texture on the page.

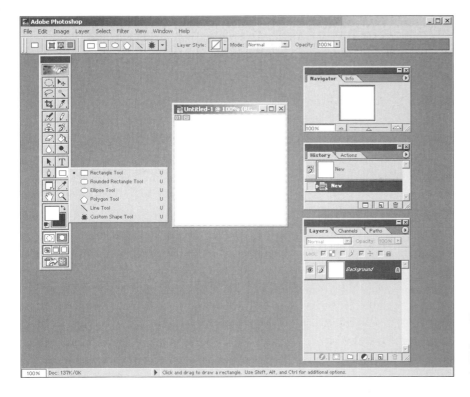

Figure 3.4

Either select the Shape tool you want to use or click the button and pick a shape from the options bar.

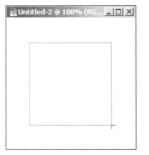

Figure 3.5

When you're adding a shape to your image, your choices are a new shape layer, or a filled region on the currently active layer.

Figure 3.6

Click to establish the shape's starting point, and then drag diagonally away from that spot.

Figure 3.7

These two shapes (one a flat square filled with color, the other a circle with 3-D effects applied to it) draw attention to the graphical text.

Wrangling Shapes with the Lasso

If you want to draw a completely freeform shape and fill it with color or a pattern, use the Lasso tool. You can draw curvy shapes or polygonal shapes and then use the Foreground color to apply a solid fill, or you can activate the Paint Bucket to apply a pattern fill.

Creating Shapes with the Marquee Tool

I still fall back on this old technique, despite the availability of the Shape tool. Why? Because it's familiar, and because I don't have to make any choices about how or where the shape will reside on my image. I can make a new layer for the marquee-created shape, or I can add it to the active layer, even if that's the background. Of course, I can do that with the Shape tool and its Filled Region option, but that's an extra step if all I want to do is create a simple rectangle/square or ellipse/circle on the active layer.

To create a shape with the Marquee tool, choose the marquee shape you want to use, and then click on the active layer and drag to draw the shape. As with the Shape tool, you can use the dragging technique (and the Shift key to maintain equal height and width). The only difference is that the resulting shape is merely a selected space on the layer, and you must immediately fill it with the Foreground color or click the Paint Bucket tool and choose a pattern fill for the shape.

Drawing a Closed Shape with the Pen Tool

The Pen tool creates Bezier curves—loops that you draw by clicking at a starting point and then at an ending point. The loops can be changed in terms of their size and curve by dragging the nodes or anchor points that are created each time you click and/or drag as you draw the shape. Figure 3.8 shows a freeform shape created with the Pen tool, and its parts are identified.

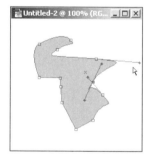

Figure 3.8
Create smooth, amoeba-like shapes, angular shapes, or a combination thereof.

You can edit your shape by dragging any existing anchor point with your mouse. Be careful not to create a new anchor point, because you'll end up adding another section to the shape or creating a figure 8 out of a single loop. If you inadvertently add an anchor point, click on the unwanted point with the Delete Anchor Point tool to remove it and the changes it applied to the shape. Remember that the Delete Anchor Point tool can be found by clicking the triangle in the lower-right corner of the Pen Tool button.

You can use the Convert Point tool (also a Pen Tool variation) to turn a smooth curve into an angular one or vice versa. As shown in Figure 3.9, whether you've rethought the shape from an artistic standpoint or simply made a mistake while drawing, you can change curves to corners or corners to curves, each time changing the overall look of the shape. Of course, if your goal was to

Figure 3.9
A freeform shape or a drawing of a recognizable object? Your mouse skills make all the difference.

draw something realistic and not to create an abstract shape, it will require a great deal of mouse skill and patience to draw it in the first place, and a lot of tweaking with the Add Point, Delete Point, and Convert Point tools.

Drawing Straight Lines

The shortest distance between two points is—that's right, a straight line. Straight lines can be very useful within images and as images themselves. You can separate sections of an image with a straight line, or, by inserting an image that consists solely of a straight line onto your Web page, create an interesting alternative to the very dull horizontal rule. Straight lines can be drawn with the Line tool (which is one of the Shape tool alternatives). Or you can draw a straight line with the Paintbrush or Pencil tools; simply hold the Shift key to keep the line straight as you drag. Figure 3.10 shows three straight lines—one drawn with the Line tool, one with the Paintbrush set to a size 9 brush, and one drawn with the Pencil, at size 3.

Pen(cil) Me In

You can draw closed shapes with the Paintbrush and Pencil tools, too. Just click on the tool and start drawing on the active layer, or stop to create a layer before drawing. After drawing the shape (be sure to come back to your starting point to close the shape), you can apply any fill color or pattern to the shape using the Paint Bucket tool. To find out all about the Pen, Pencil, and Paint Brush tools, refer to Chapter 2, where you'll find all of Photoshop's tools are covered in detail.

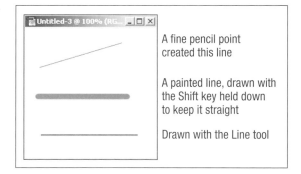

A fine pencil point created this line

A painted line, drawn with the Shift key held down to keep it straight

Drawn with the Line tool

Figure 3.10
Choose a line-drawing tool based on the look you want for the line.

Drawing Freeform Lines

The Paintbrush and Pencil tools, as well as the Airbrush tool, are great for drawing freeform lines. When you activate any of these tools, you can adjust the thickness of the resulting lines by increasing or reducing the size of the brush, and even work with a textured line if you're using the Paintbrush. You can pick a color for the line and, once the line is drawn, use the Layers palette to open the list of effects that can be applied to the line. Figure 3.11 shows an interesting map drawn with the Paintbrush and Pencil tools. This graphic could serve as the link to a page of maps and directions.

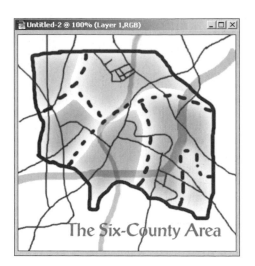

Figure 3.11
Create eye-catching graphics
with simple freeform lines.

Right Back Where You Started

Remember that freeform lines can become unfilled shapes if the starting and ending points meet. You can also fake a thick border around an object or shape within your image by drawing a line that follows its borders.

Applying Fills

Color, pattern, gradient, and style fills are applied differently, based on the shape in question and how that shape was drawn. Fills can be applied only to closed shapes or to entire layers. The layer itself is seen as a closed shape the size of the image canvas. You can apply fills using the Paint Bucket or Gradient Fill tools, or a fill is applied automatically if you draw the shape using the Shape or Pen tool. Other shapes—closed shapes drawn with the Pencil, Paintbrush, or Airbrush—are not filled automatically, but if they are truly closed (the starting and ending points meet), they can be filled. If you select an area with the marquee or lasso tools, you can fill that area with a solid color or a pattern fill as long as the area is selected.

Filling Shapes and Layers with Solid Colors

Before applying a fill color, choose one with the Color Picker. Click the Foreground Color button, and the Color Picker dialog box opens. Of course, because the image is bound for the Web, you want to make sure the Only Web Colors option is selected at the bottom of the dialog box, as shown in Figure 3.12. If you know the color number (the hexadecimal number for the Web-safe color) and/or the RGB levels of the color you want to use, you can enter them in the dialog box, or you can simply click on a color that looks right.

After you've picked a color, click the Paint Bucket tool and then click inside the shape you want to fill. This technique applies to shapes you've created by selecting an area with the marquee or lasso tools; to closed freeform shapes drawn with the Paintbrush, Airbrush, or Pencil tools; or to shapes you've drawn with the Shape tool that aren't on their own shape layer (filled regions). Figure 3.13 shows an area selected with the marquee being filled.

If you drew a shape on its own shape layer, you must use the Layers palette and open the Color Picker from there (see Figure 3.14). If a pattern or layer style has already been applied to the shape, turn off those effects in the Effects list. These extra steps are why I don't like to create shape layers but prefer to draw a filled region on a new layer I create just for that shape or on an existing layer.

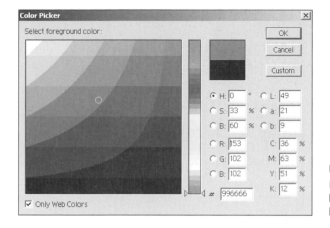

Figure 3.12

Pick a color by eye, by hexadecimal number, or by RGB levels.

Figure 3.13

Make sure the Paint Bucket mouse pointer is inside the shape or marquee before you click to fill it; otherwise, you'll fill the layer itself or perhaps an adjacent shape.

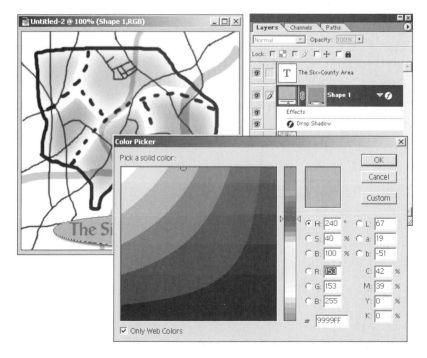

Figure 3.14

Shapes on their own shape layer require special handling if you want to change their fill color.

Applying a Gradient Fill

Gradient fills are shaded from the Foreground color to the Background color or vice versa, depending on how you apply the fill. To apply a gradient to a shape or layer, first choose your colors and then click on the Gradient Fill tool. When you move your mouse onto the shape or layer, your mouse appears as a crosshair. Drag across the shape or layer from left to right to start with the Foreground color and fade to the Background color, or drag from right to left to apply the gradient starting with the Background color. Figure 3.15 shows several shapes with gradient fills.

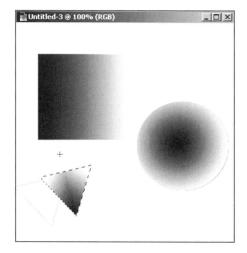

Figure 3.15
A gradient can imply a light source, especially if one of your colors is light and the other color is dark.

To apply the gradient to the entire shape or layer, be sure to drag from one side or corner to the opposite side or corner. If you start and/or end your dragging inside the shape or layer, the full effect of the gradient won't be achieved. If you drag from outside a shape to an opposite point also outside it, the gradient will begin outside of the shape (though the portions that are outside of it won't be filled), and you'll generate a more subtle effect because the entire range from Foreground to Background color won't be covered within the confines of the shape.

Using Pattern Fills

You can access a palette of patterns through the Paint Bucket options bar, and as soon as you change the Fill option to Pattern, as shown in Figure 3.16, the list of available patterns becomes available. Once you select a pattern, that pattern will apply whenever you use the Paint Bucket on any closed shape or selected area, until you reset the Fill option to Solid Color or pick a different pattern.

Applying Styles to Shapes

When you choose to create a shape as its own layer (using the Shape tool to create rectangles, ellipses, polygons, and any number of special shapes), the Layer Style option appears on the Shape tool's options bar. After selecting a

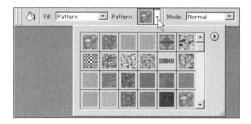

Figure 3.16
Convert the Paint Bucket to a pattern-application tool.

style, you can draw the shape and the style will be applied automatically. If you've already drawn the shape, double-click the shape's layer on the Layers palette, and click to place a checkmark next to Pattern Overlay in the Layer Style dialog box. Double-click the option (see Figure 3.17) to change the dialog box and display the Pattern Overlay options, which includes a palette of patterns you can apply to the active shape layer.

More Patterns!

If you want more than the original group of patterns, you can get more of them by clicking the right-pointing triangle on the top-right corner of the Patterns palette. This opens a submenu through which you can choose Load Patterns. Choose Patterns2.pat from the list of files and click OK to load the patterns, at which point they'll be available through the Patterns palette on the Paint Bucket options bar.

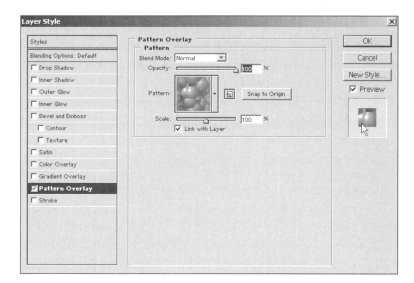

Figure 3.17
A rather lengthy process is involved in applying a pattern style to an existing shape layer—better to pick a style before you draw the shape!

Editing the Image

Editing an image you've created or are in the process of creating normally involves correcting an error or removing some of the content you've drawn or inserted. You can use the drawing tools to edit an image, adding content that you forgot or augmenting something that's already part of the image. Figure 3.18 shows the Paintbrush being used to add small vines to a drawn and filled freeform leaf shape.

If you want to get rid of something you've drawn, you can use the marquee, lasso, or Magic Wand tools to select it and then press Delete, or you can use the Eraser to literally scrub out the unwanted content. You can use the marquee to select the part of your image you want to keep and use the Image|Crop command to get rid of everything else. If the content you want to get rid of is alone on a layer within your image, you can delete that layer to eliminate the unwanted content—simply drag the layer in question down to the Garbage Pail icon in the Layers palette, or right-click the layer and choose Delete Layer from the shortcut menu.

Figure 3.18
Embellish your image with
drawing tools.

Erasing What You've Drawn

The Eraser has a few options that you can use to your advantage in editing your new image. You can erase everything in the path of the Eraser as you drag with your mouse, or you can erase only certain colors. You can also erase only the background, enabling you to remove background content and leave all the other layers intact. This technique is especially helpful if you've applied any kind of fill to your background layer, or if your background layer contained any content you no longer want to include in the image. Figure 3.19 shows the Background Eraser in action.

Figure 3.19
Wipe out that busy background
and allow the rest of your layers'
content to stand out.

I like to use the Eraser tool to remove shapes from within other shapes. If you have a shape on top of another element and you want to see that element through the top layer, use the Eraser to remove some of the fill on the top layer so that the lower layer can be seen through it. If you then apply to the top layer any kind of effects, such as a drop shadow or beveling and embossing, it looks like a 3-D layer with part of it cut away, as shown in Figure 3.20. If you think of the Eraser solely as a tool for removing mistakes, you're only beginning to tap into its value.

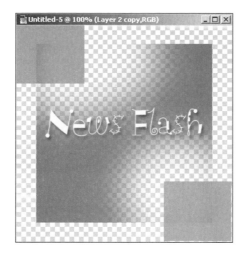

Figure 3.20
Draw with the Eraser by removing existing content in a freeform shape.

Using the Marquee to Reshape Image Content

You can cut away portions of an image with the Marquee tool (and with the Lasso, for that matter) by selecting the unwanted portion and pressing Delete. By repeatedly selecting and deleting areas around the edge of your image, you can create the illusion of a new shape for the image, as shown in Figure 3.21. By deleting round sections around the edge of the picture, it looks as though the picture itself (and not just the food it depicts) is being eaten.

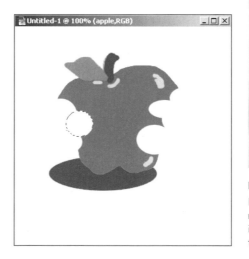

Erased... Sort Of

If you use one of the more diffused brushes for the Eraser tool, you can erase the edge of an image, creating a fuzzy, dream-sequence sort of effect. You can also change the opacity of the Eraser so that it doesn't erase anything completely; the portions of the image over which you drag with the Eraser are made less opaque, as though they're fading away. This can be very useful for graphics that need to blend in with a soft background or that need to match an ethereal or soft look found on the rest of the page.

Figure 3.21
Humor can make a rather mundane image much more interesting. Use your Photoshop tools creatively!

Cropping an Image

To get rid of a choppy edge, remove unwanted background content, or reduce the subject matter in a picture, you can crop it. By drawing a marquee around the portion of the image that should remain, you set the stage for cropping everything that's outside of the selected area. Choose Image|Crop, and the unwanted edges are gone. Figure 3.22 shows a picture with too much nonessential stuff in the background. The marquee that's drawn will reduce the image to what's important after you issue the Crop command.

Figure 3.22
Eliminate unwanted edges by cropping an image down to the important content.

You can also use the Crop tool to create the selection, after which you can use the Image|Crop command to make it happen, or you can press Enter to automatically crop the image to the space within the selection. The Crop tool can be a convenient alternative to the Marquee tool because you can alter the shape of the selected area, dragging the selected area's handles, as shown in Figure 3.23.

Figure 3.23
Reshape the crop area to a polygon that fits tightly around the desired area of the image, and press Enter to complete the crop.

With file size being so important for Web graphics, it's a good idea to eliminate all but the essentials in most images on a Web page. By reducing the excess content around the key portion of the image, you reduce the dimensions of the image and the file size at the same time.

PROJECT Create a Logo

In this project, you'll create a simple, yet effective, logo using shapes and lines. The text is provided for you in the image on the CD-ROM. You'll be adding the shapes and lines and moving the existing text layer as needed.

Start a New Image

Using the File|New Command, start a new image that's 300 pixels wide and 300 pixels tall, with a White background. Click OK to close the New dialog box and begin working on the image. If RGB is not the selected Mode, choose it from the list—all Web-bound graphics should be in RGB mode from the start.

Create New Layers

1. Choose Layer|New|Layer.

2. In the New Layer dialog box, name the layer "shape 1".

3. Create another layer called "shape 2".

4. Create another new layer, and call this one "line 1".

5. Create another layer, called "line 2".

Draw Shapes on the Shape Layer

1. Referring to Figure 3.24, draw a circle on the layer called "shape 1".

2. Draw a triangle (choose the Polygon shape and reduce it to three sides) on the "shape 2" layer.

3. Position the two shapes as shown in Figure 3.24.

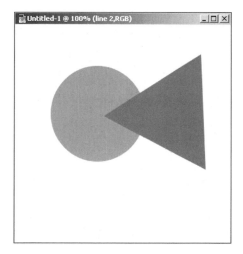

Figure 3.24
The foundation of your logo consists of two simple geometric shapes.

Draw Lines on the Lines Layer

1. Referring to Figure 3.25, draw a horizontal line on the "line 1" layer using the size 13 Paintbrush.

Figure 3.25

Move your lines to match their positions in this image.

2. On the "line 2" layer, draw a freeform line that looks like a smear of paint, as shown in Figure 3.25. You can use the textured Paintbrush of your choice, and set the opacity to 67%.

3. Position the lines as shown in Figure 3.25.

Save the File

Save the file in PSD format. Name the file "mylogo.psd". You'll save it in a Web format later.

Working with Layer Effects

Every layer in your image can be formatted with special effects—layer styles found in the Layer Style dialog box—which include a drop shadow, inner and outer glow, bevel, and embossing effects. You can apply these effects quickly and leave them applied in their default states, or you can customize them to look exactly as you want them by working with the substantial set of options for each effect. Figure 3.26 shows the Layer Style dialog box with the Drop Shadow options displayed.

Consistency Is Always a Good Thing

As you apply effects to elements in your graphic, make a note of any customizations you establish, and keep track of the combinations of effects that you apply—such as drop shadow with an outer glow, or bevel and emboss with 50 percent opacity—so that you can apply the same effects in the same way to similar graphics on the same Web page. If you're designing a button, a navigation bar, a logo, or anything else that will appear more than once or that will have companion items of a similar size and nature, make sure you apply effects the same way to all of them. You wouldn't want a shadow coming from the left on one button and coming from the right on another if both buttons are on the same page, because the inferred light source should be the same over the entire page. Consistency helps build a polished look for your Web page, and if you're designing someone else's Web page, consistency shows that person you're detail-oriented and reliable.

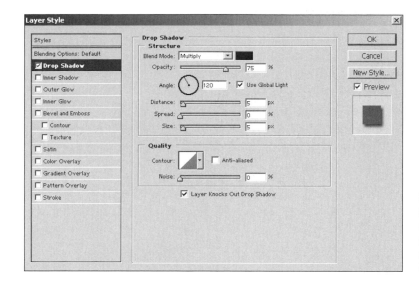

Figure 3.26
Customize the effects applied to your layer, right down to the exact angle that the drop shadow is cast beneath your layer content.

To apply effects to any layer, simply double-click the layer within the Layers palette (see Figure 3.27) to open the Layer Style dialog box. This box features a list of effects on the left and room to display the selected effect's options in the middle. As you click in the checkboxes to turn on one or more of the effects, the options for the effects appear. These options enable you to customize the depth and angle of drop shadows, the shape and depth of embossed or beveled edges, and the color and brightness of an inner or outer glow. You can apply a pattern or gradient overlay or apply a solid color to the entire layer or its selected content.

You can create your own styles for future use by applying one or more effects and customizing them to meet your needs. Then, click the New Style button and give your new style a name (see Figure 3.28). To apply the new style, click the Styles button at the top of the Layer Style dialog box to display the installed styles along with the one you've created.

Saving Your Artwork

Once you've created your work of art, you need to save it. Well, actually, you should have been saving it all along during the creation process—just a few seconds after starting it, and at every significant milestone along the way. Not saving until the image is complete is simply inviting disaster. Imagine spending hours working on a graphic and not having saved it before the power goes out or your computer crashes. Hours of work would go down the drain, with nothing, not even a graphic that's partially complete (as of your last save) to show for it.

As you work, you should save in PSD format, the default format for images created in Photoshop. The first time you save your image, the Save As dialog

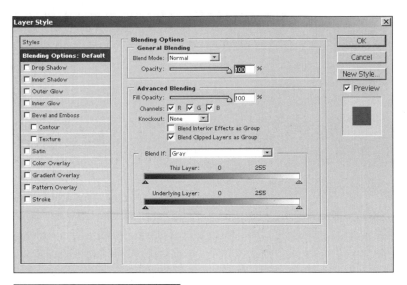

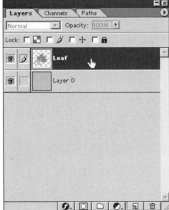

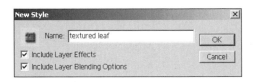

box assumes you're saving in PSD format, and if your image has multiple layers, that's the only format in which you can save the image if you chose File|Save or pressed Ctrl+S (see Figure 3.29). Even if your image is bound for use on the Web, don't skip the process of saving in the PSD format. If you don't make the mistake of failing to keep an up-to-date version of a graphic in PSD format, you can edit that image later and take full advantage of all of Photoshop's tools.

Saving a PSD File to Preserve Layers

So what's so important about saving a file in PSD format, even if you'll be using the graphic on the Web and intend to save it in GIF, JPEG, or PNG format anyway? Of course, you can always paint over parts of a GIF, JPEG, or PNG file

Figure 3.29
A multilayered image created in Photoshop should be saved in PSD format so that you can go back and work with it later.

opened in Photoshop, and you can use the selection tools to select parts of the image for deletion and editing. So why preserve the original PSD version? One word: layers.

Imagine a graphic with three layers—a white background, a layer that's a textured shape filled with a solid color, one that contains a photograph, or maybe some text. As shown in Figure 3.30, these individual components are more easily edited in their layer form than if they're combined into one flat image in any other format. If you want to edit the text or swap one photo for another, it will be much easier if the content you want to change or get rid of is on its own layer. Any edits to that content affect only that layer, and everything else is left intact.

You won't just need to edit graphics because of changes in design or errors during the creation process. In Figure 3.31, the graphic buttons on the Web page depicted in the figure are all very similar; some of them have different button colors, and all have different text. They're all based on one original PSD file, which is easily edited. This file serves as the foundation for several different Web-format files. To change "Contact Us" to "View Shopping Cart," all you have to do is open the original version of the graphic, edit the text layer, change the button color (as desired), and save the file with a new name in a Web-safe format. The original file remains intact for the next required variation.

Saving Files for the Web

Once you've saved your file in PSD format and are satisfied that the image is complete and ready for use on the Web, it's time to save it in a Web-safe format. Currently, your choices are GIF, JPEG, and PNG. In the future, other formats

Figure 3.30

(Right) Keep your layers separate in the PSD version of your graphic so you can go back and make changes easily later.

Figure 3.31

(Below) Create one graphic that can serve as the basis for many other similar graphics on your Web page. Use the PSD version to create the new graphics based on the original.

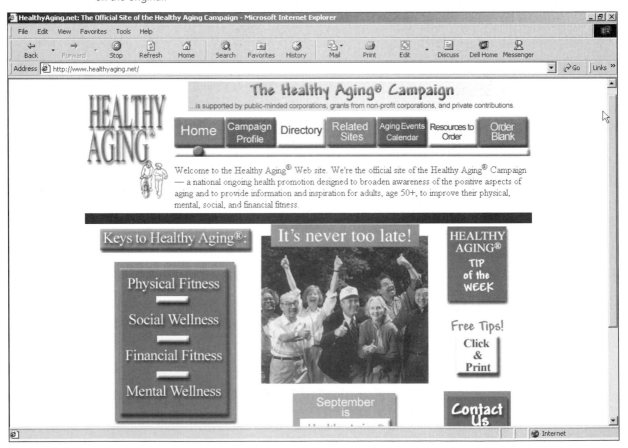

may be sanctioned and supported by the major Web browser applications, but currently, these three are the only reliable games in town. GIF and JPEG are the most frequently used.

To save a file for use on the Web, simply use Photoshop's File|Save For Web command. The Save For Web dialog box opens (see Figure 3.32). Here you can choose the file format you want to use, and make any appropriate adjustments to the file quality and color depth. You can also apply effects, such as transparency (for GIF files), or you might choose to make your GIF file Interlaced or your JPEG Progressive. These two options, as you may recall from Chapter 1, allow your image to load immediately when a page is accessed and clear up as the page continues to load. This is often preferable to the image not appearing at all until it has completely loaded in the browser window.

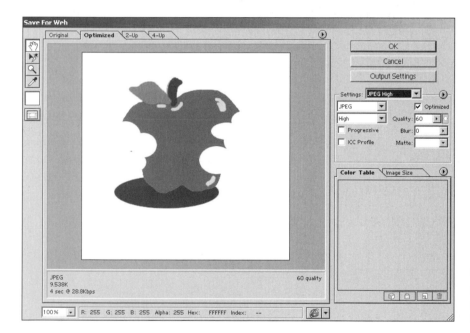

Figure 3.32
Check your image size and estimated load time, and make adjustments accordingly.

Saving a GIF Image

The GIF format is best applied to simple images—shapes and lines with no photographic content. For images with just a handful of colors and no delicate or complex shading or special effects applied, GIF is a good choice. The GIF format creates small file sizes, which translates to quick upload times, and that's essential for graphics intended for the Web.

To save your image in GIF format, click the Settings drop-down list (see Figure 3.33) to choose one of the GIF format choices. You can choose from seven different variations on the GIF format, each designed for images of varying color complexity. GIF 64 supports 64 different colors, which is fine for a very simple image, and GIF 256 supports 256 colors, more than enough

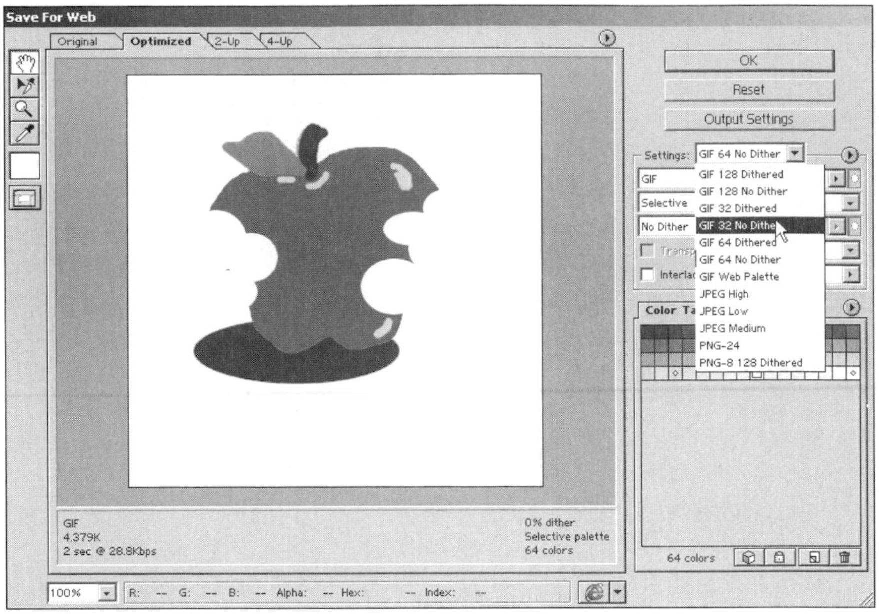

Figure 3.33

Pick a GIF format that meets the color needs of your image.

for the complete Web-safe palette. The Dither and No Dither variations of each color depth allow you to choose how colors not supported by the color table for the GIF format you've chosen are substituted or filled in. For example, if you choose to save the file in GIF 64 Dither format, if you have a color in the image that's outside the 64-color table, the Dither setting will allow the mixing of colors from the table to create the missing color. If you choose the No Dither variation, a single color will be substituted for the missing shade. This can result in clumsy-looking shading between adjacent colors, so carefully inspect the Optimized view of the image before committing to this option.

Once you've chosen a setting, you can tweak it to meet the special needs of your image. If, for example, you've selected GIF 128 Dither, you can adjust the amount of dithering by increasing or decreasing the Dither percentage option. You can enable the Interlaced option, and you can adjust the amount of image clarity lost to compression by changing the Lossy level for the image (see Figure 3.34).

As you make changes to the GIF format's option settings, you'll notice that the size of the file (and therefore the load-time estimate) changes in some cases. (These statistics appear in the lower-left corner of the dialog box, as shown in Figure 3.35.) The GIF format you select will affect these two statistics, and then whatever changes (if any) that you make will affect it further. Of course, if the changes you're making will result in a better-looking image, they're probably useful, but be careful that adjustments don't nudge your image into dangerous territory—images that are larger than 30K and that take more than 10 seconds to load. We live in a busy world, and people have lower and lower thresholds for what they consider an acceptable time to wait for images to load.

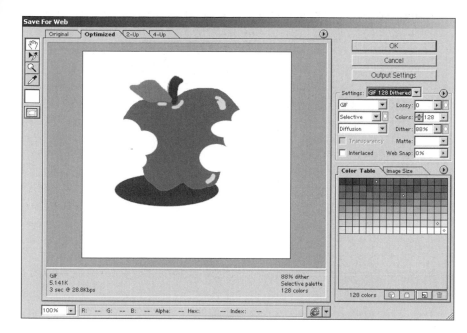

Figure 3.34
Customize the GIF format you've selected.

Figure 3.35
Keep an eye on your image size and load times. A fast load can be more useful than an absolutely perfect rendering of your image.

As soon as you're satisfied with the image quality as seen in the Optimized tab and you're happy with the file size and load-time statistics, click the OK button to continue saving the image for the Web. In the resulting Save Optimized As dialog box (see Figure 3.36), give the file a name and choose where to store it. As soon as you click Save in this dialog box, the Web-safe image is ready for uploading to the Web.

When you choose a place to store the file, consider saving it to the folder that contains the images that will be uploaded to your Web server when you're ready to post or update your pages. By saving to that folder now, you avoid having to cut or copy the file to it later, and you begin organizing your Web content, one of the first steps in the planning of any site design, redesign, or update.

Saving a JPEG File

The JPG Setting option in the Save For Web dialog box comes in three quality levels: Low, Medium, and High. Once you pick one, click the drop-down list below the format drop-down list (see Figure 3.37) and note that Maximum is available as well. The difference in file size and load time can vary as much as 100 percent between JPEG quality levels, so be careful that you don't choose

Adaptive? Perceptual? Huh?

Set to Selective by default, the color reduction setting allows you to choose how colors will be displayed and interpreted in the image, and how the color table will be created. The browser to display the image as accurately as possible uses the color table, saved as part of the image file. Your choices include the following:

- Perceptual—Creates a custom color table, favoring colors to which the human eye is most sensitive.

- Selective—Builds a color table similar to the Perceptual color table and preserves Web colors. A selective color table offers the most color integrity.

- Adaptive—Creates a custom color table based on the range or spectrum of colors found most often within the image.

- Web—Works with the standard 216-color Windows and Mac 256-color palettes. This table, also known as the Web-safe palette, prevents any browser dither if the image is displayed on low-end, older monitors. The table also customizes itself to your image. If your image has fewer colors than the available color depth (say your image has 16 colors and you've chosen the 64-color GIF format), the unused colors are removed from the table.

- Custom—Maintains the current color table and uses it as a fixed, unchanging palette.

- Mac OS—Utilizes the Mac OS 256-color table, including uniform RGB color model colors. As with the Web option, if your image has fewer colors than the number of colors allowed by the selected GIF format, the colors not being used are removed from the table.

- Windows—Uses the default 256-color table, again based on uniform RGB colors. Unused colors are removed from this table format as well.

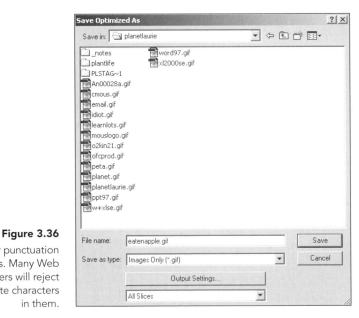

Figure 3.36
Don't use spaces or punctuation in your file names. Many Web servers and browsers will reject files with inappropriate characters in them.

Maximum or High when Medium would look just fine and the resulting image would take half as long to load.

Here are some other points you should consider when saving an image as a JPEG:

- Should the image be Progressive? If you want visitors to know that the image is there and not move on before it loads completely, enable the

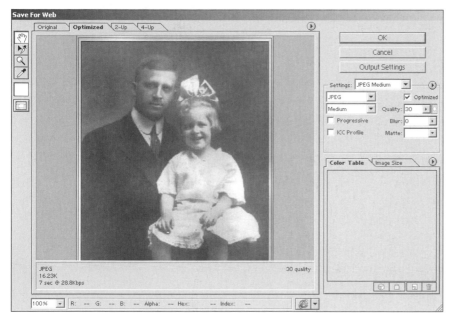

Figure 3.37
Choose the JPEG format at the quality level you think is best for your image, based on the image complexity and the role it plays on the Web page.

Progressive option. The image will appear immediately in a blurry, choppy state. As the image loads, it clears up, and the visitor can read and/or use it as intended.

- What color matte do you want to apply? When the JPEG file is placed on a Web page with a background that matches the matte color, the image appears to blend with the Web page background. This is very handy if the image has a transparent background or layers within it set to a low-opacity level.

- Adjusting the Blur option can help a lower quality image blend in with its surroundings and avoid choppy edges on curves. Increase the blur if you want to avoid the choppy edge, but don't blur it so much that it looks fuzzy to the eye.

- The ICC profile is based on color management conventions developed by the International Color Consortium (ICC). If you want your image to adhere to these conventions, turn this option on. The benefit? The ICC profile dictates how color numbers are mapped when interpreted by a scanner, printer, or monitor. By applying a color profile, you make sure colors are displayed accurately.

Remember that the JPEG format is best for photographs and complex images with lots of color, because the JPEG format supports millions of colors. A JPEG file tends to be larger than the GIF versions of the same image, so don't use the JPEG format unless the image requires it. If you find that choosing High or Maximum quality is creating too large a file, use the Quality slider to lower the quality at that setting. Sometimes you can shave as much as 50 percent of the load time by going from High at 80% quality to just 70%.

Quantity vs. Quality

If your image contains information—text, a map, a flowchart with instructions, anything that needs to be clear and legible—don't risk that the detail will be lost to a low-level JPEG setting. Although a fast load is important for site visitor satisfaction, if people can't read the instructions or make out the name of a road on your map, what have you gained by making an illegible graphic load faster? The role your image plays on the page is an important consideration when determining the quality of the image.

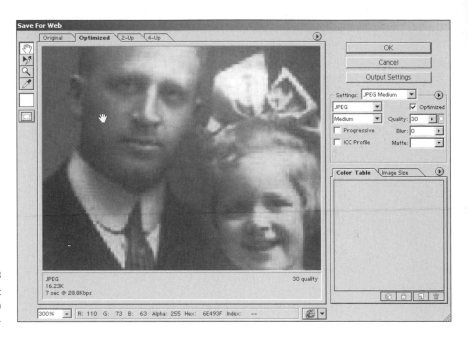

Figure 3.38
Zoom in tight to check the effect your format settings have had on the quality of your image.

PNG with Care

In order to make your pages viewable by the largest possible audience, you want to avoid using a format that's not supported by the two main browsers (Microsoft's Internet Explorer and Netscape's Navigator) in many of their versions. If you're not absolutely certain—and rarely can you be—that all of your site's visitors will be using version 5.0 and later of either or both browsers, it's best to avoid using the PNG format for your graphics files. Of the two PNG formats, PNG 24 is more widely supported, however, so if your heart's set on PNG, use that variant rather than the 8-bit.

At this point, make sure you're happy with the way the image looks. (Don't forget you can use the Zoom tool on the small toolbar in the upper-left corner of the dialog box, as shown in Figure 3.38.) If you're satisfied, go ahead and click the OK button to continue the process by naming and storing your file using the Save Optimized As dialog box.

Saving in the PNG Format

The PNG format is the most recent addition to the rather short list of Web-safe graphics file formats. If you want to save your graphic using Photoshop's Save For Web command, your two PNG choices are PNG 8 and PNG 24—the numbers referring to 8-bit color and 24-bit color, respectively. PNG 8 is quite similar to GIF in terms of the way color is handled, and it is best used for crisp, clean images such as line art, simple drawings, and graphics with text. PNG 24 supports more colors, so it is more of a parallel to JPEG, although the same image saved in PNG 24 format will be larger than it would be in JPEG format.

When you choose either PNG 8 or PNG 24 as the format for your new Web-bound graphic, the Settings options change considerably. As shown in Figures 3.39 and 3.40, when you choose the 24-bit PNG format, your only options are to supply a matte color and to make the image transparent (which means that all but the actual image content can be made transparent, allowing the page background to show through). You can also set the file to Interlaced so that the graphic composes slowly rather than not appearing on the page at all until it is completely loaded by the browser.

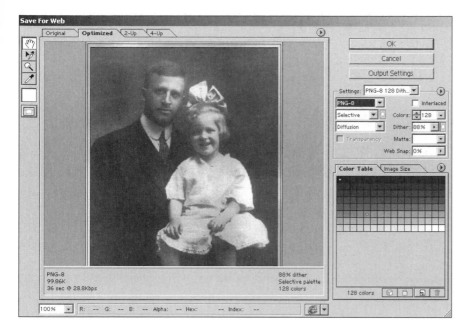

Figure 3.39
PNG 8 format's options are very similar those offered for GIF format files, yet another similarity between these two formats.

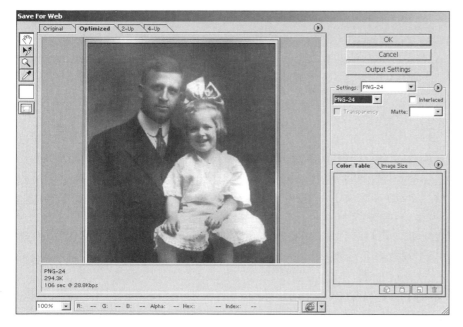

Figure 3.40
PNG 24's closest match would be JPEG, and very little tweaking is required when you choose this format.

Create and Save a JPEG Image
Open the File

Open the tree.psd file, found in the Chapter 3 folder on the accompanying CD-ROM.

Select and Copy the Tree

Using the Lasso tool, draw a rectangle around the tree in the image. You can achieve an interesting effect if you set the Lasso to 10 pixel feathering, as

Figure 3.41
The final logo now includes a
photograph of a tree.

shown in Figure 3.41. The tree will appear to have a glow around it. You can also use the Marquee tool as long as you draw the rectangle very close to the tree and get as little background as possible.

Copy the selected area to the Clipboard by choosing Edit|Copy.

Paste the Tree Into "mylogo.psd"

Open the mylogo.psd file (in the event that you didn't create the image in the first project in this chapter, open a file called laurielogo.psd), which can be found in the Chapter 3 folder on the accompanying CD-ROM.

Choose Edit|Paste. The tree appears on the logo image, in its own layer.

Position the Tree Layer

Move the tree layer so that the tree appears as shown in Figure 3.41.

Save the File

Save the file as a JPEG at High quality. The file name can stay the same—Photoshop will apply the .jpg extension automatically.

Moving On

Now that you've created your own artwork, you can edit those images or edit existing images—photographs you've scanned or clip-art images you want to customize for your own use. The next chapter will introduce you to Photoshop's considerable range of tools for retouching any sort of image. You'll learn how to use filters, actions, and other interesting special effects.

Chapter 4

Retouching Images for Use on the Web

Whether it's a graphic you created in Photoshop, a picture drawn with an illustration program, or a photograph or drawing you scanned, Photoshop offers a variety of tools for improving your Web-bound images. In this chapter, you'll learn techniques for using those tools to your advantage.

Scanning Images in Photoshop

If a scanner is connected to your computer (and was connected at the time Photoshop was installed), you can access it through the File menu by choosing Import|Twain. If you have more than one scanning device attached to your computer, choose Import|Select Twain Device first, and then choose Import|Twain after you've designated which scanner you intend to use in the current scanning session.

Scanning software is often included with your scanner, or perhaps you've found imaging software you prefer. As soon as you issue the File|Import|Twain command, the software you set as the default for your scanner will open. Figure 4.1 shows a Visioneer PaperPort window, through which typical scanning procedures can be performed.

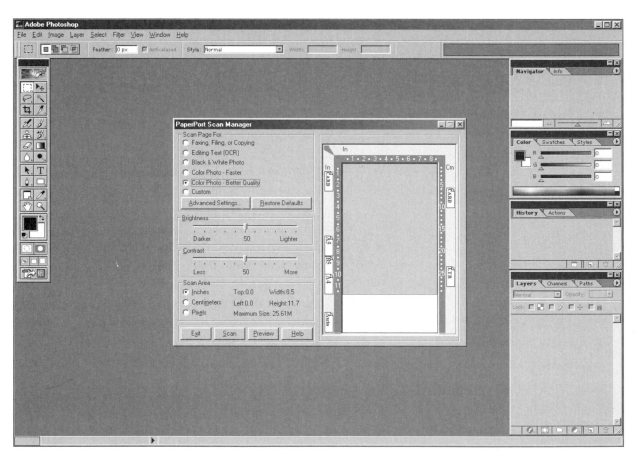

Figure 4.1

Turn printed photographs and drawings into a Photoshop file that you can edit and save for the Web.

With any scanning application, you must follow some basic procedures:

1. Select the type of scan you want to perform—a color scan, black and white, or grayscale.

2. Customize the way that scans will take place by adjusting the scan settings, as shown in Figure 4.2.

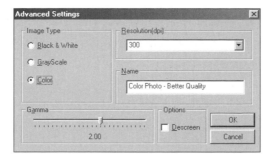

Figure 4.2

Scan at a high resolution so that you get as much detail as possible. This gives you more to work with as you edit and retouch the image.

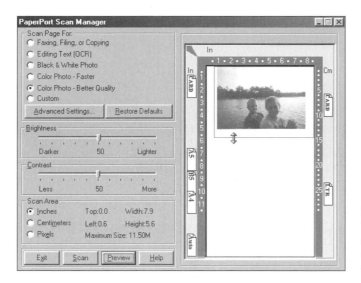

Figure 4.3

This array of photographs can be scanned as is, or you can focus the scan on just one of the pictures.

3. Preview the image. This makes the scanner take a look at what's on the glass plate and show it to you (see Figure 4.3).

4. Adjust the scanning area by moving and resizing the box surrounding the preview. Your mouse will be a four-headed arrow when you're moving the box and a two-headed one when you're resizing it. The key is to reduce the scanning area to just the parts of the image you want to scan. There's no sense scanning a white background around something or scanning an entire sheet of paper if you only want an image in the upper-right corner.

After you've set up your scan and done a preview, click the Scan button. A progress bar (see Figure 4.4) will help you keep track of the speed of the scan. Bear in mind that scanning at high dots per inch (dpi) will take a lot longer than scanning at a low dpi, and color takes longer than black and white or grayscale. When the scan is complete, the image will appear in a new file window within the Photoshop workspace, as shown in Figure 4.5.

As soon as the file window appears, you can begin retouching and editing the image. Don't reduce the pixels per inch (ppi) until you've done all your retouching—you'll have more information to work with when you move and

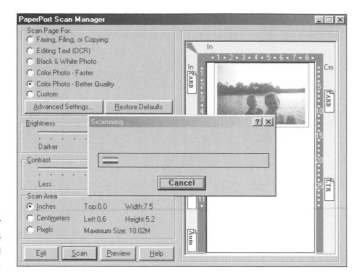

Figure 4.4

The scanning process takes more time if you're scanning at a 300 dpi.

Figure 4.5

Voila! A scanned image quickly becomes a Photoshop file, "Untitled" until you save and name it.

manipulate the image content. After the image looks the way you want it to, reduce the pixel size and then issue the File|Save For Web command to convert your image to a Web-safe format and to find the right file type and setting for quick loading online.

Rasterize?

Adobe Illustrator images are vector images, consisting of mathematical information about the shapes and lines that make up the image itself. If you want to use Photoshop to edit these images, they must be rasterized, a process that turns the vector-based mathematical information into a collection of pixels. Each pixel of the rasterized image contains color information, and that information is what you're editing as you work on the image in Photoshop. The color from one pixel is applied to another, all the pixels of a particular color are selected for deletion or copying, or a collection of pixels are added, moved, or changed to a different color.

Opening and Editing Illustrator Images

Adobe Illustrator's native file format (AI) is easily opened from within Photoshop. Simply choose File|Open, and from the Files Of Type list, select Generic EPS, which includes AI files. This change will enable Photoshop to see your Illustrator files within the drive and folder where you have them stored. After you select the specific image you want to open, click OK to open it, and the Rasterize Generic PDF Format dialog box will appear, as shown in Figure 4.6. You can change the color model (CMYK is the default in Illustrator, and you'll want to switch to RGB for a Web-bound graphic edited in Photoshop). You can also adjust the Resolution setting. Click OK to rasterize the image, and the image will open in its own file window in the Photoshop workspace.

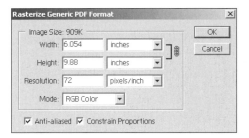

Figure 4.6
Adobe Illustrator images must be changed for use in Photoshop using the Rasterize Generic PDF Format dialog box.

The rasterizing process takes time. You'll see a progress bar at the bottom of the Photoshop window as this process occurs. The larger the AI file, the longer the rasterizing process takes. Once it's complete, the image opens in its own window in the Photoshop workspace, still in AI format (see Figure 4.7). When you choose File|Save or File|Save As for the first time, the default format for the new version of the file is PSD. Although you can save the file in a variety of formats—TIF, PCX, BMP—you should save it in Photoshop format and keep a version of it in that format as you prepare the image for the Save For Web process, the last step in creating a Web graphic.

Importing Vector Graphics

In addition to choosing Illustrator's AI format, you can open a variety of vector-format files in Photoshop, as shown in Figure 4.8. Virtually every graphics file format, both vector and bitmap, is represented in the Files Of Type list in

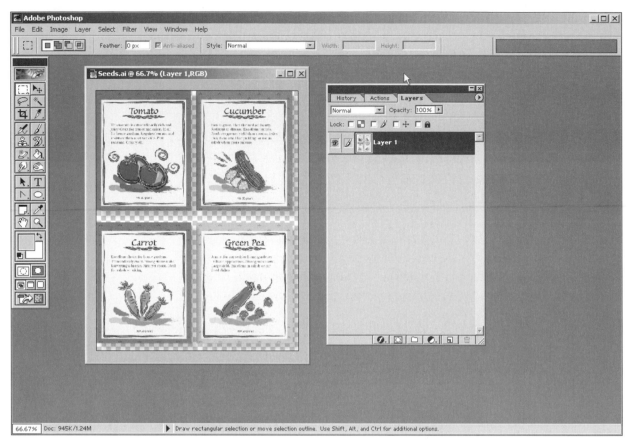

Figure 4.7

The rasterized file retains the .ai extension, and you can still open the file in Illustrator if you want to work on it there.

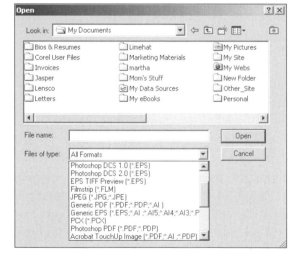

Figure 4.8

Pick a format, any format, including just about any vector-based format.

the Open dialog box. The default is All Formats, which means that a file in any of the represented formats will show in the Open dialog box when you go to the drive and folder containing the desired file.

When you choose any vector-based file and open it, a Rasterize dialog box opens. As long as your next step after the file opens is to save it in PSD format, your original vector-format file will be preserved. You can always continue to work on the file in its native illustration program, perhaps in preparation for using it in a printed document or on-screen (but non-Web) presentation.

Working with Masks and Selections

So you have an image, one you created from scratch in Photoshop, or an image you imported from another application. You're working on it in Photoshop because it needs something—you need to add, move, or delete an element, or perhaps just introduce something to make it more compelling or prettier. Whatever the image needs, you can make the change within Photoshop, and the keys to controlling the effects of the edits are *masks* and *selections*.

Masks are areas of the image that are cordoned off, made separate from their surroundings, so that whatever you do to the image doesn't apply to the masked area. Using masks in Photoshop is similar to using masking tape around a window when you paint the woodwork; you can paint around the window much faster if you aren't worried about absolute accuracy as you paint around the individual frames, because the tape is preventing paint from getting on the glass. So it is in Photoshop. If you want to paint around the edges of an image or apply an effect (brightening or darkening an area, for example), you can mask off the areas that should not be affected, and then you can use broad, fast strokes with your mouse to apply the effect to the desired area.

Unlike when you apply masking tape to a window, you use masks and selections to select the area that will be affected so that everything else won't be. For example, look at Figure 4.9. If you want to brighten the face in this picture,

Figure 4.9
Select the specific area you want to work with and the rest of the image is protected.

you select the face before using the Dodge tool. You can then use a large brush size to quickly apply the Dodge effect to the selected face in one pass, and you don't have to worry about accidentally brightening the surrounding content.

Masks can be created in one of two ways: by using the selection tools (Marquee, Lasso, Magic Wand) or by switching to Quick Mask mode and using a tool typically used for drawing, such as the Paintbrush, to mask off areas to be excluded from any changes. Figure 4.10 shows an area selected while in Quick Mask mode. The Paintbrush, using a size 13 brush, was used to create the selection. To remove a mask, switch back to Standard Editing mode and press Ctrl+D or choose Select|Deselect.

Click here to enter
Quick Mask mode

This area cannot be edited,
thanks to the mask

Figure 4.10

Draw or paint over the area
to be masked.

Once you've applied the mask, you can do whatever you want to the image—paint it, apply a fill (solid, pattern, gradient), move or delete the selection, or improve the area with the Dodge, Burn, or Sponge tools. Photoshop also offers a variety of filters, each one designed to achieve an interesting visual effect for your image or an area you designate through a mask.

Applying Filters

Filters are effects that change an image or a section of the image. Filters can have subtle effects, such as sharpening or blurring the content, or they can have drastic effects, turning a crisp, clean photograph into what looks like an abstract mosaic or watercolor painting. Here are some rules to keep in mind when you're applying filters:

- The last filter you used (in the Filter menu) will move to the top of that menu, making it easy to repeat the filter's effect.

- Repeating a filter will heighten its effect. If you mean to start over and apply the filter with different settings or to a different area of the image, undo the filter's application and literally start over.

- You cannot use the File|Revert command on an unsaved file. Before you start tinkering with filters, save your file so you have a good foundation to which you can return with the Revert command.

- Apply the filter to a small area of the image first, or perhaps to a test image. Save your image using the File|Save As command, and append the word "test" to the file name (before the extension) so that you can tinker with the image and experiment with filters without any fear of permanently damaging your image or having to navigate back with the History palette to undo the filters you've applied.

- If a particular filter doesn't work, it might be one that isn't appropriate for the file type you're working on. Some filters work only on RGB images, and others can't be applied to bitmap files or images with indexed colors in them.

- The filter you select will apply only to the active layer. If part of the active layer is selected (using a selection tool or through Quick Mask mode), the filter will apply to that area only.

Each filter has its own unique settings that allow you to dictate how the filter will be applied and the effect it will have. The settings generally affect the intensity of the filter's result, as shown in Figure 4.11. After you've specified your settings, you can see what the filter will do right inside the dialog box. If you don't like what you see there, don't click OK to apply the filter!

The exceptions to the rule that every filter can be controlled through settings in a filter dialog box are few, but they're there. Luckily, they're also easily spotted. When you select one of the filter submenus, such as Filter|Render, note that the Clouds and Difference Clouds filters don't have an ellipsis (...) after them in the submenu (see Figure 4.12). This means that if you choose those filters, no dialog box will appear, which means the filter will apply in a preset, unchangeable manner. Use these filters with care, and be sure to have a small section of the image selected so that the filter applies only to a small area. No preview is available to help you decide whether to apply the filter.

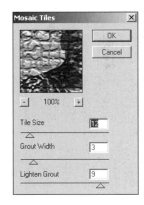

Figure 4.11
Apply filters with care, and take advantage of the preview provided in the filter's dialog box.

Figure 4.12

An ellipsis indicates a dialog box
will open to help you control the
effect of the selected filter.

Once you apply a filter, its effects become part of the image. You can edit those effects by using any of Photoshop's tools. For example, you can paint over them, smudge them, brighten them, darken them, or even clone them and apply them elsewhere in the image. Figure 4.13 shows the Artistic Watercolor filter applied to a key area of the picture. By testing the filter here, where there is the greatest amount of detail (the person's face and clothing), you can determine whether the filter will work overall in the image. If you do like the results in a section, go ahead and use the filter in other areas. Be careful to apply the same settings (where possible) so that the look you liked is the look you get the next time. If you use the first command in the Filter menu (which changes to the last filter you used), Photoshop will apply the filter in the same way.

Figure 4.13

Turn a photo into a painting
for an interesting effect on your
Web page.

Adjusting Brightness and Contrast

The most commonly adjusted aspects of any photographic image are the brightness and the contrast. Overexposed pictures, images with insufficient light, a lack of definition between dark and light areas—these are the problems you'll find in many photos, as shown in Figure 4.14. When you scan the photos, you often end up intensifying these negative aspects, especially if you scan at a low resolution or use a lower quality scanner. Fear not, however, because Photoshop makes it easy to take a picture that's too dark, too light, or just not well lit and turn it into a photograph that's worthy of your well-designed Web page.

There are two convenient ways to adjust the brightness of your image: You can use the Dodge tool to lighten or the Burn tool to darken, or you can use the Brightness/Contrast dialog box (to open this dialog box, choose

Figure 4.14
These two boys' faces are nearly unrecognizable—the sun was behind them, and the camera's flash didn't compensate.

Image|Adjust|Brightness/Contrast). The first method allows you to "paint" the light (Dodge) or dark (Burn) effect onto the image. You can use a large brush to apply the effect to the whole image or to a section, or you can use a tiny brush to apply the effect to small areas. The Brightness/Contrast dialog box allows you to set specific levels of brightness and contrast, and you can preview their effects on the entire layer or for a selected portion of it.

Using the Dodge and Burn Tools

As we mentioned, the Dodge tool (see Figure 4.15) enables you to lighten an image. You can select the brush size and the amount of light (using the Exposure setting on the options bar), and you can choose which aspects of the image to lighten—the shadows, midtones, or highlights.

Figure 4.15
Brighten the highlights or make the shadows less shadowy by using the Dodge tool.

The Burn tool does just the opposite of the Dodge tool—instead of brightening an image, it darkens the image, or at least the parts you select. The Burn tool's options are the same, however. You can choose how the darkening will be applied—intensely or subtly—or to only the highlights, midtones, or shadows. You can also specify how big the brush strokes will be as you apply the effect. When it comes to images on the Web, darker images are easier on visitors' eyes (less glare). Be careful that detail isn't lost when you darken an image or a portion of it. Figure 4.16 shows how the Burn tool can be used to darken the edges of an image and make it appear as though the image is emerging from a dark fog.

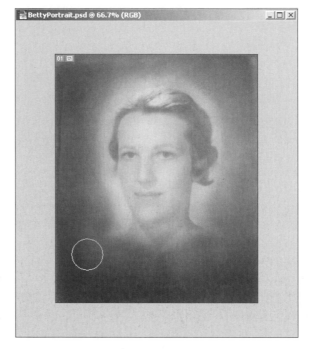

Figure 4.16
Darken the edges of your image so they'll blend in more effectively with a dark background on your Web page.

Using the Brightness/Contrast Dialog Box

You open this dialog box by choosing Image|Adjust|Brightness/Contrast. As shown in Figure 4.17, you can drag the sliders to the left to decrease the Brightness or Contrast effect or to the right to increase it. Be sure the Preview box remains checked so that you can see the effects of your adjustments without actually applying them. The change is reflected on the image itself, but until you click OK, the change won't become permanent.

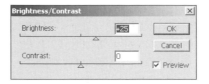

Figure 4.17
Adjust the Brightness and/or Contrast setting for an entire layer or a selection within a layer.

Editing Photographic Content

Imagine a photo of your company fleet of vehicles that includes a car that was recently damaged in a car accident, and/or that's in need of a wash. You don't want that car in the picture, but you like the picture otherwise and want to use it on a Web page. What can you do? You can remove the unwanted vehicle, replacing it with other content—trees or a brick wall if the picture was taken outdoors, or another undamaged/clean car from the lot, copied and put in place of the damaged one. You can get rid of a Dumpster or trash can in a picture of your new warehouse by pasting green grass from another area of the image onto the unwanted container, or duplicate the flowers and shrubbery from one section of an image and position the copies elsewhere in the image to expand the appearance of your garden. Figure 4.18 shows two images side by side—the left image is the "before" version, and the right image is the "after" version. In the "after" version, you can see how content from other areas of the image has been added to cover undesirable content.

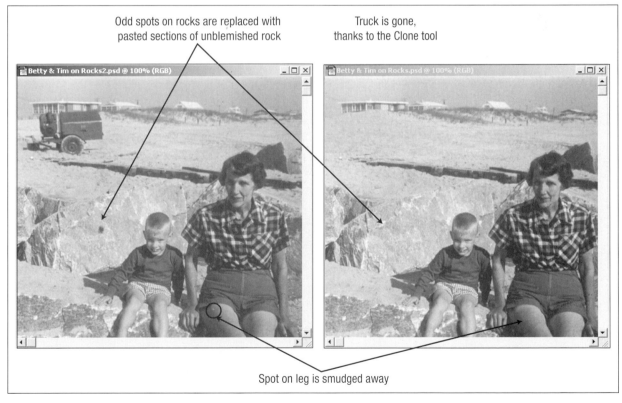

Odd spots on rocks are replaced with pasted sections of unblemished rock

Truck is gone, thanks to the Clone tool

Spot on leg is smudged away

Figure 4.18

Like sweeping dirt under a rug, pasting good content over bad is a quick and effective way to improve the overall appearance of an image.

If your image content is fine but needs some cleaning up to remove dirt, scratches, and creases from the original scanned picture, you can paint them out, smudge them away, or paste content from a clean area over them, as shown in Figure 4.19. Your options for removing, adding, and cleaning any portion of your image is virtually unlimited.

Removing Unwanted Content

It's fairly simple to get rid of things you don't want to include in your image. In the case of Photoshop (PSD) files, you need to make sure the layer containing the unwanted content is active, and then use the Eraser or a selection tool (Marquee or Lasso) to select the unwanted region. In the latter case, you'll have to use the Delete key on your keyboard to complete the removal process, deleting the content within the selection on the active layer.

Using and Controlling the Eraser

The Eraser, in its default form, erases everything in its path on the active layer as you drag it with your mouse. You can change its mode, setting it to a fuzzy-edged Airbrush, a clean-edged Paintbrush, a fine Pencil, or a Block. You can also change its Pressure setting so that you can erase lightly (50% or lower pressure), leaving much of the content behind, or erase heavily (51% or higher pressure) to erase most or all of whatever's in the path of your mouse. Figure 4.20 shows the results of both light and heavy eraser pressure in a photograph. The heavy pressure removed much of the image perimeter, and the light pressure faded some of the image out to near invisibility.

You can also use the Background Eraser, which erases just what you'd imagine—the image background layer. If you've merged all of your layers into one, or if you're working with a JPEG or GIF image that consists solely of a background layer, erasing with this tool will erase everything you drag over with your mouse.

Deleting Selected Content

If you want to remove selected areas of an image, use the Marquee tool to draw a box, oval, or thin strip and then press Delete to remove everything within the selected area. To select a freeform or polygonal area, use the Lasso tool, as shown in Figure 4.21. Of course, you'll only delete what's on the active

Poof! It's a Magic Eraser

Get rid of colors that don't match your Web page color scheme by using the Magic Eraser. Set the Tolerance and Opacity settings for the Eraser, and then click on areas of color that you want to eliminate from the image.

This corner was erased at 100% pressure with a size 19 brush

This area was erased at 20% pressure with a size 100 brush

Figure 4.20
Dim parts of the image with a light eraser touch, and eradicate other things with the Eraser set to 100% pressure.

layer, so if you want to remove everything in a particular area, merge the layers that have content in that area, and then delete what you don't want.

Cleaning Up a Photograph

As shown in Figure 4.22, scanned images can show a lot of wear and tear—the abuse that the original printed image endured through years in desk drawers, on the pages of a photo album, or languishing in an envelope awaiting use on your Web page. People touching and bending photographs, scraping them face down across a tabletop, writing on the back of the pictures—all of this results in images that need a lot of cleanup before they're presentable for Web use.

Smudging Spots and Smoothing Edges

If your photograph has some spots on it, or the subject of the photo—a person's face, for example—had some flaws to begin with, you don't have to allow these imperfections on your Web page. By using the Smudge tool, you can literally wipe away a blemish of any kind, as shown in Figure 4.23. Set the tool's brush size to a small setting (3 or 5) and then just blend surrounding colors onto the unwanted mark.

Figure 4.21
Carefully select a face, a tree, a piece of furniture—anything that you want to get rid of. You can paste other content over it later.

Other useful settings for the Smudge tool include the following:

- Adjust the Pressure setting to control how much of the surrounding color you drag onto the unwanted mark. If you use too much pressure, you could end up with a mark that's lighter than the surrounding area; with too little, some of the blemish might remain. Tinker with different pressures, using Undo after each unsuccessful experiment.

- Use the Finger Painting feature along with the Eye Dropper. Finger Painting smudges the current Foreground color onto the image wherever you

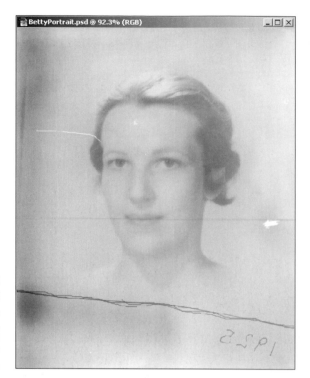

Figure 4.22

The signs of a well-loved old photograph—creases, spots, scratches—can be removed, bringing the electronic version of your image back to near mint condition.

Figure 4.23

Smudge some of the flesh tone onto the spot, and you have a perfect complexion (compare to Figure 4.22).

drag the mouse. Use the Eye Dropper to set the Foreground color to a color found right next to the blemish, and then "finger paint" the mark away with the Smudge tool.

- If you're not sure which layer the blemish is on, simply turn on the Use All Layers option.

Painting Out Errors

In the same way you smudge the Foreground color onto an unwanted spot on the image, you can use the Paintbrush to cover up something you don't want by painting a color from nearby pixels onto the spot. As shown in Figure 4.24, with the Foreground color set to the color of the girl's dress, the Paintbrush can get rid of what was a tiny nick on the surface of the printed photograph.

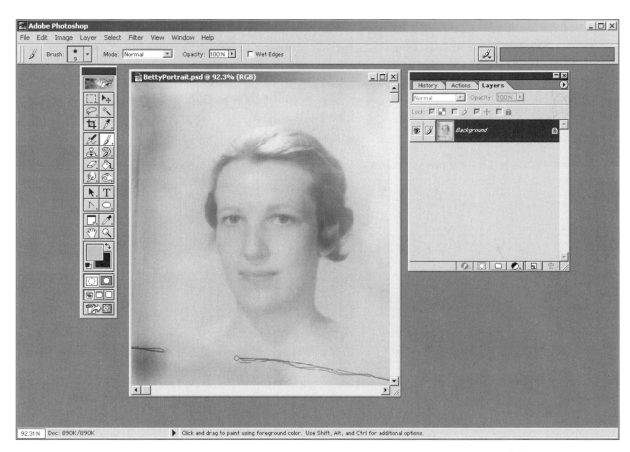

Figure 4.24
Use the Eye Dropper to select a nearby pixel, and then paint that color over the spot.

Cloning the Good Stuff

Need to get rid of a patch of dirt on an otherwise lush green lawn? Clone the grass and place the clones on top of the dirt. Figure 4.25 shows two images, one before and one after cloning the nice green grass onto a muddy patch. Even if your Web page doesn't have any pictures of gardens or anything outdoors, you can imagine a scenario where you wish there was more of one

Figure 4.25

Put your best foot forward by replacing unwanted content with the better parts of the image.

thing than another in the image. Perhaps you design kitchen cabinets and someone left a notepad on the counter in an otherwise great picture of your latest design. Don't reshoot—clone some pristine countertop onto the notepad, and it's gone, as though it was never there in the first place.

The Clone tool works by your sampling an area with the Alt key. Simply press that key and with the Clone tool in use, click on an area of your image that you want to clone to another spot. When you click while holding down the Alt key and then click where you want to deposit the first (and perhaps only) clone, you set the distance between your mouse, which will be applying cloned content, and the portion of your image being cloned.

You can also "paint" with the Clone tool by selecting the cloned content (holding down the Alt key), and then releasing the Alt key and dragging your mouse to apply the cloned content in strips or freeform areas, as shown in Figure 4.26. Be careful not to inadvertently create the appearance of a pattern, though, as this figure also shows. It's a good idea to resample the cloned area so that the area filled in with cloned content doesn't look like a patchwork quilt.

Copying and Pasting

Very similar to using the Clone tool is the process of using the Clipboard to copy sections of the image from their current location and paste them onto other areas of the image. Figure 4.27 shows a family group with two dogs sleeping nearby. One of the dogs is a fake, placed there by copying the real dog and pasting a duplicate.

Figure 4.26
If you're cloning a solid color, you can drag to position cloned content. Avoid this technique if the cloned area is patterned or textured.

Figure 4.27
Wish you had two dogs instead of one? Copy one and paste another!

To copy part of your image, use the Marquee tool to select a geometric shape, or use the Lasso tool to select something more freeform (like the dog in the previous figure). With the area selected, choose Edit|Copy or press Ctrl+C. Then, choose Edit|Paste or press Ctrl+V. Photoshop adds the copied selection on its own layer, and you can use the Move tool to position it where it's needed. Continue to use the Paste command to paste multiple copies of that content, each copy on its own layer. After positioning one or more of the pasted sections, merge the paste-created layers. To merge only the pasted layers, link them by clicking in the empty checkbox on each of the layers created by pasting (a small chain icon will appear in the box) and after all the layers you want to merge are linked, choose Layer|Merge Linked.

Smoothing Out the Rough Spots

If you can see sharp edges on spots where you placed pasted or cloned content, use the Smudge tool set to a light pressure to smooth out the edges. Just drag the Smudge tool along the unwanted edge, and then smudge lightly across the edge to completely blur it.

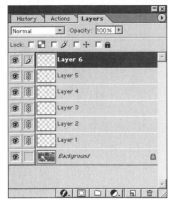

Figure 4.28

To simplify subsequent editing, link the layers created by repeated pasting, and then merge the layers.

Controlling the Image with the Layers Palette

If you built an image layer by layer, you can use the Layers palette to control the image content and appearance. The simple way to do this is to turn layers on and off: Turn off the parts you don't want to see, and leave on those you do want to see. You can also duplicate layers that have content you want more of, and then position the duplicate layers as desired. Here are two other commands you'll find on the Layers menu that can facilitate your plans for editing an image:

- *Flatten Image*—This command takes all the layers in your image, both visible and invisible, and turns them into one layer. You can then duplicate this single layer and remove content and apply filters to the duplicate. By precise positioning of the two layers, you can achieve interesting effects, as shown in Figure 4.29.

Figure 4.29

Two layers that were identical (and therefore redundant) to begin with now work together.

- *Merge Visible*—If you need to merge two or more groups of layers into separate individual layers, hide one group while you issue this command, and then make them visible again while you hide the merged layer. Repeat the command and you have two layers, each consisting of what were separate layers.

Using Actions

A Photoshop action is a series of preset steps that are performed on selected content within your image. Like a macro that you might run in a word processing program that opens a file, formats the text, and inserts page numbers, an action can apply colors, filters, and special styles automatically, eliminating the need for you to apply them individually and manually through toolbox buttons and menu commands. The Actions palette, shown in Figure 4.30, displays the series of steps that come with Photoshop. You can click the triangles next to any one of the actions to see the steps involved.

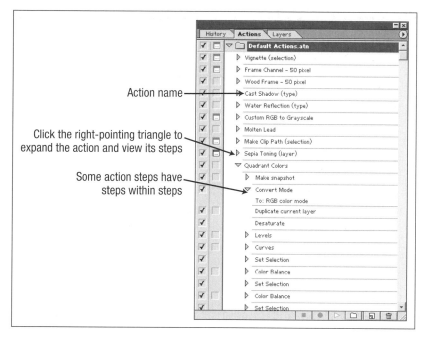

Action name

Click the right-pointing triangle to expand the action and view its steps

Some action steps have steps within steps

Figure 4.30
Action names give you some idea of what they do, but view their steps to see how it's done.

Recording a New Action

You can create your own actions by recording a series of steps, and you can access actions created by other Photoshop users by searching for "Photoshop Actions" on the Web. To build an action of your own, follow these steps:

1. Display the Actions palette and click the New Action button (see Figure 4.31).

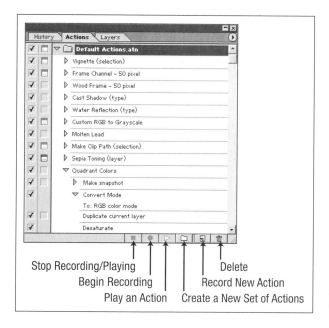

Stop Recording/Playing
Begin Recording
Play an Action
Delete
Record New Action
Create a New Set of Actions

Figure 4.31
Click the Actions tab to display the Actions palette, or choose Window|Show Actions.

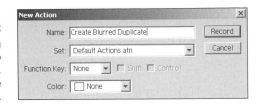

Figure 4.32

For most actions, providing a name is all you need to do before you begin recording. Make sure the name reveals the purpose of the action's steps.

2. In the resulting New Action dialog box (see Figure 4.32), give your action a name and choose a function key if you want to be able to invoke your action via the keyboard.

3. Click the Record button to begin recording your actions.

4. Perform the steps that you want to be performed by your action. Invoke tools in the toolbox and apply different options to them, fill areas with color, apply patterns, apply styles—do anything you would do to an image, in the order that you want the steps taken. As you perform the steps, you'll see them accumulate in the Actions palette.

5. If your action requires user input—such as selecting a color, using a tool that the action has invoked, or making a selection so that the next step is applied to only a part of the image—you can add a pause to the action. Click the Actions palette menu (see Figure 4.33) and choose Insert Stop.

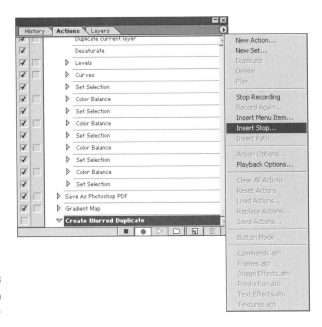

Figure 4.33

Choose Insert Stop to add a pause for the user.

6. In the Record Stop dialog box, enter instructions for the person using the action, such as "Delete everything that should not be blurred." Make sure the Allow Continue option is turned on (see Figure 4.34) so that after the user performs the task indicated in the stop message, the action will proceed when the user clicks the Continue button in the resulting prompt (see Figure 4.35).

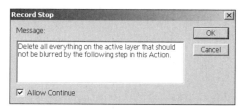

Figure 4.34
Make your instructions clear and concise, especially if other people will be using the action.

Figure 4.35
After the stop occurs during an action's process, if you enabled the Allow Continue option, this prompt appears for the user.

7. When your steps are complete, click the Stop Recording button at the bottom of the Actions palette.

Testing and Troubleshooting Actions

The first thing you should do after recording an action is test it. To do so, select part of your image and click once on the action name in the Actions palette. Click the Play Selection button, and Photoshop will perform the action. If you don't like the results, you can delete the action and re-record. To get rid of an action, simply drag it onto the Delete button on the Actions palette.

Of course, if only a particular step in the action is the problem, you can delete just that step or move it to another point in the action. To remove a step, drag it onto the Delete button at the bottom of the Actions palette. Then, retest the action to make sure the deletion solved the problem. If you think the order of the steps is the culprit, drag the potential offender(s) up and down within the action's steps to rearrange them, testing after each rearrangement. You might also find that your actions require more stops for user intervention than you imagined—if only to use tools you invoke in the action or to make selections that allow users to customize how the action is applied.

To add a stop to an existing action, click on the existing step that should precede the stop, and then click the Actions palette menu button. Choose Insert Stop, enter the directions for the user, and make sure Allow Continue is selected. You can always move the stop to another point in the action if after testing you find that the stop occurs too early or too late.

Storing Actions in Sets

You can create sets and store your actions in them, making it possible to create and group actions that do similar things. Click the Create New Set button at the foot of the Actions palette, and in the resulting dialog box, provide a name for your new set. Click OK to store the name. The next time you record a new action, you'll see the new set listed in the New Action dialog box, within the Set list. To move existing actions to a new set, simply drag your actions by name into the set on the Actions palette, as shown in Figure 4.36.

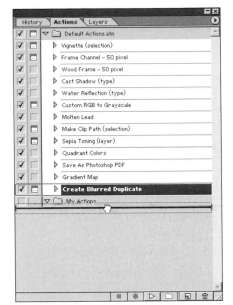

Figure 4.36

Organize your actions—the ones you've created, the ones you've downloaded, and the ones that came with Photoshop—in sets that you create and name to help categorize actions that achieve similar results.

PROJECT Edit a Photograph for Use on the Web

In this project, you will take a vintage photo and clean it up, removing spots and scratches, and then you'll use the Clone tool to edit the image content.

Open the File

On the CD in the Chapter 4 folder, find and open the image named afternoontea.psd, shown in Figure 4.37.

Use the Eye Dropper and Paintbrush to Edit Scratches on the Image

There are several scratches and spots on the image. Use the Eye Dropper to select colors near the unwanted marks, and then paint the marks out with the Paintbrush tool.

Use the Clone Tool to Replace Image Content

To cover a big spot on the grass in the picture, use the Clone tool to apply grass from the unmarred portions of the lawn in the image to the large mark on the far right side of the picture. Use the Smudge tool to eliminate a patchwork or pattern effect you might end up with after cloning the grass.

Duplicate a Portion of the Image

Use the Lasso tool to select the dog, and copy him to the Clipboard. Paste the duplicate dog into the image, and move to another spot on the ground near the table. The choice is yours.

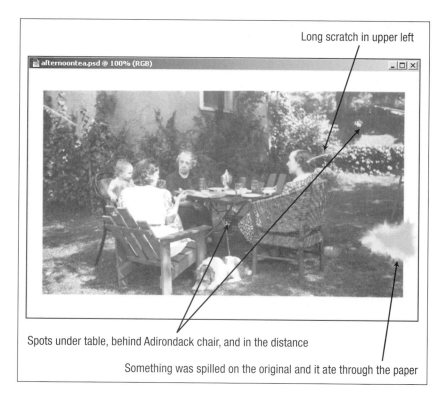

Long scratch in upper left

Spots under table, behind Adirondack chair, and in the distance

Something was spilled on the original and it ate through the paper

Figure 4.37
A picture you might find on a Web site for an outdoor furniture supplier, this image presents a variety of problems.

Merge the Pasted Layer

Using the Merge Visible command, merge the layer created by pasting the dog with the single background layer you started with. When the image repairs are completed (see Figure 4.38), the image should look clean and the additional dog should blend right in and be a believable addition, save the fact that he's sleeping in the same position as the other dog.

Figure 4.38
Vintage photos need not look tattered and old—at least in their electronic versions.

Save the Image in JPEG Format

Save the file as JPG, High Quality. You can keep the file name (afternoontea) and allow Photoshop to apply the .jpg extension automatically.

Moving On

Now that you know how to build, edit, and save images for the Web, you're ready to fine-tune your images to meet specific needs. In the next chapter, you'll learn to match print colors from your existing marketing materials to Web-safe colors and to maintain the effective look and feel of your current marketing pieces in your Web pages and across your site as a whole.

Chapter 5

Matching Print Colors and Style to Web Pages

*Most organizations have printed marketing materials—
business cards, brochures— before they have a Web site.
Because consistent marketing themes and images are most
effective, this chapter shows you how to match the colors,
content, and tone of your printed materials in your
Web page designs.*

Working with the Web Palette

By now, you're aware that the colors you use in a Web page—applied to graphic elements, backgrounds, borders, and simple text—must be found within the Web-safe palette. Photoshop supports Web colors, making it much easier for you to build images that, when viewed online, will display as you designed them.

But what if you already have a considerable visual presence through printed materials, and those materials weren't designed with Web-safe color limitations in mind? Don't worry—most companies' printed materials weren't designed to do anything other than look great in print. Photoshop can be a significant tool in your pursuit of a cohesive set of marketing pieces, even if your Web page is the latest in a series of brochures, color print ads, business cards, and other printed stuff. Through Photoshop, you can find the Web-safe colors that will closely match your printed materials so that you don't have to come up with a new color scheme for your Web site.

Understanding Color Models

Color models help us see colors as the sum or their parts. Let's say your logo consists mainly of a conservative, stately shade of slate blue, but how is that slate blue made? How much green is in that color? How much red? Is there any yellow? Not that you'd stay awake at night pondering these things, but when you use a slate blue color in your Web page (or attempt to), the browser that displays your page will see the color as levels of other colors—a lot of blue, a little bit of green, perhaps some red. Browsers see colors through the RGB (Red, Green, Blue) color model, and Photoshop lets you look at them that way, too. As shown in Figure 5.1, the Color Picker dialog box displays the RGB levels for each color you click on in the palette.

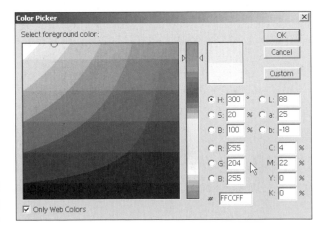

Figure 5.1
View the color ingredients that make up a particular shade.

Finding the Closest Web-Safe Match

So how do you use that information to find a match for the color from your printed materials that you now want to use on your Web site? You simply find the RGB levels of the print color, enter them in the Color Picker, select the option

The Nine Times Rule

In marketing, it is said that customers must see your mailing or ad nine times before they'll respond to it. Of course, there are exceptions—if a potential customer has a need for your services at the very moment he or she sees your marketing materials, a quick response is much more likely. Overall, however, consistency is key to any marketing plan, and to the materials that support it. While your Web site should stand out and not simply act as an electronic version of an existing printed brochure, the look and feel of your site should match your printed materials, and color plays a significant role. If you've selected a specific shade of blue, for example, that appears in all of your printed materials, that shade of blue (or the closest Web-safe match) belongs on your Web page. People respond to consistency, to things they recognize. Let your Web site be one of those things!

Only Web Colors, and the closest match is selected within the palette. You can click OK to select the color as your new Foreground or Background color. You can determine the RGB levels of your print color in one of several ways:

- If you use a professional printing company to produce your marketing materials, call your contacts at that company and ask them what the name or number of the color(s) used in your materials is and if they know the RGB levels.

- Look at a printed color chart that lists the RGB (and perhaps other color model) levels for each color. You can find these charts at many printing and duplication services, as well as in some books and on the web. A color chart of the entire Web-safe palette appears in the Photoshop Studio section of this book.

- Find your color in Photoshop's Custom Colors dialog box (click the Custom button in the Color Picker), and when you've selected the color, view its color levels, as shown in Figure 5.2.

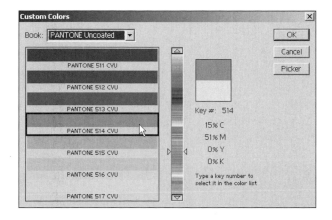

Figure 5.2
Find your custom color and view its color ingredients.

Note that when you view your colors in Photoshop's Custom Colors dialog box, you'll see CMYK levels, not RGB. Why? Because traditionally, the CMYK (Cyan, Magenta, Yellow, and Black) model has been used for print. This isn't a problem, however; the Color Picker displays both RGB and CMYK levels, so you can enter the CMYK levels and find the closest RGB (and Web-safe) match.

Let's take that step-by-step. To find your custom color, of course you need to find the name or number of the color first. As stated previously, that information is probably available from the company that prints your materials. Once you have that name or number in hand, follow these steps:

1. Open the Photoshop Color Picker by clicking the Foreground or Background color tools in the toolbox.

2. Click the Custom button (see Figure 5.3).

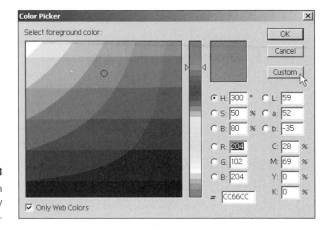

Figure 5.3
Go from a Web-safe palette to a tool for finding just about any print color you can imagine.

3. In the resulting Custom Colors dialog box, click the drop-down arrow to display the Book list, as shown in Figure 5.4. Then, select the color system that contains the color you need.

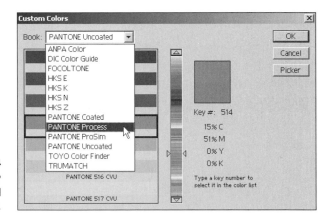

Figure 5.4
Pantone? Focoltone? Trumatch? Pick a color system and then find your specific color.

4. After selecting a color system, find the specific color for which you need RGB-level information. You can scroll through the colors to find it, or if you know the name or number of the color, type it. The list will automatically move to the color and display its levels.

5. Note the CMYK levels and click the Picker button to switch back to the Color Picker dialog box.

6. Back in the Color Picker, note that the CMYK levels you just noted (or numbers very close to them) appear in the Picker's C, M, Y, and K boxes, and a color very similar to the color you want is selected in the palette.

You can now note the RGB levels so that you can use them in other RGB-only color charts or in a Web design application such as Macromedia's Dreamweaver or Adobe's GoLive (where you'll pick solely from a Web-safe palette and see RGB levels for those colors as you design your page). For more information about working in these applications, see Chapter 16.

Building Web Content to Match Printed Materials

Photoshop is not a Web design tool—it's a tool for creating graphic images and retouching images and photographs, many of which end up on the Web these days. Although you can't build a Web page in Photoshop, you can create graphics that mimic the layout of your printed materials, which results in a greater consistency between your printed materials and your Web page.

As shown in Figure 5.5, a list of bullet points found in a brochure is much easier to create graphically in Photoshop. Inserting bullet graphics and text (and having the text look like the text in the brochure) would be a time-consuming process if done directly in a Web page design tool such as GoLive or Dreamweaver (or directly through HTML). Simply placing the graphic created in Photoshop on the page or in a table cell is much easier than creating a whole table construct to house the bullets alongside each line of text.

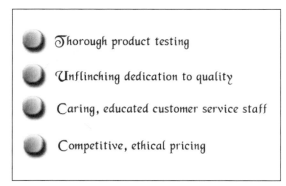

Figure 5.5

If you built this on the Web page, you'd need a table with a column for bullets and a row for each line of bulleted text.

There's another reason to rebuild content from your printed materials in Photoshop rather than retyping text and trying to manipulate page layouts to match printed layouts: Some of the effects are difficult, if not impossible, to achieve on the Web. Referring again to Figure 5.5, the watermark image that appears behind the bulleted text would have to be placed as a table background on the Web page if the bullets and text were applied individually and

---

Yours, Mine, and Ours

The scanner attached to your computer probably came with its own software. However, since you installed the scanner, you've probably found specific scanning software you prefer to use. The figures in this section of the chapter depict the scanning software on my computer, for a Visioneer PaperPort scanner. The basic techniques, as also shown in Chapter 4, are the same in any scanning application. So if yours isn't exactly the same as mine, don't worry—you can apply the basic concepts to whatever software you have.

---

directly to the Web page. This image might not appear in all versions of all browsers. Designing it in Photoshop eliminates that issue altogether; the watermark is part of the graphic, as are the text and bullets, and the entire image works as a unit.

Scanning Printed Materials

When scanning printed materials, always use the best quality originals you can. If the designer of the logo or brochure is available, find out if he or she can provide the electronic versions of any of the artwork (to eliminate much or all of the scanning) and, in the absence of that, a sheet of camera-ready images on bright-white glossy paper.

If you can't get camera-ready originals from the designer, obtain the cleanest printed versions possible: a brochure that hasn't been handled a lot, or a copy of a flyer that's as clean and crisp as possible. If the image is in color, make sure the colors are dense and evenly printed. Skip using anything that's a color copy (created on a color photocopier) or printed on an inkjet printer, because these devices can create slight defects in the image quality that the scanner might only emphasize.

Good on Paper

It's often tempting to use a business card as the original, but you should avoid doing so if the card was printed with raised (embossed) lettering, or if the card has a linen finish. In the case of the raised letters, the 3-D aspect can result in unwanted shadows and highlights on the scan. The linen finish will create a background texture that you probably don't want.

When you scan through Photoshop, after you've previewed the image, set the scan area, chosen the scan type (black and white, grayscale, text, color), and done the scan itself, the image opens in Photoshop. If you follow the scanning suggestions from Chapter 4, you know that you should scan at a high resolution—300 pixels per inch (ppi) is a good setting—so that you get as clean and detailed a scan as possible. You can always reduce the image size later, but having as much visual content as possible from the original scan makes it much easier to retouch the image by adding, removing, and cleaning up its content. Figure 5.6 shows a panel from a brochure that was scanned at 300 ppi, with the Color-Good Quality setting through my scanning software.

After you scan the artwork, you'll probably have to clean it up—removing stray marks, replacing content that didn't survive the scan well (tiny text, fine detail in drawings and maps), and making up for any deficits in the original, such as faded colors, blotchy fills, and textured paper. You can use any of Photoshop's tools for editing the scanned image so that it's as clean and clear as possible.

Figure 5.6

Scanning at the best possible settings can still give you an image with problems.

Once you've retouched your image, save it in PSD format and then use the File|Save For Web command to save the file in a Web-safe format. You can refer to Chapter 1 if you aren't sure which format to use (GIF, JPEG, or PNG). It's important to save it in each format because having the PSD file makes it easier to make new versions of the image later, for other uses, with layers added, content edited, and so on.

Maintaining a Consistent Look and Feel

If you're the person who designed the printed materials for your organization (or for your client), you have a significant advantage in maintaining the look and feel of your printed materials in your Web pages—just do again whatever you did the first time. However, if you weren't involved in the design decisions, you have to observe the materials that exist and ask some questions:

- What was the tone the designer was shooting for? Was he or she trying to achieve a conservative, structured look, or a high-tech, freewheeling appearance? Was "fun" a word on the designer's mind, or was it "serious"?

- Did he or she achieve the goal? If the tone of the printed materials matches the desired tone of the organization, company, or person to which the materials pertain, then the answer is yes.

- How can you use the printed materials to help build the Web page? Of course, only if the materials are successful in conveying the desired tone should their content be perpetuated on the Web page. If your materials strike the wrong tone entirely, it might be time to forge a new trail and make the Web site stand on its own, including only a few key elements to tie the printed and the online marketing materials together.

Blah, Blah, Blah

Many times, your client or employer will hand you a stack of brochures, flyers, ads, and business cards and you'll look at them and think "Boring!" A lot of organizations are timid in their designs for printed materials, either due to a lack of imagination or a desire to keep printing costs down (multiple-color printing is much more expensive than two-color printing), or both. If you're staring at a pile of white pages with black or blue text on them and some unappealing clip art and charts thrown in at odd locations, don't think you have to capture that on the page you've been tasked with designing. Take what you can—logos, text content (not the look, but what it says), and the order in which topics are presented—and perpetuate that on the Web site. Two wrongs don't make a right!

So you've ironed out what the goal was, you think the designer achieved it, and now you're ready to mimic it in your Photoshop designs. What's next? Scavenging. Your next step is to figure out what you can use from the printed materials and how much time and effort you can save. Can you scan the logo from the brochure? If the materials are text-heavy, can you scan that text into a word processor and then paste it onto the Web page as editable text? If the brochure is text-light, should you create graphical text for some of it rather than typing it directly onto the Web page? Make a three-column inventory list—what you have within the printed materials, what you need that can't be taken directly from the printed materials, and for those items in that second column, how you're going to go about getting or creating them.

Your Web page content will fall into two main categories: text and graphics. Some graphics contain or are made up predominantly of text; others are drawings, shapes, or photographs. Text is the words you'll type directly onto the page through your HTML text editor or a Web design program such as Dreamweaver or GoLive. Obviously, it is the graphics you'll create in Photoshop.

To maintain the same look and feel in your Web graphics that was found in the printed materials, follow these basic guidelines:

- Use the same colors, or the appropriate Web-safe versions. Many organizations have a favorite color, a single shade that they feel is "theirs." The color will be found on letterhead, business cards, perhaps even their carpeting. If the printed materials feature a dominant color, make sure you use it prominently on the Web page.

- Stick to the same overall layout. If the brochure or flyers have a linear layout, stick to that on the Web page. If there are no borders or colored bars separating sections on the printed materials, avoid using them on the Web page.

- Use the same fonts. This is where some of the printed text has to become graphic text rather than text that is typed directly on the page. Why? Because, as you'll remember from the first chapter, when it comes to text on a Web page, you want to use fonts you know everyone has, such as

Times New Roman, Arial, or Helvetica. If visitors don't have the font you used, their computer will select a substitute, and it may not be one that looks right with the rest of your page. If the fonts on your brochure are fairly esoteric, especially when it comes to titles and headlines, create graphic text instead, and your font choices are virtually unlimited.

PROJECT Use Scanned Images to Build a Graphic That Matches Existing Marketing Materials

In this project, you will open an image that was scanned from printed marketing materials. The company had a logo created for the materials, but the designers did not provide the image electronically; they only provided sheets of camera-ready versions of the image in various sizes. To create an electronic version for use on the Web (and to have one that can be added to documents in a word processing program, too), the company scanned the image into Photoshop. Your job is to remove parts of the image that didn't scan effectively and reproduce them using Photoshop's tools. After doing so, you'll save the image in a Web-safe format.

Open the File

Open the file called companylogo.psd, which you'll find in the Chapter 5 folder on the CD. This image was scanned from the camera-ready artwork for a logo.

Remove Text from Scanned Image

The fine text under the shapes and company name didn't survive the scanning process too well. Crop the image as shown in Figure 5.7 to exclude this text. If you're good with the mouse, you can try erasing it with the Eraser tool, instead. If you do use the Eraser tool to remove the text, skip the next two steps in this project, because they apply only to those who cropped the image.

Figure 5.7
Crop out the bottom of the graphic, where the sketchy text appears.

Increase Canvas Size

If you chose to crop the image to exclude the text below the logo itself, you now need to increase the size of the canvas (not the image) to allow room for the text to be retyped. Increase the canvas height only, adding an inch to its current vertical dimension by issuing the Image|Canvas Size command.

Move the Image Up within the Canvas

Use the Marquee tool to select the graphic portion of the image (see Figure 5.8). Then, use the up arrow on your keyboard to move the selected portion up within the canvas, stopping when the image appears as it does in Figure 5.9.

Figure 5.8
Using the rectangular Marquee, select the graphics in preparation for moving them.

Figure 5.9
When you've moved the graphics up, they should be at the top of the canvas.

Add Company Information to the Logo

In the original logo, the company's slogan appeared below the name and the graphical portion of the logo. Because the text was so fine on the printed original and the scanner was not set to scan at a high resolution, this text looked terrible and had to be removed. You will now replace it:

1. Click on the Type tool and then click to position your cursor on the image, as shown in Figure 5.10.

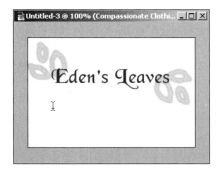

Figure 5.10
Place your cursor where the slogan line should begin.

2. Type "Compassionate Clothing Since 1978".

3. Select the text with your mouse in preparation for formatting it to match the original text.

Format the Company Slogan

Apply Caslon Open Face (or a reasonable facsimile) to the slogan text, and set the font size to 24 points. Figure 5.11 shows the result.

Figure 5.11
Graceful fonts with varying thicknesses within the characters often fail to scan effectively. Retyping the text in Photoshop is the best solution.

As needed, use your arrow keys (with the Move tool activated) while on the Type layer to move the slogan up, down, left, or right to position it to match its location in the scanned original.

Moving On

In this chapter, you learned how to capture the color, look, and feel of printed materials in your Web graphics. The project in this chapter provides a segue to the next chapter's topic: the designing of graphic text for Web pages. You'll put to use what you've learned about using Photoshop's tools to type, format, and apply interesting effects to text meant for the Web.

Chapter 6

Designing Graphic Text for the Web

A picture's worth a thousand words, right? Well, a picture of a word is worth millions in terms of increased flexibility and design potential. With Photoshop's tools for designing graphic text, you can create great text for your site while circumventing any browser's font limitations!

Why Create Graphic Text?

When you type text directly onto a Web page you're designing, you should choose from a very limited list of fonts—Arial, Helvetica, Times New Roman, or Verdana being the most popular and accepted. Why such a short list? Because you don't want to use a font that your visitor doesn't have on his or her computer—if you do, the visitor's browser will substitute a font, and the results could be less than appealing from a visual standpoint. Figure 6.1 shows the default list of fonts offered by Macromedia Dreamweaver—a rather limited list to be sure.

Figure 6.1

The text you type onto your Web page should be in a "vanilla" font that every potential visitor will have on their system.

A Blessing in Disguise

It's actually a good thing that Web page text has to be in a simple font such as Times New Roman or Arial. Were it not for that limitation, all the people who can't resist using five or six very ornate fonts in the same flyer (thus making it impossible to read and creating a design nightmare) would be doing the same thing to Web pages, rendering many of them illegible and unpleasant to look at.

With so few fonts to choose from, many Web designers decide instead to create graphic text—single words, phrases, sentences, even whole paragraphs typed into a Photoshop image and saved as an image or part of an image. The text is legible on the Web page, and it can even be divided into hotspots (using your favorite Web design application) so that visitors can click on individual words or phrases and be linked to other pages and sites, just as though they were pointing to hyperlink text.

In addition to escaping the aforementioned font limitations, you'll find that graphic text is just better looking. You can apply shadows, 3-D embossing, and highlights, and place the text on top of pictures, patterns, and solid colors. To do that on a Web page, you'd have to fill table cells with color, or apply a background image to the entire Web page (which usually means a long wait for the image to compose). Graphic text, on the other hand, is typically small in size (less than 35KB) and therefore loads quickly.

Creating a Text Object

Photoshop's Type tool can be used for typing anything—a single character or digit; a word, phrase, or sentence; or one or more paragraphs. Using the options bar that appears when you activate the Type tool (see Figure 6.2), you can apply fonts, sizes, and colors to the text. Text you type into a Photoshop file is automatically placed on its own layer, so moving the text within the image is easy. Accessing tools for applying interesting effects, such as drop shadows and highlights, also becomes easy.

Figure 6.2

Click the Type tool and you'll see a variety of formatting options that you can apply before or after you type.

Well, That's Great, But...

If your Web page is entirely (or even predominantly) made up of graphic text, it might be harder for Web search engines to find it. Pages are indexed based on their metatags (keywords established at the beginning of the page's HTML code) and the first 150 words on the page itself. Graphic text is a picture, not text, in the eyes of the search engine, and it isn't "read." Therefore, be sure to include keywords and important text, typed directly onto the page—even if you have to hide the text by changing its color to blend in with the background so no one knows it's there—except the search engine.

Typing the Text

You can type on an existing image, such as a scanned photograph or a drawing you've created in Photoshop. You can also type in a new, blank image, creating a type layer on top of a solid color or transparent background. Typing the text is easy: Just click on the Type tool and click inside the image window to position your cursor. Then, type the text you want. The text appears right on the image (see Figure 6.3), rather than in a dialog box as in previous versions of Photoshop.

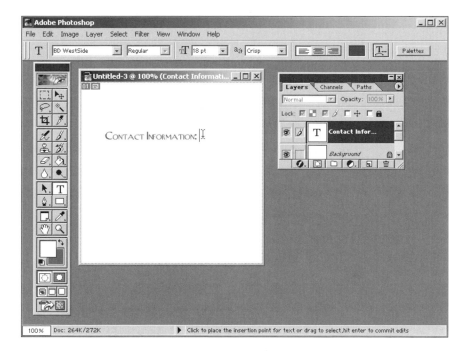

Figure 6.3
Text appears on the image in the font, size, and color displayed on the Type tool's options bar.

If the text consists of a sentence or paragraph, you have to press the Enter key to force a word-wrap effect. If you don't press Enter, the text will continue in one endless string. The text will be left-aligned by default, but you can change that—along with just about anything else about the text content and appearance.

Editing Text

After you've typed your text (and even during the typing process), you can edit it by pressing the Backspace key (to remove text to the left of your cursor) or the Delete key (to remove text to the right of your cursor). You can also select text with your mouse and press Delete to remove it. You can use drag and drop within a string of text to rearrange the words. You'll find that using the Type tool is very similar to using a word processor in terms of how you select and edit text. The overall process of typing and editing text in Photoshop is familiar to people who use such programs as Microsoft Word. Figure 6.4 shows some editing in process.

Figure 6.4
Use your mouse to select the word you want to change or remove.

Moving and Resizing the Type Layer

Once you type even a single character, you create a type layer that is represented on the Layers palette. You can move the text within the confines of the image window by activating the type layer and then using the Move tool to drag the text with your mouse. To activate the type layer, choose one of the following methods:

- Right-click the text itself and choose the layer by name from the shortcut menu. The type layer name will match the text on the layer, as shown in Figure 6.5.

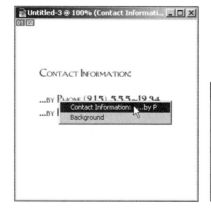

Figure 6.5
Activate a layer by right-clicking it and selecting it by name.

- Click the layer to select it on the Layers palette, and it becomes the active layer in the image.

- Activate the Move tool and then click once (with your left mouse button) on the text to make it the active layer.

Moving Text Around

Once the layer is activated, you can use the Move tool to move it around on the image. Just drag the text with your mouse, releasing the mouse when the text is in the desired position. Be careful when you click to begin dragging, because if you inadvertently click the background or the content on a nearby layer, you'll activate that layer and the text won't move.

Changing the Layer Order

If the image includes other item—shapes, lines, photographic content—and they're on one or more other layers, you can rearrange the items and adjust their stacking order by clicking and dragging the layers within the Layers palette. Figure 6.6 shows a type layer dragged to the top of the list of layers on the Layers palette, which results in the text appearing on top of all the other content in the image.

The Text That Wouldn't Move

If you find that you keep selecting the background layer each time you go to click on and move your text, try using the arrow keys to move it instead. Use your mouse to select the type layer (click the layer on the Layers palette), and then remove the mouse from the process. Rather than dragging the text up, down, or to the left or right, use the arrow keys on your keyboard to nudge the text into place.

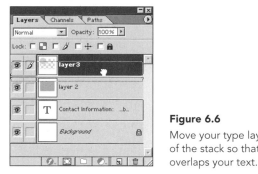

Figure 6.6
Move your type layer to the top of the stack so that nothing overlaps your text.

Transforming the Type Layer

As with any line or shape you draw in Photoshop, you can resize text with the Edit|Transform or Edit|Free Transform command. You can make the text larger or smaller, rotate it, skew it (stretch it horizontally or vertically), or flip it. If you choose the Edit|Transform command, you have to pick what you want to do from a submenu, as shown in Figure 6.7. At this point, the layer's content (the text, in this case) is surrounded by a perimeter of handles, as Figure 6.8 shows. When you click and move your mouse on the image and drag one of the handles, the desired effect occurs. Figure 6.9 shows an image skewed horizontally.

The Free Transform command works very much the same way, except you don't have to pick what you want to do first. By choosing this command from the Edit menu, you cause handles to appear around the perimeter of the layer's

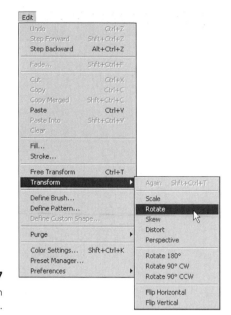

Figure 6.7

Pick the transformation you want to perform.

Figure 6.8

Side and corner handles appear, giving you something to grab as you resize, rotate, or skew the image.

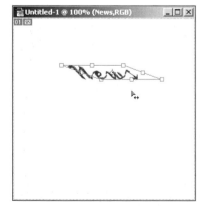

Figure 6.9

Each transformation has its own mouse pointer. The skew mouse points left and right or up and down, depending on which handles you point to.

Figure 6.10
If you're using Free Transform, watch your mouse pointer carefully to avoid surprises—a resize when you meant to rotate, or a skew when you meant to resize.

content. Then, you can rotate, skew, or resize the image depending on where and how you click and drag on the handles. Again, the appearance of your mouse pointer tells you which transformation effect you're about to apply. By pointing just outside the corner handles (see Figure 6.10), you enter a rotate mode. Pointing directly on the handles puts you in resize mode, and pointing just outside a side handle makes it possible to skew the selected text.

If you enlarge or reduce your text with the Edit|Transform|Scale command or by dragging a corner handle while in Free Transform mode, your text will resize in proportion, maintaining its width and height ratio. The font will also be updated (observe the options bar while the Type tool is active and after you've just applied the transformation). If your formerly 12-point text is now twice the size, the Size field will display a larger font size, as shown in Figure 6.11. This is a great feature for people who don't have a specific point size requirement and know how big the text needs to be simply by looking at it.

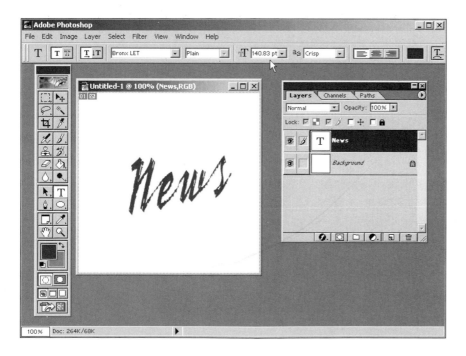

Figure 6.11
Resize your text with the Transform or Free Transform tools, and automatically adjust the font size as well.

After using your mouse to spin or stretch your type, press Enter to apply the transformation permanently (of course, you can always reverse your actions with Undo or by using the History palette). If you click on another tool without committing to the transformation, a prompt appears, asking if you want to apply the transformation. Click Apply if you do.

Working with Type Formatting Tools

You can apply fonts, sizes, and colors to all of the text in a particular layer, or you can select a part of the text and apply different effects to that bit of text. For example, as shown in Figure 6.12, applying a different font and size to the first letter of a word makes it stand out. Use this process to create the look of a drop cap; you don't have to change the position of the character to achieve this effect.

Figure 6.12
Choose a completely different font for the first letter of a word to make your graphic text stand out.

What's a *Drop Cap*?

Remember those fairytale books you read as a kid, where the "O" in "Once upon a time..." was bigger than the rest of the text and was usually very ornate or at least in a fancy font? That's a drop cap. In typesetter's lingo, a drop cap is literally a capital letter at the beginning of a paragraph that is dropped below the baseline (the invisible line that the text sits on) and enlarged to stand out.

Changing the appearance of text has special importance on a Web page—much more so than in many printed documents. Although designers who create printed materials might argue with me, consider the volume of printed marketing or informative materials one potential customer, volunteer, or donor might have on his or her desk at any one time. Ten pieces? Twenty? One hundred? Now think about how many Web sites he or she has on that same desk via the Web. A thousand? Try millions. With that much competition for the attention of site visitors, text that does more than simply impart information is key. Your site has to grab a visitor's attention and keep it—and a spiffy headline, button, or other text-based graphic can do just that. The information is there, but instead of appearing in boring old Times New Roman or Arial font, it's there in something equally legible but much more interesting, such as Bank Gothic or Renaissance. Figure 6.13 shows two bits of text on a Web page. They both say the same thing. Which one would you notice first?

Figure 6.13

Grab them with graphic text and they'll follow your links and maybe even come back later, simply because they remember your site.

Displaying a Helpful Text Palette

You can click the Palettes button on the options bar to display a two-tab palette offering character and paragraph formats galore. Some of the options are also available on the options bar itself, but most of them are unique to the palette, such as those for adjusting the leading between lines of text and the kerning and tracking between characters. Figure 6.14 shows the Character tab, and Figure 6.15 shows the Paragraph tab.

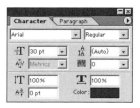

Figure 6.14

Choose a font, size, color, tracking, kerning, baseline shift, and horizontal and vertical scaling for selected text.

If you click the triangle on the upper-right side of either the Character or Paragraph palette, a menu displays, offering more options for changing the format of selected text. For example, if the font you're using can't be made Bold (Bold isn't in the Font Style list, or that list is dimmed), choose Faux Bold from the menu. Faux means "fake," and what's happening is that the text is being made bold by adding pixels around each letter rather then a bold version of the font being applied.

Choosing the Right Font

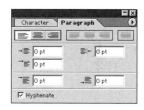

Figure 6.15

Set the alignment, indents, and add space before and/or after lines of text.

The phrase "the right font" sounds a lot like "the right shoes" or "the right school." Highly subjective selections, I'd say. Who can tell you which is the right font for your Web page? Well, I can try, and I'll give you a few guidelines to think about as you decide what's right for you. In the final analysis, though, it's you who must decide which font is right for your page.

Fonts are a lot like pictures: They can say more than you think. A picture of a boat on a lake can say much more than "Here is a boat on a lake." It can say, "Here's a lovely way to spend the summer" or "What a relaxing afternoon." Fonts are very similar. The words you type can say, "Click here to begin planning your boating vacation on Lake Whatever," but the font you choose can invoke feelings in those who visit your site. As shown in Figure 6.16, the same phrase says very different things in different fonts. From classic to casual, from dignified to dizzy, each font makes an impression, yet the words never change.

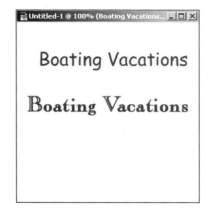

Figure 6.16

Should "boat" say "yacht" or "dinghy"? Pick your font accordingly.

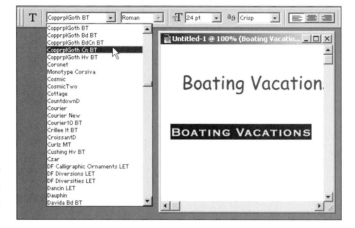

Figure 6.17

Pick a font and observe the change within the type layer on your image.

Regrettably, Photoshop's Font list (on the Type tool's options bar) doesn't show each one graphically. You have to apply it to see what it will look like. Luckily, you can place the image window so that you can watch the text change as you make selections from the list (see Figure 6.17).

Applying Font Sizes

Size is important, especially when it comes to text. Text should be big enough to be read, but not so big that it takes up valuable real estate within the image and then on the Web page when the graphic is inserted. When you're choosing a font size for your text, be sure to view the image on a test page using at least two monitor resolutions: 800×600 (the "standard" for most Web designs these days, mercifully increased from the previous standard of 640×480) and 1024×768 (the popular choice of designers themselves as well as serious Web surfers). When you test the graphic text at these settings, make sure it's not too small (consider far-sighted people who forget their glasses!) and not too big (so that it doesn't overwhelm the page).

Testing Your Resolution

To change your monitor's resolution, if you're using Windows, select Start|Settings|Control Panel and choose Display. You can also right-click on any empty spot on the Desktop and choose Properties. Either method opens the Display Properties dialog box. On the Settings tab, you can increase or decrease your monitor's resolution, dragging the gauge in the Screen Area section of the dialog box. Click OK to apply the change, and then accept the new setting when prompted. View your page at the new setting, and then try another setting to see if the text still looks okay. Of course, once you've created a few graphic text images, you'll have a sense of font sizes and how they look on the Web and you won't have to test each one to know if it's right for a given situation.

To apply font size, select the text (after you've activated the type layer containing it, of course), and then use the options bar's Size setting to change the size of the text. You can choose a size from the list, or type a size into the field directly. If the size you pick makes the text too big for the image (see Figure 6.18), reduce the size, or, if the size is what you want and the image needs to grow to hold it, edit the canvas size.

Figure 6.18
Text that runs off the edge of the image is only a temporary problem.

Note that I said you'd need to increase the *canvas size*, not the image size. It's a common mistake, almost a reflex, to increase image size when what you really need to do is make the *canvas* (the area on which your current content lives) bigger. To change canvas size, choose Image|Canvas Size and enter new measurements. As shown in Figure 6.19, you have no protection from a change in the canvas's proportions—no lock that prevents increasing the width more than the height or vice versa. You can enter any dimensions you want in either the Width or Height box, and you can choose how the dimensions will be measured (inches or pixels are your best bet for a graphic bound for the Web).

Having It All

If you're trying to select all of your text, including the characters that have run off the edge of the image, press Ctrl+A. You'll get all of the text on the active layer, even the letters you can't drag through with your mouse. Then, reduce your font size on the Character palette or the options bar, and the entire text layer is resized.

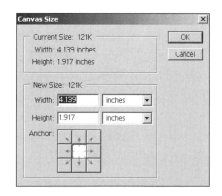

Figure 6.19
Give your graphic text a little more elbow room by increasing the width and/or height of your canvas.

Note the Anchor option in the Canvas Size dialog box. This nine-block box allows you to choose where the added canvas area will appear. By default, the center block is selected, meaning that the added canvas will be evenly distributed around the edges of the current canvas size. If you click a corner block, say the upper-right corner block, the added canvas will appear at the left and bottom of the image.

Changing Text Color

Of course, no matter which color you pick, it has to be Web-safe if your graphic text is bound for the Web. You apply the text color by using the Type options bar. Simply click the Text Color block two buttons to the left of the Palettes button to open the Color Picker dialog box. Within the Web-safe palette, the color you choose is up to you, but keep these guidelines in mind:

- Don't forget the background color. Whether it's the background color of the image itself or the page background appearing behind a transparent GIF, its impact on the legibility and effectiveness of your text cannot be denied. Obviously, light-colored text is best on a darker background, and darker text is more effective on a lighter background.

- Don't use red and green together. Approximately 15 percent of the male population is colorblind, and to them, red and green are just shades of gray when seen next to each other. This goes for all the shades of both colors, so pinks and pastel greens aren't good choices together, although if it's a holiday graphic, you're forgiven.

- Avoid the "Star Wars" effect. A black background with white or yellow text seems like a good combination—it's legible, right? Well, at first glance it is, but after a while, it's rather hard on the eyes. For a graphic that doesn't contain a lot of text or for any graphic that includes large text, white or yellow text on black is fine. If your graphic text consists of a paragraph or paragraphs, however, or if the text is smaller than 12 points, it can be visually taxing for your page visitors.

Changing Text Alignment and Orientation

By default, all text you type is left-aligned, an attribute that becomes relevant only if you type more than one line of text in a single text layer. You can change the alignment by using the options bar or the Paragraph tab on the Type palette. Choose from Center, Right, and Justify All (the latter is available only on the Paragraph palette, as shown in Figure 6.20), in addition to the default Left alignment.

If you don't like the direction your text is going—horizontally, that is—you can change it so that it runs straight up and down. Figure 6.21 shows a string of text running vertically, achieving the look of a sign on the side of a building.

The Color Wheel

If you're not sure which colors go together, consult the color wheel graphic found on the CD that accompanies this book. The image consists of four wheels—one showing the primary colors (red, blue, and yellow), one the secondary colors (the colors made by mixing primary colors), a third showing the tertiary colors (the colors made by mixing secondary colors), and a fourth showing a full spectrum with the complementary colors for each color pointed out on the wheel. Working with these wheels will help you make confident color combination choices from now on! The graphic is named colorwheels.jpg, and you'll also find a printed version of it in the Photoshop Studio section of this book.

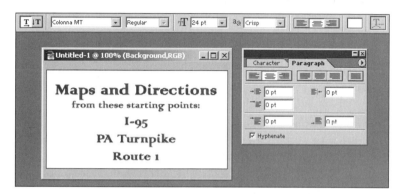

Figure 6.20

Text alignment changes the horizontal position within the space defined by the text itself—not over the width of the entire image.

Figure 6.21

Rather than always making your viewers read left to right (how dull!), try running your text from top to bottom.

Of course, you can type vertical text only if you enable that option before you start typing. As soon as you click the Type tool in anticipation of typing your text, click the Vertically Orient Text button (see Figure 6.22) on the options bar. Then, click on the image and start typing. Your text will start at the cursor and flow down, one character at a time.

Figure 6.22

Click the Vertically Orient Text button to run your new text from top to bottom.

Warping Text to a Shape

Need your text to follow a path or conform to a geometric shape? The Create Warped Text button is your ticket to text that looks stretched, bent, or melted, as shown in Figure 6.23. You apply the tool to existing text and expect a minor

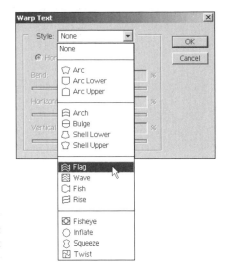

Figure 6.23

Click the Create Warped Text tool and choose a warp effect from the dialog box.

delay while the font in use is reconfigured for the type you're warping. The duration of the delay is dictated by the speed of your computer and the amount of memory you have available. Your warp options include shapes and paths, and the results depend on the font you're using, the size of the text, and the tracking, kerning, and leading you have in effect. Figure 6.24 shows a few different warp effects, including Fisheye, Wave, and Arc.

Figure 6.24

As if cool fonts aren't enough, warping your text makes it even more attention grabbing than ever.

Of course, not every Web page is an appropriate place for warped text. Like any other visual effect, use it judiciously, and only where the effect matches the tone you're trying to set or the message you're trying to send. You don't want warped text on a page that requires lots of structure and straight lines to communicate a sense of reliability and stability. You do want warped text on a page that uses freeform shapes and layout to communicate flexibility and creativity.

When you do use warped text, you can control the intensity of the shape and path, and your text's adherence to it. In the Warp Text dialog box, use the Bend and Distortion sliders to reduce or increase the warp effect (see Figure 6.25).

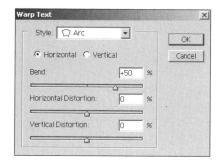

Figure 6.25
Drag to the left to reduce the effect; drag to the right to increase it. The Bend effect is intensified at higher percentages.

Using Text as a Mask

Text can be used to cut away portions of your image, or to mask an area for painting or deletion. Click the Create A Mask Or Selection button prior to typing your text (the button is available on the options bar as soon as you click the Type tool before you type any text). Once you finish typing, switch to the Move tool if you want to drag the selected area away, taking the content within the selection from the active layer with it. Or you can click on the Marquee tool if you want to simply delete the masked area. Figure 6.26 shows text as a selection that we moved from one area of the image to another.

When you click the Create A Mask Or Selection button, your image turns orange, and the entire active layer is masked. When you click your mouse on the image to position your cursor and begin typing, every character you type becomes a selected area, and the mask is removed from that selection (see Figure 6.27).

Cutaway Text

You can cut your selection to the Clipboard and paste it onto another image, creating two effects—the removed text on one image, and text with a pattern or photographic fill on another image. You can also paste the cutaway text onto another layer, where it will cease to be text but will create an interesting, legible shape.

Figure 6.26
(Left) Text that serves as a selection allows you to both communicate and decorate with type.

Figure 6.27
(Right) Mark an area for deletion, or create a selection in the shape of a word or phrase that you can fill (using the Paintbrush or Paint Bucket) or simply move to another spot on the image.

Applying Effects to the Type Layer

As I mentioned earlier, as soon as you type your text, you create a type layer that is visible on the Layers palette. By double-clicking that layer on the palette, you open the Layer Style dialog box, which lets you apply all sorts of interesting visual effects to your text. As shown in Figure 6.28, you can apply shadows, glows, 3-D bevels, and embossed effects, as well as color, gradient, and pattern overlays.

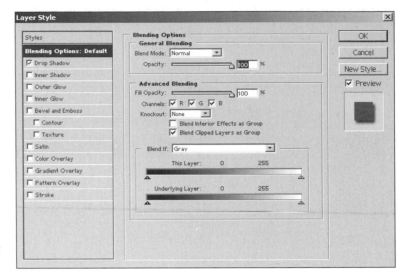

Figure 6.28
Display the full assortment of effects for your active type layer.

Turning various effects on and off is easy: Just click in the checkboxes at the far left of the dialog box. As you click on a checkbox, if you move the dialog box aside so that you can also see your image, you can watch the effect(s) being applied to your text. When you've added all the effects you want (the default settings for each one are often quite acceptable), click OK to apply your changes and close the dialog box.

Adjusting Effects

What if you want a drop shadow but you want it to be very diffused and spread out around the image? Or suppose you want to change the implied light source from the left of the image to the right. Within the Layer Style dialog box, double-click the effect in question and simply tinker with the Blending and Advanced Blending options, as shown in Figure 6.29. You can change the Blend Mode and adjust the opacity of the effects. In the Advanced Blending area, you can choose which of your text's colors are blended by picking a color (Gray, Red, Green, or Blue) from the Blend If drop-down list.

Note the Preview block on the right side of the dialog box (the Preview option is on by default). The effects and the adjustments you make are applied to the gray box in the Preview area. However, there's no substitute for seeing the effects and your adjustments to them on the actual text, so be sure to move the dialog box aside and preview the effect on your text before you commit by clicking OK. To move the dialog box, simply drag it by its title bar.

Applying Styles

Just above the Blending Options: Default button at the top of the list of effects on the right side of the dialog box, you'll see the Styles button. If you click that button, the dialog box changes and displays a palette of colored pattern/picture fills that you can apply to your text (see Figure 6.30). Like the blending effects, styles can be applied to entire layers and shapes, in addition to text.

When to Say "When" to Effects

A little bit of 3-D is great on the Web. The Web is a medium that isn't confined to a flat surface (like printed materials are confined to paper), and the illusion of depth and texture is very effective onscreen. Resist the temptation, however, to make all of your graphic text 3-D with shadows, beveling, and embossing. A little bit goes a long way, and the parts that you do make pop through the use of Photoshop's considerable assortment of effects will have much more impact if they're used sparingly on the page.

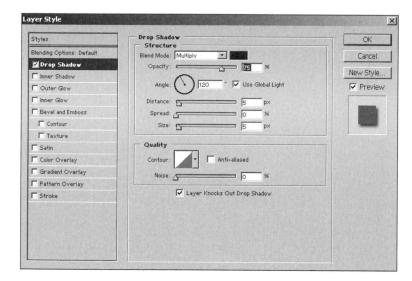

Figure 6.29
Make changes in the way your chosen effects are applied.

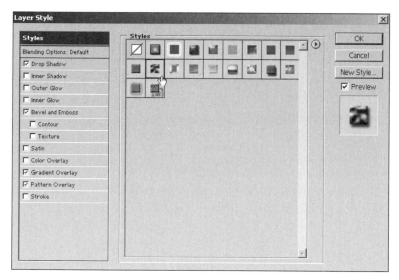

Figure 6.30
Apply a style to your text for a multicolored effect.

To apply a style, simply click on the style you want and watch as Photoshop applies it to your text. The blending options still appear in the dialog box—Drop Shadow, Bevel and Emboss, etc.—so you can tinker with those options after you've applied the style.

You can also create your own styles by applying various effects to your text and then clicking the New Style button. In the resulting dialog box (see Figure 6.31), give your new style a name, and then click OK. To delete a style you've created, right-click it and choose Delete Style from the shortcut menu.

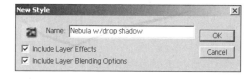

Figure 6.31
Come up with something snazzy you think you'll use again? Save that style and give it a descriptive name.

Saving Graphic Text for the Web

Like any Web-bound graphic you create in Photoshop, your graphic text needs to be saved in a format that's safe for the Web. Your choice from the available options (GIF, JPEG, and PNG) will be dictated by the content of the image. I don't tend to use the PNG format because only the latest browsers recommend it, and I'd counsel you to restrict your choice to either GIF or JPEG. With that in mind, consider these points as you pick which format to apply to your graphic text images:

- If you haven't applied any effects to your image—no drop shadows, no glows, no embossing—GIF might be the way to go. A simple text-based graphic (as shown in Figure 6.32) with only a couple of colors and no shading will be smaller in terms of file size and faster in terms of loading on the page if you choose the GIF format.

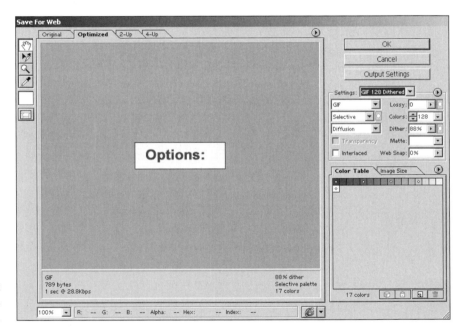

Figure 6.32
Simple images require a simple GIF format.

- An image with any shadows, embossing, or other effects applied might be better off as JPEGs so that all the colors are supported and you get a cleaner image after it's saved for the Web.

- If there is any kind of photographic or complex pattern behind your text, go with JPEG. The image in Figure 6.33 includes effects and photographic content behind the text and is therefore a good candidate for the JPEG format.

When you choose a format, watch the file size, and make adjustments to image quality to achieve the cleanest image with the fastest estimated load time—the same rules you'd follow when saving any sort of image for the Web. However,

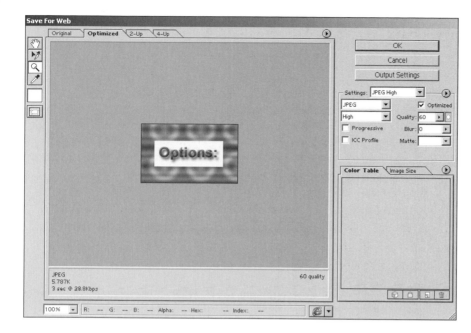

Figure 6.33
A more complex image needs a
format that supports all the
colors your shadows, glows, and
3-D effects require.

one area where you don't have to follow the rules is when using the Progressive
(for JPEGs) and Interlaced (for GIFs) options. As you might recall from earlier
coverage of this topic, Interlaced and Progressive images appear blurry and
choppy at first, and clear up as the image loads. This is in contrast to images
that don't appear at all until the image has completely loaded. When the image
is a picture that doesn't serve as a link or doesn't contain any linked hotspots,
it's fine to let it appear only after the image file has completely loaded; it's not
essential that the visitor see the image before following links on your page or
reading page text. If, on the other hand, an image has information in it and/or
serves as a link to other pages, you want it to show up as soon as possible so that
visitors know it's coming and will be willing to wait (but not more than a few
seconds) for the image to compose so they can read it.

Think about the role your graphic text plays on the page. If it's instructional,
you want people to know it's there as soon as possible. If it contains links to
other pages that you don't want people to miss, again use the Progressive or
Interlaced option so that the image appears early. Just make sure the file size is
small enough that the image composes quickly.

Build a Graphical Text Object

In this project, you'll create a list of items that will become a series
of links. This graphical menu will be more visually appealing than a list of
words typed onto a Web page, and you can chop it up into hotspots (desig-
nated areas on the graphic, each associated with a specific file or URL) using a
Web design application such as Adobe GoLive or Macromedia's Dreamweaver.

Start a New File

Use the File|New command to open a new file. In the resulting New dialog box, set the dimensions of the new image:

- Width: 200 pixels

- Height: 400 pixels

- Resolution: 72 pixels/inch

- Mode: RGB Color

- Contents: White (because the image will be placed on a page with a white background)

Type the Text

Activate the Type tool, and type the following series of menu items:

- About Us

- Our Mission

- Products and Services

- News and Events

- Contact Us

Be sure to press Enter after typing each item.

Format the Text

Apply a single font to every word in the list, and choose any color you want for the text. The size of the text should be close to 18 points, although you might be able to use a larger size for certain fonts.

As needed, tinker with the kerning within the words so that combinations of letters—r and i, or r and n and i, for example—don't visually blend into n and m (respectively). You should also adjust the leading so that adequate space appears between each item, which makes it easy to draw the hotspot rectangles around the words later on. If the menu items are too close together, even after you create the hotspots, visitors could accidentally click on the wrong item by shifting their mouse just slightly.

Figure 6.34

A menu of links to other pages is made more compelling through the use of Photoshop's tools for creating and formatting graphic text.

Apply Effects to the Text

Double-click the type layer and apply a drop shadow to the words. The resulting graphic may look something like Figure 6.34, although yours will vary based on the fonts and colors you chose for your image.

Save for the Web

Save the image in JPEG format, and call it pagemenu.jpg.

Moving On

In this chapter, you learned to create text for the Web that enables you to break free from the browser restrictions on fonts. The next chapter will build on this one, and you'll learn to create navigation bars that contain both text and shapes.

Photoshop
Web Graphics
Studio

*Here are some examples of Photoshop Web graphics
in full color—including original artwork and photographs.
On this book's CD-ROM, you'll find a complete HTML
chart of the 216 Web-safe colors.*

This image is a sample logo, demonstrating Photoshop's shape, line, and type tools. You'll find more about using these tools in Chapters 2 and 3.

Another logo, this one includes special effects, such as drop shadows and embossing. The Gradient fill and the Paint Brush have been used to achieve a 3D look and to provide the illusion of depth and texture. You can explore the tools that enable you to create an image like this one in Chapters 3, 4, 6, and 7.

This scanned business card contains the information that a client wanted on their Web page. As the designer, I had to match the fonts and colors and create a home page that echoed the design of this printed marketing material. Read more about matching Web colors to print colors in Chapter 5.

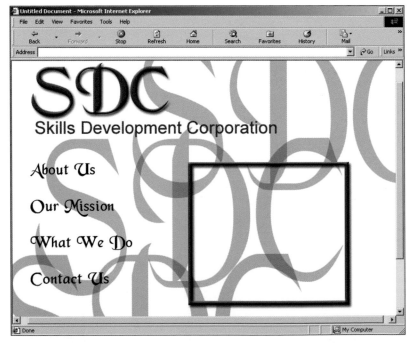

I created a logo from the tiny sample, matched the colors and fonts, and laid out a home page that resembles the business card, satisfying the client's need to have a cohesive set of print and Web marketing materials. This image also shows Photoshop's tools for enhancing even the most basic content, and how graphic text can be inserted where Web-safe fonts won't do—a technique you can master in Chapter 6.

This scanned photo needs a great deal of work; it shows how bad an image can be and still be considered salvageable with Photoshop's retouching tools.

It's amazing what can be done with an image that seems beyond repair. The scratches and stains are gone, and the dark parts of the image are now brought out through the use of Photoshop's retouching tools, including the Smudge tool, Paint Brush, Clone Stamp, and Dodge tool. Learn how to use these tools in Chapter 4.

While the image is in pretty good shape, this photograph needs some cropping to remove unwanted edges, and some filter effects to make it more interesting.

The image frame has been removed, and the radial blur filter has been applied to the background. A section of the original also was enlarged, and its edges were blurred with the Blur tool to make it blend with the filtered area surrounding it. Find out more about applying filters in Chapter 4.

This image shows a graphic text menu, with each word/phrase mapped and turned into a link. Learn how to build your own image maps in Chapter 10, and see how to create hotspots in Dreamweaver in Chapter 15.

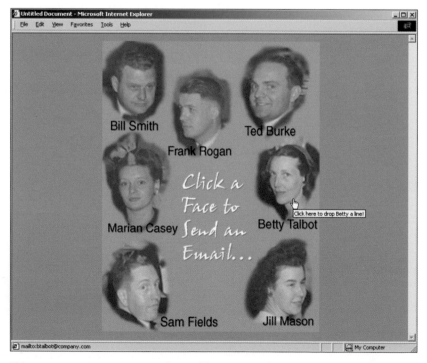

This contacts page contains a collage of faces merged into one image. Each face is mapped and linked to an email address. The image-mapping process is discussed in Chapter 10, and you can find out more about using photographic content in your Web graphics in Chapter 4.

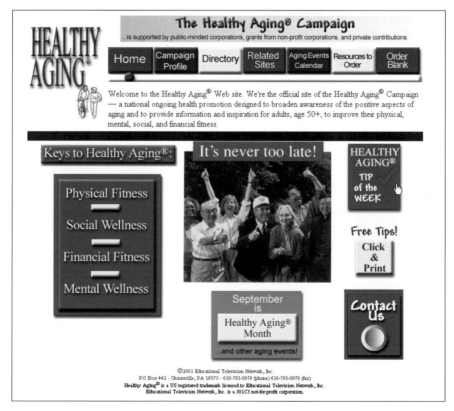

Don't spend time developing a sample page for client review in HTML code or through a WYSIWYG application such as Dreamweaver or GoLive. It's faster and easier to set up a page prototype in Photoshop—you're free to design your graphics and lay out your page with the same tool, and changes are easily made if you keep all the parts on separate layers. Learn to create your own page prototypes in Chapter 9.

This image can be placed on a page with Dreamweaver and used as a blueprint for positioning text and graphics, designing structural devices (a table, in this case) and making sure that the page works in an 800×600 resolution environment. Tracing images is discussed in Chapter 8.

This Web page was built entirely with Photoshop-created elements—the logo, the ad banner, the navigation bar, and the buttons. The photograph was retouched in Photoshop and the file size was reduced for fast loading. To see the page live and check out the other pages in the site (which also contain graphics created in and photos retouched with Photoshop), go to **www.healthyaging.net**.

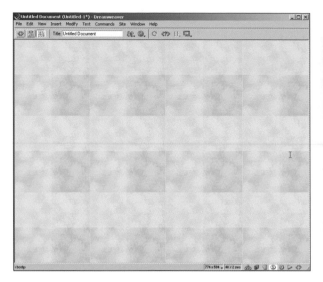

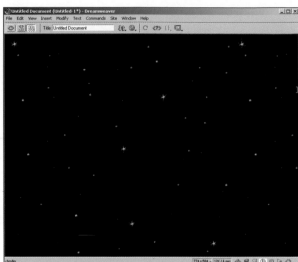

A background image should complement the page, not overpower it. This lovely pattern provides a beautiful backdrop for a wide variety of Web pages and topics; it is simply the repetition of a small image, designed and sized to work in either an 800×600 or 1028×764 display resolution. The fact that the image file is small (less than 35KB) means that the background will load more quickly than a single screen-size image would—just one of the useful tidbits you'll find out about background images in Chapter 8.

Rather than use a boring solid color for a background, try something like this starry night sky. The placement of the stars appears random across the page, yet it is based on a small image that's repeated over the width and height of the page. In addition, the stars are small enough that they won't compete with white, yellow, or some other light colored-text, nor will it overpower graphic images on the page.

With the use of color, 3D effects, and an interesting font, a simple Home button can be an artistic addition to any Web page. You can use Photoshop's tools to make a simple graphic more compelling, drawing attention to it so people will notice it and click it. The variety of skills involved in creating this button are found in Chapters 3, 6, and 7.

This button beckons visitors to click it through the use of freeform shapes, an informal font, and the visually interesting use of textures, highlights, and shadows. The button informs, making it clear what will happen when visitors click the link, and it draws attention to itself, so that the visitors don't have to waste time searching the page before they can place their order.

This navigation bar is static, and derives its visual appeal from vivid colors, 3D effects, and a variety of interesting shapes and fonts, each communicating the tone of the overall site and the page to which the individual tab links. Chapter 7 covers the creation of navigational graphics in detail.

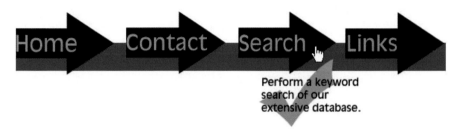

This navigation bar relies on good design and movement to attract and maintain visitor attention. It contains rollovers for each tab, and as shown, as the visitor mouses over the tabs, a shape and a bit of text appears, describing the content of the linked page. Taking navigation tools (covered in Chapter 7) a step further, discover more about creating rollover effects in Chapters 10, 11, and 12.

Rather than just the same old "Contact Us" or "Send an Email" text, this button includes a drawing. When a site visitor mouses over the image, it changes to show an alternate image, seen in the next figure. Master drawing tools in Chapter 3, and the creation of rollovers (to display an alternate image in response to a visitor's mouse) in Chapter 12.

When a visitor mouses over the original image, it changes to this slightly different version of the original. This compels a visitor to click the link, and shows some creativity—something that's important on the Web, as millions of pages vie for your visitors' attention.

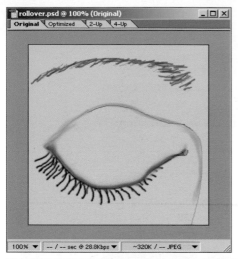

This image and the other three images on this page show the four states of a rollover image created in ImageReady. This first state is how the graphic looks when no mouse is near it. You'll find out how to make rollover images in Chapter 12.

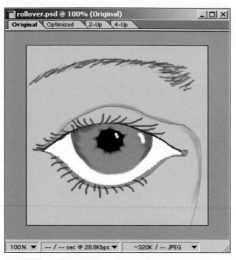

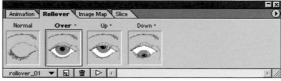

When the a visitor moves the mouse onto the Normal image, this image appears. The eye opens, as though the mouse awakened it.

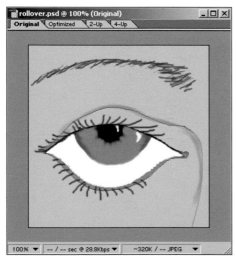

Should the visitor's mouse move up and away from the image, this image appears.

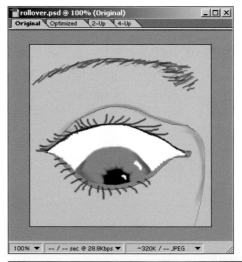

As the visitor's mouse moves down and away from the image, this image appears.

Chapter 7

Creating Web Navigation Tools

Web sites that consist of a single page and contain no links to other sites or files are rare. Consequently, you'll need to create navigational tools to both assist your visitors in moving around within your site and to make your pages more visually interesting.

Building Buttons from Shapes and Lines

A button built in Photoshop can consist of a geometric or freeform shape; perhaps a line around, on, or through the shape; and probably some text. The shapes and lines, however, are the backbone of the button, so we'll work with that part of the button first. As shown in Figure 7.1, you can build buttons in virtually any shape or size. You can even create buttons that don't look like traditional buttons; a smear of paint can be a button on the Web.

Figure 7.1
Traditional round and square buttons are great, but freeform buttons can be a nice change, especially on a page with other nontraditional elements.

Creating Layers for Button Elements

A good first step before you begin to build your button is to think about how many actual parts it will have and create a layer for each one. Having a layer for each part of the button makes it possible to hide certain layer parts, edit the button text, change the color of shapes on different layers, and resize some or all of the parts for use in the future. You know consistency is good on a Web site, so having similar buttons would be desirable, right? Building a button that's easy to reuse with different text and in different sizes and colors will save you a lot of time in creating similar-looking buttons for an entire site.

To create your button's layers, create a new Photoshop file (which starts with a Background layer and nothing else) and choose Layer|New|Layer. In the New Layer dialog box (see Figure 7.2), type a name for your layer so you can easily tell one layer from another (which is not always easy to do by just looking at the layer thumbnails if some of the layers contain very similar-looking content), and then click OK.

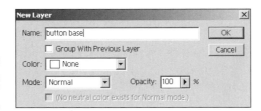

Figure 7.2
Give your layers clear, concise names such as "button base" and "button center".

Repeat this process for every part of your button (except the text, which will be placed on its own layer automatically), no matter how seemingly insignificant a part might be. For example, if your button will have a sparkle on it—a tiny star shape on the edge to indicate a flash of light glinting on the button—put even that tiny item on its own layer. By doing so, you make it possible to easily move the sparkle (and thus vary the implied light source) without adversely affecting the content on which the sparkle currently sits.

Drawing Shapes and Lines

Once you've created the preparatory layers, go to the layer for the first part of the button you want to build. You don't necessarily have to build the button from the ground up. For example, you can build the center or top of a button before you build its base, because you can always rearrange the layers' stacking order later.

With the layer selected, use the appropriate tool for creating that layer's content. For example, suppose your button will have a rectangular base with a circular indentation in the middle, as shown in Figure 7.3. You can use the rectangular Marquee tool or the Rectangle tool (in Create Filled Region mode, because you don't need a shape layer in addition to the one you've already created) and draw the button's base. After drawing the base, switch to the layer for the circular indentation and draw that shape.

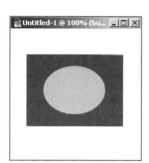 

Figure 7.3
Before its text (if any) is added, this button consists of three layers: a background, a button base layer, and a button center layer.

Aligning and Distributing Shapes

If you don't trust your eye to tell you whether a shape is centered within another shape, or that an element is lined up on the left side of another element, use the Align and Distribute tools that appear on the options bar when a layer is selected (and no specific toolbox tool is in use). You can click on one layer and then link it to the layer or layers with which you want to align and/or distribute content. To link layers, you use the Link checkbox next to each layer in the Layers palette. In Figure 7.4, we've linked the button base and button center layers and used the Align Vertical Centers and Align Horizontal Centers buttons to make sure the ellipse is exactly in the middle of the rectangle.

If your button will have any lines on or in it, draw those, too, using the Paintbrush or Pencil tool. You can also create the illusion of a bar by drawing a very thin rectangle with the Marquee or Rectangle tool. Remember that if you want to draw a straight line (to create the illusion of a bar, as shown in Figure 7.5), you can press and hold the Shift key as you draw the line. Bars drawn with the Marquee or Rectangle tool will already be straight, and you don't want to hold the Shift key down as you use them. If you do, you'll create a perfect square, which isn't what you're looking for here.

Applying Colors to Button Elements

You can apply Foreground color to your shapes and lines as you create them, or you can apply colors after the shapes and lines are drawn. I prefer to apply colors as I draw my button elements, if only so that I can see each of them

Inching Along

It can help to display the rulers in your Photoshop file window. If you know how wide your button needs to be, it's easy to draw the shape if you have a ruler to guide you. Choose View|Show Rulers, and horizontal and vertical rulers appear on the top and left sides of your window. Select View|Hide Rulers to get rid of them if you don't need them anymore for the active image.

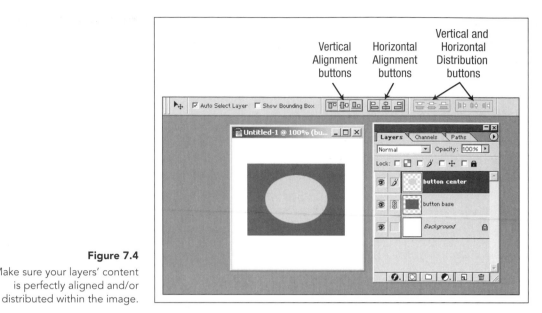

Figure 7.4
Make sure your layers' content is perfectly aligned and/or distributed within the image.

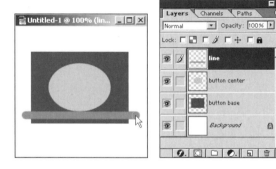

Figure 7.5
Add texture and additional color to your button by adding lines—straight or wavy—to the mix.

Figure 7.6
A white-to-black gradient on the bottom shape and a black-to-white gradient on the top shape creates the illusion of a button with a depressed center.

separately. If your Foreground color is set to the default (black), two or more shapes occupying the same spot on the image will blend visually. You can also apply gradients and patterns, although if the buttons will be very small, it's probably best to stick to solid colors. Figure 7.6 shows a larger button with gradient fills used to create the illusion of depth and shape, and a smaller button that works best with solid fills so that the button's design isn't lost to a busy fill.

Positioning Image Content

If you didn't build your layers and their content in the order in which they should stack within the image, you'll have to restack the layers in the Layers palette and perhaps position the individual layers so that the button is put together properly. To restack your layers, simply drag them up and down in the list, as shown in Figure 7.7.

The only layer you can't move is the Background layer; it has to remain at the bottom of the image. If you want to move the Background layer up in the image stack, duplicate the layer (it will be called Background Copy by default), and you can move that new layer up in the stack. You can then delete the content on the original Background layer, essentially removing it from the image, or just hide it by clicking its Eye icon.

Applying Effects

Your button's component layers can be enhanced through the use of Photoshop's effects, accessed by using the Layer Style dialog box. To open this dialog box, double-click a layer on the Layers palette. You can apply drop shadows, embossing effects, glows, colors, and textures. You can also apply preset styles, including elaborate picture fills, by clicking the Styles button on the left side of the dialog box above Blending Options. Figure 7.8 shows the Styles options.

Figure 7.7
Move your layers up and down in the stack until all your button parts are in the right order.

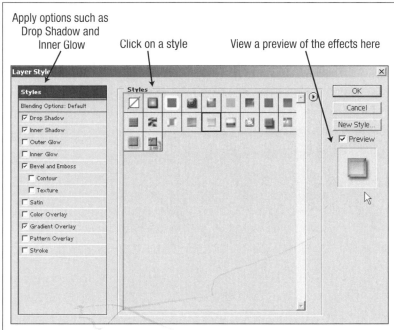

Figure 7.8
Need a cool fill that looks like bubbles or a psychedelic tie-dye? Choose from a variety of styles and apply them to the selected layer.

As you apply an effect from the Blending Options list, you can customize the way that effect is applied to the layer by clicking the effect (not its checkbox—that's merely used to turn the effect on and off). Figure 7.9 shows the Bevel And Emboss settings.

When applying effects and styles to your buttons, be careful not to make the button look too "busy." Buttons are usually relatively small (an inch or so in width at the most), so you don't want to render the button's text illegible by putting a patterned background behind it. Nor do you want a drop shadow to make small type very hard to read. It is effective to apply drop shadows and embossing to your buttons, creating a 3-D look on the page. This can make buttons stand out from other graphic elements, drawing visitors' attention to the buttons so that they're more likely to click them and explore the page or

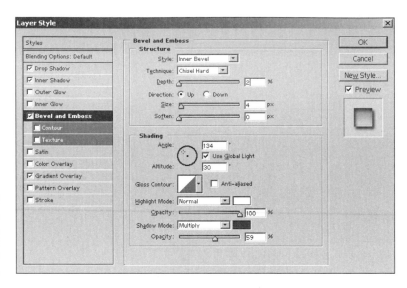

Figure 7.9
Although the defaults for each effect are great in most cases, there will be times that you want to tweak the way a particular effect is applied.

Figure 7.10
Take advantage of the visual depth of art viewed on screen and make your buttons look 3-D.

Life Needs a Little Texture Sometimes

The Texture option (a sub-option under Bevel And Emboss) can be tweaked to mimic anything from burlap to crinkled paper to a pebbled sidewalk. Double-click the option and view the patterns you can embed in the colored fill you've already applied. Figure 7.10 has a subtle pattern applied, adding some interest to what was a solid color fill.

site to which the button is linked. Figure 7.10 shows a button that looks like solid plastic, raised off the page, thanks to some subtle use of shadows and embossing.

Linking and Locking Layers

When your button parts (each on its own layer) are carefully positioned within the image, you can link some or all of them to ensure that nothing is accidentally dragged or nudged out of place. You can take this further by locking key layers so that they can't be deleted or edited.

To link layers, click once on one of the layers to be linked, and then click in the boxes to the left of the layer names. A Chain icon appears, as shown in Figure 7.11. Continue clicking in the boxes to link as many layers as you want. A typical process would be to link the type layer to the button shape on which the text appears to rest so that these two items are never separated,

Figure 7.11

Chain your button's elements together, especially those that must maintain their current relative positions.

even if they're both moved up, down, left, or right by an accidental (or purposeful) drag with the mouse or nudge with the arrow keys. Once you've created those links, any time you click on any of the linked layers, the chains will appear on the layers linked to the selected layer.

To lock a layer, click once on the layer to select it, and then click the Lock All checkbox at the top of the Layers palette (see Figure 7.12). As soon as you click the checkbox, a small Lock icon appears on the selected layer. While a layer is locked, you can't remove it or edit its content. If you try to draw or paint on it, or to delete anything on the layer itself, a prompt appears indicating that you can't proceed (see Figure 7.13). You can rearrange locked layers, moving other layers on top of or behind them, and locked layers themselves can be dragged up and down within the stacked layers in the palette.

Figure 7.12

(Left) Lock a layer to preserve its content and keep it from being deleted.

Figure 7.13

(Right) Once locked, a layer won't let you or anyone else add, change, or remove its content.

To unlock a layer, just click on the locked layer to select it, and then remove the checkmark from the Lock All box. To unlink layers, click on any layer in a linked group and click on the displayed Chain icons—these icons toggle off if they're on, and on if they're off.

Typing and Formatting Button Text

Text on a button is essentially the same as the graphic text discussed in the previous chapter. You use the Type tool to activate the Type options bar, and you click on the image to type your text. The text you type appears on its own layer automatically, and you can rearrange that layer within the stacking order. You can also apply effects to the text by double-clicking the type layer on the Layers palette, which opens the Layer Styles dialog box.

What makes button text different from other image text is the demands made on the button text. The word or words on the button have to be clear and concise. If the button will be set up as a graphic link to your contact information page, the text on the button should read, "Contact Us" or "Get in Touch". It shouldn't say, "Click Here to See a List of Phone Numbers and Email Addresses". That long string belongs, if anywhere, in the Alt text associated with the hyperlink. (You can set up Alt text through a WYSIWYG Web design application such as Dreamweaver or GoLive, or you can set it up through HTML code directly.) Button text should make it clear what the button does, but in as few words as possible. By using fewer words, you can make the text a little larger, resulting in more legible text.

Creating Text for the Button

To create your button text, simply click on the Type tool to activate it, use the options bar to set your font and size (preferably the same as any existing buttons or navigation tools with text so that your pages have some consistency), and then click on the image and start typing. As you type, you can tell if you need to reduce or enlarge the text to fit on the button, and you can make those alterations after the text is typed. Figure 7.14 shows button text in progress.

Figure 7.14

Don't worry about starting the text at exactly the right spot; you can always move the text later so that it's properly positioned among your other button elements.

Remember that you don't need to create a type layer ahead of time; the very process of activating the Type tool and typing text on the image creates a type layer automatically. Many users end up with extra, blank layers resulting from creating new layers for text because they forget that, unlike with other image elements, Photoshop will create the layers for you.

Formatting Button Text

Button text can be formatted with the options bar that appears whenever the Type tool is active, or by using the Character and Paragraph palettes, as shown in Figure 7.15. You can adjust the spacing between letters and lines of text, specify the alignment of your text, and even change your fonts, sizes, and colors, all from these tiny palettes. Just be sure the text is selected before you make your choices in the palettes or on the options bar so that Photoshop knows where to apply your settings.

Figure 7.15
The font you chose is a little hard to read—no problem! Just select the text and pick a different font.

Positioning Button Text

To move your text from its current location to a better spot on the button image, first activate the type layer, and then use your Move tool to click on and drag the text to where it belongs. You can also use the arrow keys on your keyboard to nudge the text into place. (The type layer must be active, and you must click the Move tool before the keys will work.)

If your text is overlapped by another button element, drag the type layer up within the Layers palette until it is above the overlapping content. Figure 7.16 shows type that's partially obscured by part of the button, with the type layer in transit.

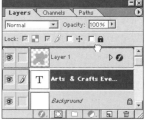

Figure 7.16
Don't hide your text! Drag it out into the open if another element is covering it up.

Linking the Button and Its Text

It's a good idea to link your text and the button element directly below it (in terms of stacking order) so that these two visually related items remain in their relative positions. To do this, click once on the type layer, and then click the Link checkbox on the right side of the other layer. As shown in Figure 7.17, this button text sits on top of what looks like a computer key. Linking the text and that embossed shape (on its own layer) will keep the text centered on the shape, no matter where you drag or nudge either of the two layers.

Figure 7.17
Keep your text and its closest neighbor chained together.

You can also lock your type layer and the layer on which it sits by clicking the Lock All checkbox for each of the layers. If they're also linked, then they can't be removed or edited, and they can't be separated in the stacking order within the Layers palette.

Creating Button Versions for Rollovers

A *rollover* is a graphic that changes in some way when a site visitor moves his or her mouse over the graphic. The use of rollovers can help draw attention to smaller, less noticeable buttons, and it also helps visitors realize that the graphic is a link. Rarely are graphics that aren't connected to anything—another page, another site, a file—set up as rollovers, also known as *interactive images*.

Of course, you can use ImageReady to build a rollover, creating an image that appears in different forms in different states: when it's idle (no one's touching or pointing to it), when a mouse has moved on top of it, and when it's clicked. You'll find out more about that in Chapter 10, in which you'll get a tour of ImageReady and its tools, and in Chapter 12, where you'll use ImageReady to create a rollover. You can also create rollovers quickly and perhaps more easily in Photoshop by creating two versions of the same image: one that's the idle version, one that's the moused-over version. I prefer this method to using ImageReady for quick rollovers, because I end up with two files, both of which I can edit later if the client asks for a change or if I feel the need to redesign one or both of the images.

Using Save As to Create Two Button Versions

The process of creating two button versions is simple. First, create one of the image versions—say, the idle version. Save that file in both PSD and a Web-safe format, and then resave it (use the File|Save As command) in PSD format with a different name (I like to add a "2" to the original file's name). Then, make some change in the new version, such as changing a background color or making the text italic. Save the new version in a Web-safe format, and resave the PSD format file. That way, you have editable versions (with layers intact) of both the non-moused and moused-over versions of the file, and you also have Web-safe versions of both files. As shown in Figures 7.18 and 7.19, the only difference between the two images is the change in shadow and embossing effects.

Figure 7.18

(Left) The idle version looks like a button that's standing up, awaiting a click.

Figure 7.19

(Right) The version that appears when a visitor mouses over the button looks as though it's been pressed or pushed into the page.

Tweaking Effects to Create a Pressed Button

If you want to achieve results like those seen in Figures 7.18 and 7.19, follow these steps:

1. Create the first button, the one that appears when the button is idle.

2. Apply a drop shadow to the bottom layer of the button—the part of the button that looks like it's sitting on the page.

3. Use the Bevel And Emboss effect on any shapes or thick lines if they're supposed to look 3-D or as though they have weight.

4. Leave the text alone—don't shadow or emboss it, because it's supposed to look like text printed on a keyboard or typewriter key.

5. Save the file in both the native Photoshop format (PSD) and in a Web-safe format, preferably JPEG because of the multitude of colors employed in creating the shadows and highlights.

6. Immediately save the PSD file with another name, using the File|Save As command. Add a "2" or a "B" to the original file's name.

7. Remove the drop shadows applied to the original file, and remove the Bevel And Emboss effect as well.

8. Apply the Inner Glow and Inner Shadow effects. The second version of the file now looks like the button has dropped into the page, as though someone has pressed the key.

Keep It Simple!

If the idle version of the button is named "contact.jpg", I name the rollover version "contact2.jpg". It's easy for me to remember that the one with the "2" is the second version, the file that will appear after the visitor mouses over the first image. Keep your file names short, and use "A" and "B" or "1" and "2" to keep versions clearly separate.

9. Save the file again in PSD format to save your latest changes, and then save it in a Web-safe format, again preferably JPEG.

PROJECT Create Home and Back buttons for a Web page

In this project, you'll create two buttons. They'll look the same except for their text; you'll create a Home and a Back button.

Start a New File

Use the File|New command to create a 2-inch-square image in RGB mode, with a white background. The resolution should be 72 pixels per inch.

Add a New, Blank Layer

Add a new layer (Layer|New|Layer) and call it "button base".

Draw a Button Shape on the New Layer

Draw a rectangle or ellipse (your choice) on the button base layer. It will automatically fill with your current Foreground color, and that's fine—you can change it later, and it will be replaced in the next step, anyway.

Apply a Gradient Fill to the Shape

1. Select the shape you just drew by using the Magic Wand tool (click on the shape, and all of its uniformly colored pixels will be selected).

2. Choose new Foreground and Background colors.

3. Click the Gradient tool in the toolbox.

4. Move your mouse onto the image, and drag across the selected shape. The gradient you apply will fade from Foreground color to Background color if you drag from left to right, or from Background color to Foreground color if you drag from right to left.

Duplicate the Shape on a New Layer

Right-click the layer with the gradient-filled shape on it, and choose Duplicate Layer from the shortcut menu. This makes a new layer with the same shape on it.

Transform the Shape, Scaling It to Be Smaller Than the Original

On the new layer (it will be named "button base copy" because it was a direct duplicate of the button base layer), choose Edit|Scale. Your mouse pointer turns into a two-headed arrow, which you can use to drag from a corner handle. Drag toward the center of the shape, making the shape smaller. Aim for an approximately 30 percent reduction, as shown in Figure 7.20.

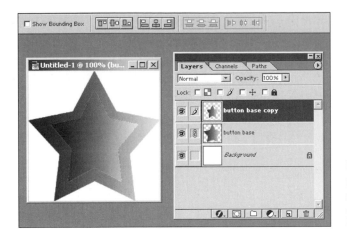

Figure 7.20
Make the duplicate shape a little smaller so it will fit inside the original shape on the button base layer.

Position the Smaller Shape on Top of the Larger One

Activate the button base copy layer, and move the shape so that it is centered on top of the original button base. You can use the Align buttons to assist you in placing the smaller shape in the exact center of the larger shape.

Apply a Gradient Fill Going in the Opposite Direction

Use the Marquee tool (the Elliptical Marquee if your button is a circle or an oval, the Rectangular Marquee if your button is a rectangle or a square) to select the shape inside the button base copy layer. You can also use the Lasso or Magic Wand tool to select the smaller shape, but be prepared to use the Shift key with the Wand to make sure you grab all of the shape.

Next, use the Gradient tool and drag across the selected shape, but drag in a direction opposite that which you dragged when you applied the gradient to the original shape on the button base layer. As shown in Figure 7.21, this creates the illusion of depth and height on the button, and a shape to its center.

Figure 7.21
When you create opposing gradient fills on the two stacked shapes, the button begins to look like a 3-D object.

Apply Effects to the Bottom Shape

Return to the button base layer and double-click it, which opens the Layer Styles dialog box. Apply the following effects:

- *Drop Shadow*—Feel free to tinker with the depth and angle of the shadow if you don't like the default settings.

- *Bevel And Emboss*—This will create the illusion of a curved edge to the button's base, making it look like a solid object, raised above the surface of the page. Figure 7.22 shows the results of these effects on a button in progress.

Create a Type Layer

Activate the Type tool, and then type the word "Home" on the image. Photoshop creates a Home type layer automatically, as shown in Figure 7.23. A font size of 22 points should create text that's small enough to fit on the button but

Figure 7.22
Your button is taking shape.

Figure 7.23
The text you type on the button tells page visitors where they'll end up if they click the button.

large enough to read. Use black as the text color, but consider adding an outer glow to the type layer so that the black text is visible on top of the darker end of your gradient fill. We've done this to the text in Figure 7.23.

As needed, use the Move tool to position the text so that it is centered on the button, inside the smaller shape. If the text doesn't fit inside the center shape, reduce the font size.

Save the Button Image in Both PSD and Web-Safe Formats

1. First, save the file in PSD format by choosing File|Save.

2. Name the file "homebutton.psd".

3. Using the File|Save For Web command, save a JPEG version of the file, keeping the file name the same. The extension (.jpg) will be applied for you.

Save the Button File with a New Name

To create a Back button that looks just like the Home button (which will take visitors back to the previous page), follow these steps:

1. Use the File|Save As command to create a new version of the Home button.

2. Save the file as "backbutton.psd". The homebutton.psd file will close, leaving its new version open.

Edit the Type Layer

On the new file's type layer (currently called Home), edit the text to read "Back" instead. The layer should automatically be renamed "Back" as well. Press Ctrl+S or issue the File|Save command to update the backbutton.psd file to reflect this change. Figure 7.24 shows the new Back button, which is identical to the Home button except for the text.

Figure 7.24
Voila! New button, no major effort.

Save the New File for the Web

Use the File|Save For Web command to create a Web-safe version of this new file. Choose the JPEG format again, and leave the file name (backbutton) the same. You now have two buttons that can be used to link site visitors to two different places, but you only had to create the button itself once!

> **Read All About It**
>
> You can find out more about using applications like GoLive and Dreamweaver in Chapter 16.

Creating a Navigation Bar

Unlike individual buttons, which can be placed anywhere on the page—in table cells, in a series down the left side or across the bottom of the page, at the end of paragraphs—a navigation bar is a solid unit that contains several navigational tools. The bar itself becomes a tool for linking to several different pages, sites, or files through the use of *hotspots*, or areas selected and assigned to Web addresses or to paths to particular files.

You create hotspots in programs like Dreamweaver or GoLive, or you can type the HTML code that divides an image into one or more link areas, directly in your Web page document. Figure 7.25 shows a navigation bar divided into

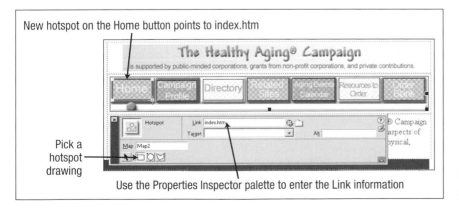

New hotspot on the Home button points to index.htm

Pick a hotspot drawing

Use the Properties Inspector palette to enter the Link information

Figure 7.25
Take the navigation bar and chop it up into hotspots.

hotspots in Dreamweaver. Using what looks like drawing tools, you draw shapes on the surface of an image, and each shape becomes a spot that, when clicked, takes the visitor to a URL or file.

Creating Layers for Bar Components

Just like a button, a navigation bar requires several layers, one for each of the bar's elements. For the bar shown in Figure 7.26, the following layers are required:

- Main bar—the long colored strip on which the individual navigation tabs will sit

- Four tabs (each on its own layer)

- An active page indicator (the colored dot) for each tab

- Type layers, one for each tab (these are created when the text is typed, not beforehand as the others are)

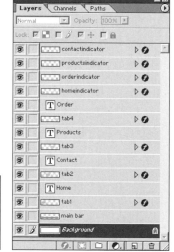

Figure 7.26

The navigation bar isn't terribly complex, but its use as a navigation tool is extensive.

Drawing the Bar

The main bar can be drawn with the Rectangle or Rectangular Marquee tool. Be sure to activate the Main Bar layer before you begin drawing. If you decide to draw the shape with the Rectangle tool, choose the Create Filled Region option, because you should already have a layer created for the shape. It's much easier to deal with layers that just happen to contain shapes than to deal with shape layers as Photoshop 6 creates them. Check out Chapter 2, for more information about this issue.

Using the tool of your choice, draw a long, horizontal rectangle, approximately 4–4.5 inches (about 400 pixels) in width and about half an inch (32 pixels) high. If you use the Marquee tool, give the selected shape a fill color by using the Paint Bucket to apply the Foreground color of your choice. If you choose to

Your Navigation Mileage May Vary

The navigation bar created in this chapter is just a sample, intended to give you ideas for creating your own, and to demonstrate Photoshop's tools for creating original artwork for Web sites. You might need a longer bar to accommodate more tabs, or prefer a vertical bar, placed on the left or right side of the page rather than running across the page top. You might prefer not to use actual tabs, or to use photographs or drawings for each page represented in the navigation bar. There are no rules! All that a navigation bar has to do is provide multiple graphical images that are linked to pages, sites, or files. The actual design of the navigation bar is entirely up to you, and I hope that after you read about the building of a rather simple one, your imagination will be unleashed to design something really snazzy.

Figure 7.27

The main bar is the navigation bar's foundation.

use the Rectangle tool to draw a shape, the current Foreground color will fill it automatically, so it's a good idea to pick a color before you draw the shape. Figure 7.27 shows the finished product.

Adding Tab Shapes to the Bar

On each tab layer (Tab1, Tab2, Tab3, and Tab4, or whatever you choose to call yours), draw a 1-inch rectangle, as shown in Figure 7.28. Fill the rectangles with a color that's either a lighter shade of the main bar's fill color or a complementary color. In this sample, I've applied a drop shadow to each tab for added visual impact.

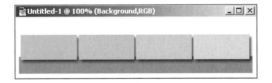

Figure 7.28

If your bar is at least 4 inches long, four 1-inch tabs will fit very nicely along the bar's length.

Creating Active Tab Indicators

On the Tab Indicator layer, draw a small circle and fill it with a color that will stand out on (but not clash with) the bar and tabs. Figure 7.29 shows the indicator dot under the first tab shape.

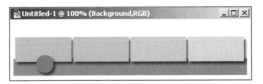

Figure 7.29

The indicator will move on each version of the bar graphic, appearing below the tab that represents the page the visitor is looking at.

Duplicate the indicator layer three times so that you have an indicator for each tab. These will be used on the multiple versions of the original navigator bar, with each individual tab having its own indicator and all the other tabs' indicators hidden.

Adding Text to the Bar Tabs

Without text on the tabs, your site visitor wouldn't know which tab was linked to which page in the site. As with the individual buttons, keep the text to a minimum so that it fits on the 1-inch tabs. You want to create separate type layers for each tab, rather than typing a long string of words with spaces between them on a single type layer. By creating separate layers, you make it easier to position each one exactly in the middle of each tab.

Typing on Each Tab

When you're ready to type on a tab, click the Type tool, and then click to place your cursor on the tab. You're not actually typing *on* the tabs, but on top of them. Type the word or short phrase for a single tab, and then click the Marquee tool to deselect the Type tool. This disassociates the first tab's text from the text you're about to type.

As you move to the next tab, click the Type tool again, and click on the tab to begin typing. Repeat this process for each tab on the bar. When you've created all of the tabs' type layers, use the Move tool to position them exactly. You want the text to be centered both horizontally and vertically within the tabs, as shown in Figure 7.30.

Figure 7.30

Type and position your text on each tab.

Formatting the Text to Fit the Tabs

As needed, you can change the font, size, and color of the text on each tab. It's best for all the tabs' text to look the same, but if you want a more free-wheeling feel for the Web page on which this bar will be placed, try using a different font on each tab. Figure 7.31 shows a series of tabs, with various fonts and font sizes.

Figure 7.31

Consistency is great, but on a page that can handle some eccentricity, try breaking up the monotony of a single font on your entire bar's tabs.

Creating a Version of the Bar for Each Represented Page

After you've built the navigation bar—the main bar, the tabs, the active tab indicators, and the text for each tab—you're ready to create duplicates of the bar. The duplicates will appear on each page in your Web site, providing a consistent navigational tool on every page and helping visitors concentrate on page content rather than finding their way around.

To make the duplicates, simply use the File|Save As command three times, naming each new version of the original file so that you can tell which bar goes on which Web page. For example, name the bar that will go on the Products page "productsbar.psd" and the bar that will go on the About Us page "aboutusbar.psd". Don't get fancy with an elaborate file-naming scheme; choose names that say exactly where the image will be used.

Hiding and Displaying Active Tab Indicators

Remember that whenever you save a new version of an existing, saved file, the original file is closed. This means that on your third File|Save As procedure, you'll end up with the last version open and all the previously created versions closed. Reopen them so that all four versions of the navigation bar image file are open and on screen. You can minimize all the windows but the one you're about to work on.

With all of the files open, go to each one and hide all but the active tab's active tab indicator. For example, in the aboutusbar.psd file, hide the active tab indicator dots for all but the About Us tab. Make sure that tab's indicator is centered just below that tab. Resave the file (File|Save) to reflect this change, and then repeat these steps for each of the other three bar images. Leave only one indicator dot visible, and position it appropriately for each version of the file.

Saving Web-Safe Versions of the Bar for Each Active Tab

After you've created four PSD files, each with the same bar and tabs but with a different tab indicated as active, save each file in a Web-safe format. Because these bars have no shadows or embossing effects, you can save the files in GIF format, which creates much smaller files. Figure 7.32 shows the Save For Web dialog box and the optimized version of the image displayed in GIF format.

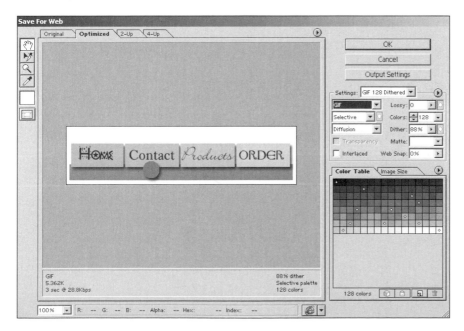

Figure 7.32

For a page element as important as the navigation bar, you want a quick load time, as estimated here (as shown in the lower-left corner of the dialog box, this image will take just 3 seconds to load at 28.8Kbps).

PROJECT Create a Navigation Bar

In this project, you'll design a horizontal navigation bar that consists of a strip of shapes and text, each pointing to a different page within a Web site. The shapes, colors, and text formatting are up to you, and you needn't create something that looks exactly like the bar in the project's figures. Feel free to use your own good taste and design sense to create something totally unique.

Start a New Photoshop File

Using the File|New command, create a new file that's 500 pixels wide by 100 pixels high. Set the mode to RGB and the resolution to 72 pixels per inch. The background should be white.

Create Layers for All the Elements of the Navigation Bar

This project requires at least 11 layers:

- The main bar itself, on which the tab shapes sit or hang
- Tab shapes for each of the five pages to which the sample bar navigates
- Active tab indicators for each tab—a total of five—that will appear beneath or above (your choice) the tab for the active page

Note that the text on each tab will be in five separate type layers. Remember that you cannot create those layers ahead of time—Photoshop creates them automatically when you type the text onto each tab.

Draw the Bar Shape

Draw a bar using the Rectangular Marquee or Rectangle tool. Fill the bar with any color you choose. Figure 7.33 shows a bar that's 25 pixels high and 450 pixels long, though it may appear smaller in the figure.

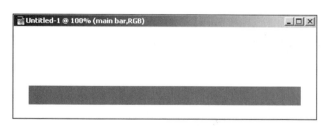

Figure 7.33
The main bar should be long enough to serve as a foundation for all the tabs you need.

Draw Tabs on Each Layer

On each of the tab layers you created ahead of time, draw a tab shape. It can be rectangular, elliptical, or freeform in shape (use the Lasso tool to draw the shape, and then copy it to each of the tab layers). You can even create tabs from pictures: Just copy portions of photographs or drawings onto the tab layers. Figure 7.34 shows a tab layer that contains a freeform tab, filled with a gradient fill. We've also applied a drop shadow.

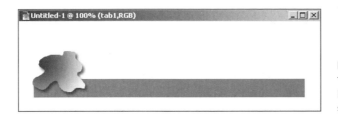

Figure 7.34
To make sure your navigation bar loads quickly, keep the images simple.

Add Type Layers for Each Tab

Using the Type tool, type text onto each tab. Each tab's text will be on its own type layer. Keep the text short, as shown in Figure 7.35. The fonts and sizes you use are up to you, but make sure the text is legible.

Figure 7.35
You can vary the fonts on each tab to add a bit of whimsy to your navigation bar, or choose one interesting font for all the tabs, as shown here.

Link Tabs with Their Text

Use the Link boxes next to each layer to chain each tab layer to its type layer.

Draw Indicator Shapes for Each Tab

As shown in Figure 7.36, each tab has a shape under it (you can place yours above the tabs, or even on the tabs, as long as the tab text won't be obscured) to indicate which tab represents the active page. The navigation bar will appear on every page in your site. When, for example, you're on the About Us page, that tab should appear to be the active tab. Having a shape under/on/above that tab (and on no other tabs) will let your visitors know they're on the About Us page.

A Whimsical Stockbroker?

Well, maybe not. Use fonts and colors that are in keeping with the tone or feeling you want for the page that will house your navigation bar.

Figure 7.36
You can draw a different shape for each tab, but for simplicity's sake, it's better to draw a single shape and paste it onto each indicator layer.

Save a Version of Your Bar for Each Tab

Your navigation bar should be repeated on each page in your site so that visitors find a common navigation tool no matter which page they're on. Of course, you don't want to create a new bar for every page, so you can simply use the File|Save As command to create multiple versions of the original bar image. I prefer to name my versions according to the page they'll live on—contactusbar.psd, placeorderbar.psd, and so on.

Hiding Inactive Tab Indicators

On each of the versions of the bar image, hide all but one tab's indicator. The displayed indicator should be under the tab for the page on which that bar will appear. For example, if the bar is placeorderbar.psd, only the indicator for the Place An Order tab should be visible, and of course, the indicator should be under/on/above that tab.

Saving Web Versions of the Bar for Each Tab

After setting up all the versions of your bar, save each one in a Web-safe format. If your navigation bar includes simple shapes with no shadows or embossing, use the GIF format to create very small, quick-loading image files. If your bar and tabs contain any shadows, embossing, photographic content, or a lot of colors (if you used any patterns to fill the tabs, for example), select the JPEG format.

Moving On

In the next chapter, you'll learn to build background images and images used to help map out the content of a new Web page. Both elements serve a pivotal role in Web page design: They provide a foundation for the page that speeds and simplifies the development of the Web page, providing either a permanent backdrop or a temporary blueprint for building tables, frames, and layers and inserting page content.

Chapter 8

Creating Backgrounds and Tracing Images

Photoshop's graphic tools play a role that goes beyond creating navigation buttons and graphic text. Designing a page background that enhances without overwhelming and tracing images that speed the design process are key skills for any Web designer.

Why Use a Background Image?

Although it's not necessary to have a background image, if you choose to use one, it can make or break your page. A background that's too dark, too bright, too busy, too *anything* can detract (if not completely overwhelm) your page content. Photos and artwork can be visually lost, text can be rendered illegible, and the entire page can fail as a tool for selling, sharing information, or conveying any sort of message. A completely ineffective background image is shown in Figure 8.1.

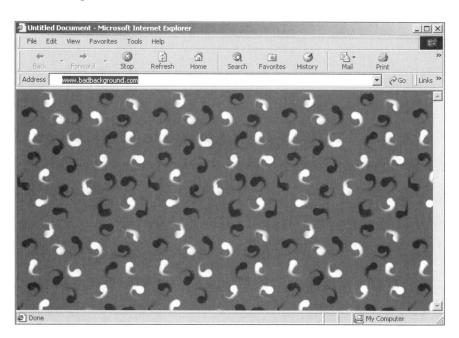

Figure 8.1
Even a powerful and elegant design tool can be used to create a hideous mistake.

On the other hand, a subtle and relevant image can be an effective backdrop for a page that has a lot of text and few graphics, or one that needs some visual "punching up" without adding a lot of pictures and graphic text. As shown in Figure 8.2, a background image that echoes the theme or topic of the page is a great addition to any Web page, provided that the background image doesn't compete with the page content.

Background Image Guidelines

If you feel your page needs a background image, it's important that you choose one that helps maintain the look and feel you want for the page, and that the background itself doesn't detract from the page. Keep these basic guidelines in mind, and you should have a more positive result from any background image:

- Keep it simple. A busy pattern will compete with text and graphics on your page. If you have an actual pattern (as opposed to a picture or logo)

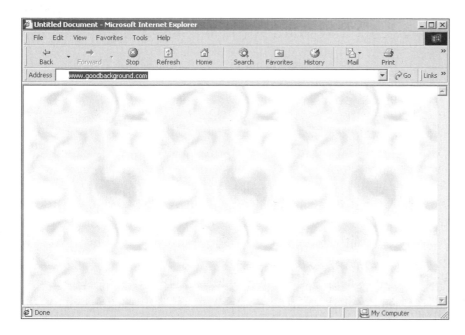

Figure 8.2

When it comes to background images, less is definitely more.

for your background, make sure it's very basic, along the lines of a checkerboard or Greek key design, as shown in Figure 8.3. Textures are also fine, as long as they're not complex—for example, a sand texture or other granular or simple fabric texture is fine, but something like river rocks or a multicolored, tweed-y fabric texture might be overwhelming.

Figure 8.3

A repeating pattern should be simple and vaguely geometric. Avoid busy paisleys and florals.

- Keep it light. Even if your Web page is dark, don't let the background be darker than a solid color you'd use. Why? Because if you'd planned, for example, on a bright blue background with dark blue or black text, a background image with any content darker than the bright blue will render dark text illegible. Always use muted, faded shades, and reduce the opacity of an image to at least 20%—anything more opaque is bound to compete with the page content. Figures 8.4 and 8.5 show the same background image—the first with too much intensity and color depth, and the second at the right opacity for effective use on a page with text and graphics.

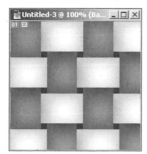 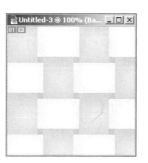

Figure 8.4

(Left) It's a simple pattern, and it matches the tone and topic of the page—but it's too dark and intense!

Figure 8.5

(Right) Ah, that's better. Fading into the background is what a background image is *supposed* to do.

Adjusting Opacity

To adjust the opacity of your image, adjust the opacity of all the layers in the image. You can do this from the Layers palette, dragging the slider down to the opacity you want. Not all of the layers have to be at the same opacity, but the overall effect, when the layers are viewed together, should be faded enough to achieve the subtle background effect you're looking for.

- Keep it subtle. This is really the result of adhering to the first two guidelines. If your colors are light and your images simple, your background effect will be subtle. Of course, subtlety doesn't come naturally to everyone, so if you're not sure whether you've achieved it, or maybe you're thinking your particular page background can ignore these guidelines, have someone you trust, whose taste you respect, review your page with the background in place.

Designing an Effective Background Image

An effective background image works like wallpaper in a room: It enhances the overall design without drawing attention to itself. As you approach the process of designing the background for your page, plan the image accordingly. If your page will contain several linear construction devices, such as frames or tables, you might want a softer background image, perhaps one with curves and more natural, visceral shapes, like leaves, vines, or even people (see Figure 8.6). If, on the other hand, your page is rather freeform, making use of layers and tables with a variety of column and row heights/widths for an unstructured layout, you can use a linear design for your background (see Figure 8.7). One of the keys to good design is knowing when to use a *foil*, which is a feature with attributes that are the direct opposite of another feature in the same space. Employing opposites allows the background to enhance the page.

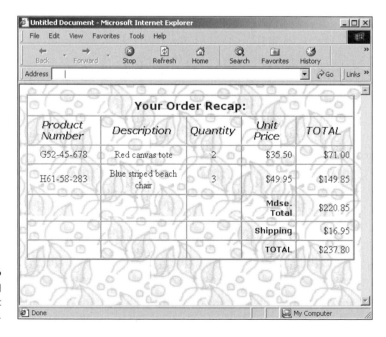

Figure 8.6

Complement your structured layout with a background that has soft, round edges within it.

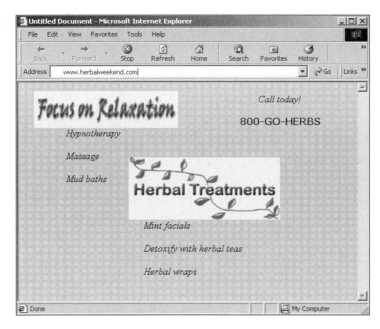

Figure 8.7
Make the most of a freeform layout by using a straightforward, structured pattern for your background image.

Controlling Image Tile Effects

Another key point to keep in mind as you begin designing your background image is the fact that the image will probably have to be *tiled* in order to fill the Web page. For example, if your image is 200 pixels square (just under 3 inches by 3 inches), it will have to tile four times across the page and three times down the page to fill a page viewed at 800×600 pixel resolution (see Figure 8.8).

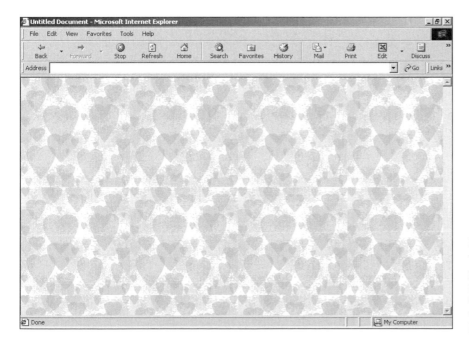

Figure 8.8
Think about the resolution of your visitors' monitors and plan to have your image tile, or repeat in a structured array, enough times to cover the page background.

Load-Time "Guesstimates"

Remember that you can see the estimated load time for any image in the Save For Web dialog box. When you save your image in a Web-safe format, check the lower-left corner of the dialog box to see the file size for the format and quality you've chosen, and to see an estimate of the load time as experienced by a visitor using a 28.8Kbps modem. The time it takes your image to load once is the time it will take for an entire screen filled with tiled versions of the image to appear on the page.

You can make your image 800×600 so that it fills the page without tiling, but that results in an image that's so big it takes too long to load. Visitors will have read the entire page, clicked a link, and moved on to another page before your background image loads. Just like any image on a Web page, your background image file shouldn't be more than 35KB, or take more than 6 seconds to load; the maximum people are willing to wait for a picture or other Web content to appear on screen. You can push the edge of that envelope slightly, using an image that takes 10 seconds or so to load, simply because it's the background. Although the page itself doesn't need the background to be read or to have the visitor follow links on the page, it is nice to have the background show up long before the visitor has left the page.

Sizing the Image for Tiling

After you design the image, use the Image|Image Size command to reduce or enlarge it to the size you need. You know what size you need if you have requirements for how the image will tile. For example, if the image is your organization's logo, you don't want it to tile 50 times on the page; it would probably look too busy. If, on the other hand, your image is just a pattern—a field of leaves or a textured effect—you can make it as tiny an image size as you want, because the number of tiles required to fill the screen will be invisible to the site visitor. Figure 8.9 shows an image that's just a texture—sort of a burlap—that's only 25 pixels square, but it fills a screen quite nicely.

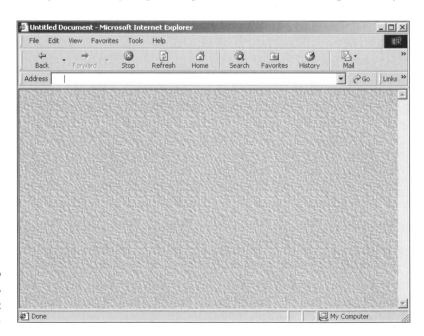

Figure 8.9
Patterns can repeat as many times as needed, so you can start with a very small image.

If your image is a picture that won't weather the tiling process well, or that should tile a very few times (four or five maximum), try increasing the canvas size rather than the image size. As shown in Figure 8.10, the logo itself is rather

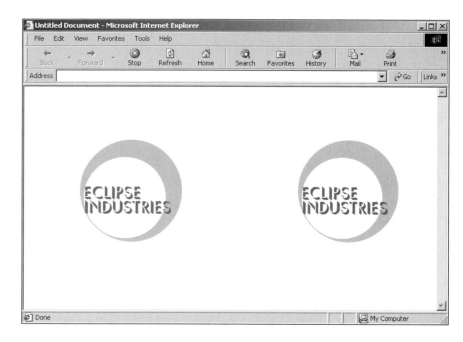

small, but on a larger solid-color field, an image of this size will tile only twice across and once down. You can tweak the canvas size as you test the image on a Web page, reducing or enlarging it until the tiling effect is agreeable.

Saving the Image for the Web

As you would save any other Photoshop image bound for the Web, you need to save the image in a Web-safe format. The same rules for choosing a format that apply to any other Web graphic apply to graphics intended for use as a background graphic:

- A lot of colors and subtle shading requires the JPEG format. So do images that contain photographic content.

- Simple shapes and just a handful of colors with no shadows or embossing applied are better off as GIF images.

To save your image for the Web, use the File|Save For Web command. In the resulting Save For Web dialog box, choose the format and quality for that format. If you go with JPEG, you can choose from Low, Medium, High, and Maximum quality, and at each of those levels, you can adjust the quality to a specific percentage. If you go with GIF, you can choose the number of colors, and therefore the quality of the image. Figure 8.11 shows the Save For Web dialog box with JPEG Medium selected. Because the image is quite faded, the details become less important than they would at full opacity, where High or Maximum might have been required in order for the image detail to be displayed clearly.

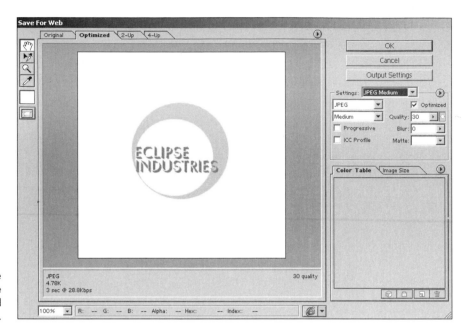

Figure 8.11
If it looks good here and the load time is acceptable, you've found the right format and quality for your image.

Testing the Background Image on a Web Page

Once you've saved your image for the Web, you're ready to add it to a page. You have to designate it as the page background rather than set it as a graphic on the page. First, set the image up on a page to test it, making sure the image looks okay when tiled and that the tiling frequency is what you expected it to be. It's a good idea to add some page content, too, so you can see if the background will compete with text and graphics. Figures 8.12 and 8.13 show a background in place on a blank Web page, and then a page with the same background and

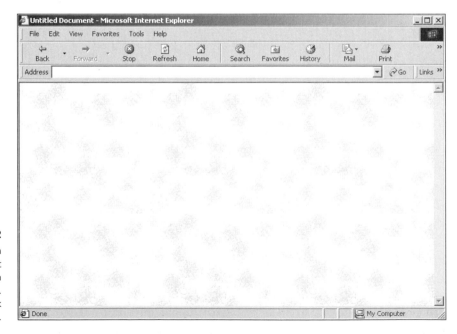

Figure 8.12
A page with only a background image doesn't completely troubleshoot a potential background graphic. Just about any image will look good on its own.

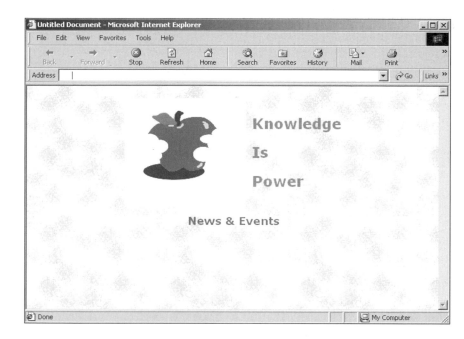

Figure 8.13
Once you add text and graphics, you find out if your background image is really doing its job. White background on the apple graphic needs to be removed so that the background shows through.

some heading text and a sample graphic in place. An effective background won't look better on a blank page than it does when you add content.

Create a Background Image

In this project, you'll create a patterned background image using an existing image. By adjusting image opacity and size, you can turn virtually any image into a background, but troubleshooting it on the Web (also part of this project) is the final test of any effective background image.

Open an Existing File
Open the Chapter 8 folder on the CD that accompanies this book and open the file called wallpaper.psd.

Reduce Opacity of All Layers to 20%
Select each of the image layers individually, and reduce their opacity to 20%.

Adjust Canvas Size to 200×200 Pixels
Using the Image|Image Size command, make the image 200 pixels tall by 200 pixels wide. This is makes it slightly smaller than its original size.

Preview Size of File Using Save For Web Command
Save the file as a JPEG file, and check the load-time estimate for the file at High quality.

Test the Background on a Web Page
Open Dreamweaver, GoLive, or the WYSIWYG application of your choice and add the image as the background image on a blank page. If you prefer, you

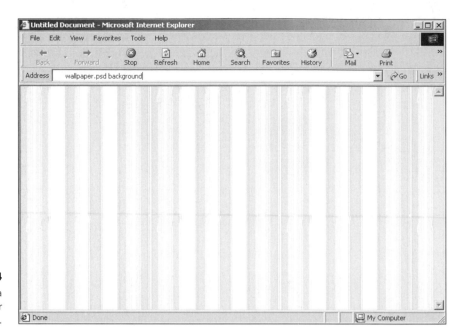

Figure 8.14
The wallpaper.jpg file creates a very pleasant background for virtually any Web page.

can create an HTML document, and add a background attribute to the **<body>** tag. After inserting the image, preview the page in a Web browser. Figure 8.14 shows the image in use on a blank page, viewed through Microsoft Internet Explorer, at 800×600 resolution.

Working with Tracing Images

A tracing image is a blueprint that sits on your Web page during the design phase, but falls under your page background and any text, graphics, or structural devices you add to the page, such as tables, layers, or frames. The image is meant to act as a guide, to remind you of the overall structure of the page and indicate where major (and perhaps even minor) elements should be placed.

Photoshop is a great tool for creating tracing images because it makes building an image the size of your page or a portion thereof quick and easy. You can draw shapes and lines, type text, and apply colored fills—all the basic elements that make up an effective tracing image. Figure 8.15 shows a simple tracing image in progress. It's currently at 100% opacity, but you can reduce that setting in Photoshop before saving the image in a Web-safe format, or afterward, by using the WYSIWYG application you use to design your page.

Creating a Tracing Image

Tracing images aren't difficult to build, and creating them is no different from creating any other image you might build in Photoshop. If you're designing a tracing image that should fill a Web page, it will be a much larger file than you're likely to design for any other Web purpose. This is because, generally, Web graphics are small files in both dimension and file size. Other than that, though, the planning and execution of the image requires no specialized Photoshop skills or tools.

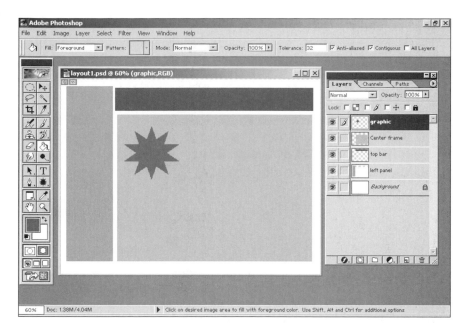

Figure 8.15
Simple shapes can indicate where layers or table cells go, and drawings indicate where graphics should be placed on the page.

Drawing Page Elements

It's best to create each element—shapes, lines, text, small drawings, or even pasted photographs or clip art—on its own layer. This makes it possible to quickly edit the image and move its pieces around. Rarely does a Web design remain the same from inception to implementation, so you'll want your Photoshop file to be easily manipulated. As your design goals change, often after you get started literally putting your Web page together, you might want to reinsert the tracing image with changes made so your design plans and the blueprint for them are in sync. Figure 8.16 shows a tracing image in progress, with layers for each part of the image—each shape, line, graphic, and even paragraph text.

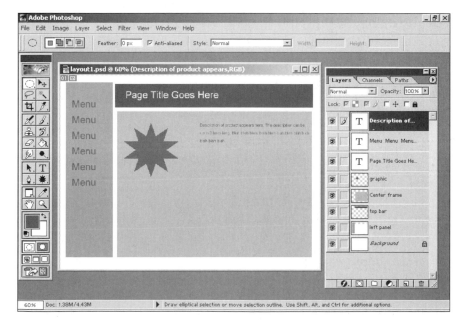

Figure 8.16
Your tracing image text can be truly representational, or simply instructional—"this goes here, that goes there"—to increase the effectiveness of the image.

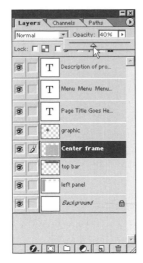

Figure 8.17

Optimally, a tracing image should be just opaque enough to suggest a design, just dark enough to be legible. Anything darker or more intense will overpower the page content.

Darken This, Lighten That

If your tracing image contains text, you might want that to remain opaque enough to read, while reducing the opacity of shapes and lines more. In most cases, those elements only need to be dark enough to see them so they help you map out layers, size frames, and adjust table widths and heights. You can always use the design application's tools to reduce opacity further should the intensity of any element in the tracing image interfere with the design process.

Changing Image Opacity

WYSIWYG design applications like Dreamweaver allow you to adjust the opacity of the image after you've inserted it as a tracing image. For this reason, there is no absolute need to reduce the opacity of the image in Photoshop. If you don't want to be bothered tinkering with it through your Web design application, however, or if you want to be able to see it in its faded, tracing state right away, go ahead and use Photoshop's Layers palette to reduce the opacity of some or all of your image layers and their content. Figure 8.17 shows the opacity of a large rectangle being reduced to 40%.

Remember that when you preview the page you're designing in a Web browser, the tracing image won't show. This makes it possible to keep a fairly opaque image on screen during the design phase, because you can keep skipping out to a Web preview to see how your design is coming along without the tracing image getting in the way.

Saving the Image for the Web

Even though the tracing image won't be uploaded to the Web server along with your page and its images, you need to save it in a Web-safe format before adding it to the page through your WYSIWYG design application. The format you choose—JPEG, GIF, PNG—is only important if one of them gives you a better quality image than another. The quality of the image need only be good enough so that you can see the image elements and read any instructional or representational text.

As you will for any Photoshop file bound for the Web, choose File|Save For Web, pick your format, and give your image a name. Be sure to save it to the same folder as your other page images, if only to make finding it easier when you're in your WYSIWYG application and ready to insert the image.

Applying a Tracing Image to a Web Page

Dreamweaver creates its own specialized HTML code (**tracingsrc**= "___" is added to the **<body>** tag) that is ignored by Web browsers (which explains why you can't see the image when you preview your page in a browser). The code is added when you specify the tracing image options in Dreamweaver's Page Properties dialog box.

To use an image as a tracing image, you must be in a Dreamweaver document (it can already have content), and then choose Modify|Page Properties. In the resulting Page Properties dialog box, click the Browse button next to the Tracing Image text box, or if you know the path to and file name of the image file, type it directly in the box. Figure 8.18 shows an image path and file name already chosen.

After you choose an image, click the Apply button to keep the dialog box open but also to see your image in place. You can then set the opacity (using the Image Transparency slider) so that the image is faded enough to serve as a

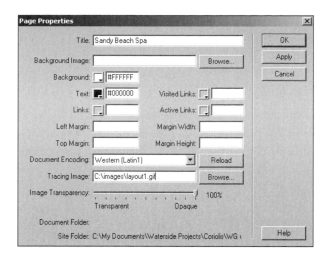

Figure 8.18
Choose an image and then set its opacity, as needed.

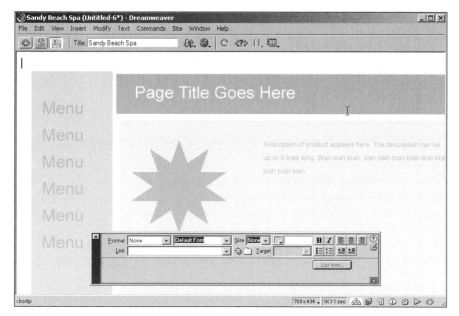

Figure 8.19
See the image in place on the page while you tweak its transparency setting.

blueprint, but vivid enough to be seen. Figure 8.19 shows an image in place and its opacity set to 30%. The image was not made less opaque in Photoshop, so all adjustments to opacity are through Dreamweaver's tools.

At this point, you can begin using the tracing image, setting up your page with tables, layers, frames, and the content placed inside them. You can preview your page in Dreamweaver by pressing F12 to see the page in the browser you have set as your default. To view the page in an alternate browser, choose File|Preview In Browser, and then select the browser by name from the resulting submenu.

Repositioning and Hiding the Tracing Image
Sometimes your tracing image won't fill the page (by design or by accident). This means you have to move it a bit so that it falls underneath the portion of the page with which you need guidance in placing page elements. To adjust

Figure 8.20

Need the tracing image in the upper-left corner of the page? Set the X and Y coordinates to 0. Refer to the ruler to set other coordinates for other desired positions.

Out of Sight, Out of Mind

There's no harm in leaving the image on the page even after you've finished your design and are ready to upload the page to a Web server. You can skip uploading the tracing image, because it won't be displayed online (the Web browser won't know what to do with the **tracingsrc=** attribute in your page **<body>** tag anyway), and leaving the image information in the HTML code makes it possible to see the image when you view the page locally—you might need to do a redesign at some point.

the position of your tracing image, choose View|Tracing Image|Adjust Position, and use the resulting dialog box to set new X (horizontal position) and Y (vertical position) coordinates, as shown in Figure 8.20. If you no longer want to see the tracing image within the Dreamweaver window, choose View|Tracing Image|Show (the command is checked when the image is visible) and toggle the image visibility off.

PROJECT Create a Tracing Image

In this project, you'll build a tracing image for a Web page and then apply it to a page through Macromedia's Dreamweaver and its Page Properties dialog box. If you don't have Dreamweaver, you can download a trial copy through the Macromedia Web site, at **www.macromedia.com**.

Plan the Tracing Image

Typically, you'd plan the design of a Web page, perhaps sketching it on paper, and that plan would dictate the content and layout of the tracing image. To make your life easier, refer to Figure 8.21, which shows a Web page already built and viewed through a Web browser. With this page in mind, make a list of the elements you'd need to include in a tracing image that would assist the designer in creating that page.

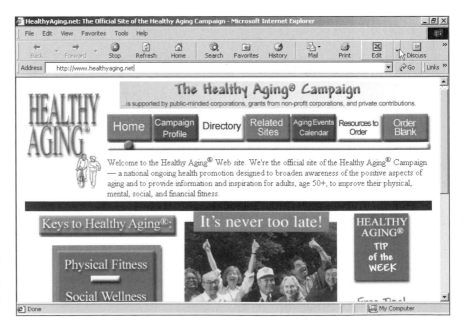

Figure 8.21

The creation of a Web page that requires a rather freeform table to hold text and graphics is simplified with a good tracing image acting as a blueprint.

Start a Photoshop File

In Photoshop, start an image that's 800 pixels wide by 600 pixels tall. This will create a large image in terms of file size, but that's not important because the image won't load with the Web page anyway.

Build Tracing Image Layers

You'll need multiple layers for the tracing image that helps build the page shown in Figure 8.21. Create and name each of them before you create any of the image content. When naming the layers, consider using names that indicate the placement of the layer's content. Names such as "left side top" and "bottom right" will help you identify and select layers later.

Draw Tracing Image Elements

Each visual section of the page needs to be mapped with a shape that helps show the width and height of each table cell, and that reminds the designer which cells should have a background color and which color to apply. Don't forget shapes and type layers to indicate where graphics and paragraphs will go on the page.

Adjust Image Opacity

Select each layer and reduce the opacity to 15%, resulting in a very faded image. Don't merge the layers and then reduce the opacity of the single layer you're left with, because in real life, chances are you'd need to keep your layers separate in case something needed to be changed or moved later.

Save a Tracing Image for the Web

You can save the file in any Web-safe format—JPEG, GIF, PNG—and name it anything you'd like. Remember, the size of the file (in kilobytes) is unimportant, as is estimated load time—the tracing image won't be loaded with the page.

Use a Tracing Image to Design a Web page

Open a WYSIWYG design application such as Dreamweaver or GoLive and insert a tracing image. In Dreamweaver, you use the Modify|Page Properties command and work through the Page Properties dialog box. Click the Browse button to select the image, and click the Apply button to see the image on screen. If the 15% opacity is too faded or not faded enough for you, use the slider to adjust it through the dialog box.

Moving On

In this chapter, you discovered how Photoshop can be used to design large-scale Web content—from backgrounds that display online behind your Web page content to tracing images that help you set up frames, layers, and tables to house that content. In the next chapter, you'll learn to design entire pages in Photoshop, creating page prototypes quickly so that you can show your plans to a prospective design client without spending time actually building a page in HTML or a WYSIWYG product. Assuming the client will love your design plans, you'll have plenty of time to build the real pages later!

Chapter 9

Building Page Prototypes with Photoshop

You know how you want the Web page to look, and you want to quickly share your vision with a client or coworker. How do you design a page without setting up an actual Web page? Create a page prototype in Photoshop.

Using Photoshop as a Page Layout Tool

First, let's get one thing straight. You're not designing a Web page in Photoshop. You're designing a *prototype*. A prototype is a dummy, a model, a for-demonstration-only version of the real thing. Photoshop doesn't have tools for creating tables and layers and setting up links. It does allow you to draw shapes, add images (by pasting them from existing artwork or designing them within the prototype image itself), and include text. So, you're able to create a mock-up of the page you have in mind and show it to a client, a coworker, your design-business partner, your mom, anyone you want to dazzle with the design you have in mind.

Rather than sketching your ideas on paper, which can never really capture the page as you're picturing it in your head, you can draw, paint, and fill a Photoshop image that looks like a Web page but acts like a picture. Figure 9.1 shows a prototype of a page that contains colored table cells with pictures, graphic text links, and paragraph text.

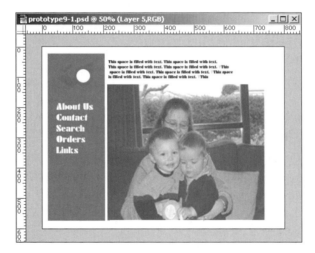

Figure 9.1

Show them what you have in mind by building a page prototype.

You might be thinking that if you're going to create the page anyway, why not simply design it in Dreamweaver or GoLive or write the HTML code directly and just be done with it? Well, if you're not the final decision maker or must consult with someone else about how the page looks—how it's laid out, what colors and fonts are used, what content is included—you don't want to spend the time doing that just to have someone say, "Can we move this over here? I don't really like blue. Can that text be in a different font?" If you're a freelance Web designer, or if you work for a Web design firm, you don't have time to waste, especially if you're paid for finished pages, not the process of brainstorming or presenting ideas.

Photoshop's a great tool for expressing what you have in mind without wasting time or energy building an actual Web page that might end up looking nothing like what you originally imagined. Making major changes to page layout through a Web design application will take almost as much time as your original design would. Photoshop can be handy during the design discussion phase of a project. As people ask you to move things around and change colors and fonts, if you've placed all of your prototype elements on separate layers (see Figure 9.2), that will be easy to do, and you'll be able to show them the results of their requested changes in just seconds!

Figure 9.2
Put each page element on its own layer so you can move and recolor things later as changes are inevitably suggested or requested.

Designing a Prototype Page Layout

Your prototype layout is, of course, entirely up to you—with some limitations. You don't want to design something that's not physically possible on the Web. If you're also a Web designer (as opposed to a graphic designer whose role ends with creating images for the Web), you know that there are constraints in terms of the placement of items on the page that are imposed by existing Web design tools and/or the Web browser software used to view the pages online. You don't want to design a prototype for a page that can't be built through an application like Dreamweaver or GoLive, or through the direct writing of HTML code. If the people who must give their approval love the prototype, you'll only end up disappointing them if you can't actually make the prototype happen.

Choosing an Image Size

When starting the prototype image, you don't have to make the image the same size as a real Web page, but it should be in proportion. For example, if you, like most Web designers, base your page layouts on an 800×600-pixel depth display (for visitors whose computer monitors are set to 800×600 resolution), you can start with an image that's 800 pixels wide by 600 pixels tall, or you can make a smaller image that's 500 pixels wide by 200 pixels tall—300 pixels smaller in both dimensions. Of course, if you go with a smaller image size, you'll have to scale back all of the page elements—text, images, and shapes that represent structural tables, layers, or frames—so make this page size decision with care.

I prefer to start the prototype image at 800×600, design everything—insert the text and graphics, draw the shapes that represent the page structural devices—and then as needed, resize the image to a smaller, yet proportional, size (using the Image|Resize Image command). You can save the smaller version(s) with different names so that your original full-sized image is left intact. By working in an image that's the same size as the page you'll be creating from the prototype, you know that you can work in the same font sizes you'll be using when you go to design the page in a Web design program or through HTML. In addition, you know that if you draw a shape or insert a graphic that's a particular width and height, your actual page will support the same-sized elements and the overall page will look very similar, if not identical, to the prototype image.

Creating Page Element Layers

Like many other Web-bound images, your page prototype should be designed with each of its elements on its own layer. This will make it possible to move and edit different parts of the page quickly. For example, the image shown in Figure 9.3 consists of five layers in addition to the ubiquitous background layer. Each layer can be moved, transformed, recolored, or edited at any time. Text layers can be edited for content. Even if you end up saving the prototype image in a non-Photoshop format, it's a good idea to keep the PSD version around just so you can go back and shuffle things around when someone has a bright idea about your design.

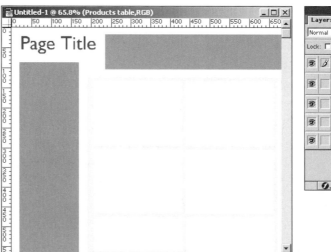

Figure 9.3

Plan all the parts of your page and create a layer for each one.

Remember, of course, that text is on its own new layer by default. Each time you use the Type tool and add a new text element to the page, a new layer is created. You therefore needn't make layers for text in advance, unless you want to make layers that will hold shapes that represent where text will go, as shown in Figure 9.4.

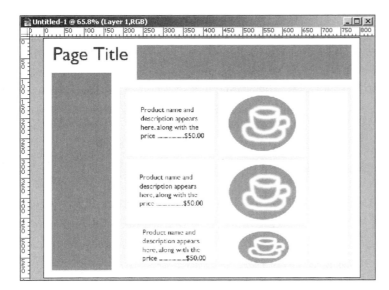

Figure 9.4
Don't have time to type page text? Just show where it will go by placing a rectangle on the image that represents one or more paragraphs.

Using Rulers and Page Guides

When you design a Web page, you typically map out where things will go and how big they'll be based on pixel dimensions. For example, you might decide that you want a vertical strip down the left with navigation tools on it—text links, graphics—and you want it to be roughly a quarter of the page in width. On an 800×600 page, that's 200 pixels. The width of the strip also allows you to design or choose graphics (graphic text images, for example) that will fit within the 200-pixel width of the strip. If the strip is a table cell, you'll want to allow for any cell padding (space inside the cell, creating a margin of sorts to keep table content from literally running into the cell's walls) in your measurements of the strip and/or its contents.

If you're working in an HTML environment, typing your code into a text editor, you can simply specify the width of the table cell (or layer or frame) as part of the HTML code. If you're working in Dreamweaver or GoLive, you can use the various dialog boxes and palettes that allow you to create and format page elements to set the size of things on the page. How do you do it in Photoshop? Simple: with the ruler and guides.

Displaying the Rulers

To turn on the ruler in Photoshop, choose View|Show Ruler. Rulers appear across the top and down the side of the image window, as shown in Figure 9.5. You can use the rulers to measure sections of the image window or existing graphic content, or to measure shapes and lines as you draw them.

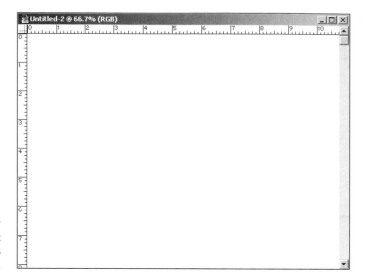

Figure 9.5
Turn on your rulers so that
you can see the width of items
in your image.

Of course, the rulers are in inches by default, and that can be a problem for those of us who don't know the pixel-to-inch conversion equation right off the top of our heads. To convert your rulers to pixels, follow these steps:

1. Choose Edit|Preferences|Units And Rulers.

2. In the resulting dialog box (see Figure 9.6), change the Rulers setting to Pixels.

3. Click OK to apply your change.

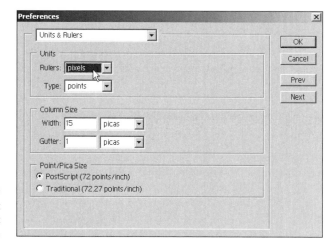

Figure 9.6
Click the Rulers drop-down list
and change from the default
Inches to Pixels.

Setting Ruler Increments

After you change the Rulers setting to Pixels, if the ruler is already displayed it changes to pixels. If you had not yet displayed the ruler, when you do display it, it will appear in pixel increments. Figure 9.7 shows a pixel ruler on an image in progress.

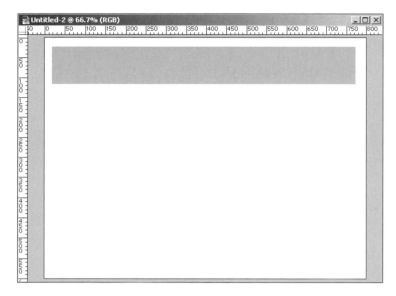

Figure 9.7
Ah, that's better. If you're designing for the Web, work in the Web-preferred units: pixels!

Adding Page Guides

Once your rulers are displayed and converted to pixels, you can begin inserting guides on the page. Guides are nonprinting colored lines, running horizontally or vertically, that help you map out areas of the image. When you're designing a page prototype, guides are indispensable tools for making sure that the parts of your page, even representational shapes and lines, are the right size for the page.

To display guides, you must have your rulers displayed, and from there it's easy. To add a vertical guide to your image, point anywhere on the vertical ruler, click and hold down your left mouse button, and drag the guide onto the image. A vertical blue line follows you, and you can drop it off anywhere on the image by releasing your mouse. Figure 9.8 shows a vertical guide being added to an empty image window.

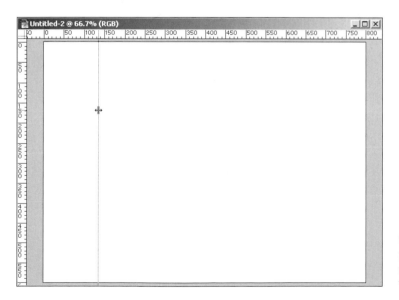

Figure 9.8
Need help setting up vertical sections of the page? Drag a vertical guide onto the image.

Using Guides

If you need to define sections of horizontal space, drag a horizontal guide onto the image, using the same technique, except that you drag the guide from the horizontal ruler, as shown in Figure 9.9. Watch both rulers to make sure you're dropping your new guide off at the right spot.

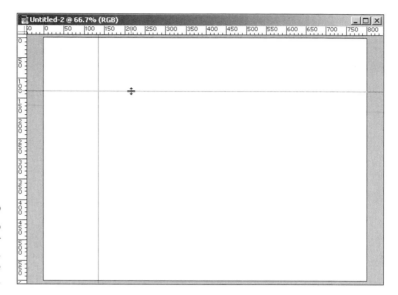

Figure 9.9
A horizontal guide can help define the area for a banner across the top of the page, or where a mid-page frame will be created.

Moving and Deleting Guides

You can add as many guides to the pages as you want, and you can move existing guides simply by pointing to them and dragging them to new locations. You know you're on one when your mouse pointer turns into a two-headed arrow, as shown in Figure 9.10. If you want to drag a horizontal guide, look for a two-headed arrow pointing up and down; if you're trying to move a vertical guide, look for a two-headed arrow pointing left and right.

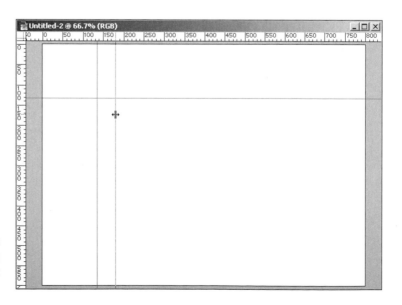

Figure 9.10
Drag your existing guides around on the page until you've got them right where you want them.

If Your Attitude Is Exactitude...

You can insert guides at precise pixel positions, both horizontally and vertically. Just choose View|New Guide. In the New Guide dialog box, choose the Orientation (Horizontal or Vertical) and then enter an exact pixel location. Click OK, and voila! You have a new guide. Guides created in this way can be moved with the mouse if you decide later that the original spot is no good. You can also delete a guide that's in the wrong place, and use this more exacting method to insert a replacement.

To get rid of a guide, drag it back up and onto the ruler from whence it came—horizontal guides to the horizontal ruler, vertical guides to the vertical ruler. If you want to get rid of all guides all at once, choose View|Clear Guides. Every last one of them will be removed, so use this command with care.

Inserting Shapes and Lines

With your guides in place, now you can begin building and positioning the shapes and lines that indicate your page design's structural devices. If your design proposes the use of a table, draw a large rectangle and divide it up into cells with lines, or draw a series of rectangles, arranged as the table's individual cells would be. Figures 9.11 and 9.12 shows these two approaches and how you might create them with shapes or lines.

Now, Don't Move

You've positioned your guides "just so" and you don't want them to move. What to do? Choose View|Lock Guides. You can't move or delete them (nor can anyone else) unless you choose View|Lock Guides again (note the check mark next to the command if the guides are already locked).

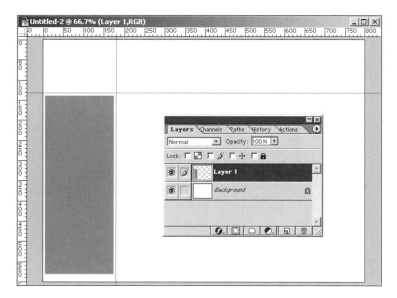

Figure 9.11

A single rectangle with lines to represent its role as a table is a quick and easy way to show your design's structure.

Of course, the page may have multiple structural devices in place—frames with tables and layers inside them, layers that contain tables, nested tables (tables inside tables)—and you'll therefore need to employ a variety of shapes and lines to faithfully represent them. Figure 9.13 shows a series of shapes that indicate the frame structure of a page, as well as the tables and layers within the frames.

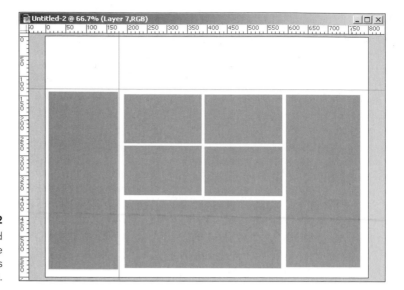

Figure 9.12

If your table will have colored fills or there will be space between cells, draw rectangles for each cell in the table.

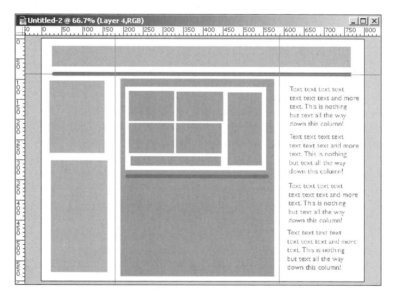

Figure 9.13

Vary your shapes, lines, and their configurations to indicate different structural devices on the same page.

Adding Text and Graphics

When it comes to the way your prototype depicts the pictures and text that will be included on your page, you can take one of two approaches (or a combination thereof):

- Be exact and literal. Use the same graphics you'll use on the page, and type the text exactly as it will appear. This takes more time, obviously, especially if you have to create the graphics for the page. Further downsides include the fact that what you want feedback on from those viewing the prototype is the overall page design—not the content—and including anything other than representational images and text invites more input than you may be looking for.

- Use symbolic content only. Create or find simple graphics that merely represent what will be used on the page. A group photo taken from any CD collection of images or a family photo of your own can be inserted to represent where an office group photo will be placed. A picture of a store-front—any storefront—can be inserted to show people where a picture of their business will go. Any repeated line could represent text, such as "This is the text that will be used on your Web page," so you don't have to ask the client for the page content. Figure 9.14 shows a page prototype that employs sample content only.

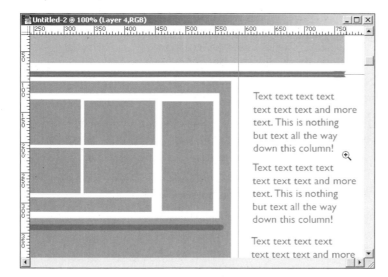

Figure 9.14

You can show where text and graphics will appear without creating or locating the actual images and text the page will contain.

Earlier I mentioned that combining these two approaches could work: Consider using real pictures (if they're available and don't require you to spend time creating them) and representational text, as shown in Figure 9.15. This approach delivers a prototype that asks as little of viewers as possible—they don't have to imagine their graphics, and how the page would look with them in place, because the graphics are already there. The text (as long as it's in the font and size you're proposing be used) doesn't have to say anything. Sample text formatted properly serves its purpose quite well in a page prototype.

Positioning Page Elements

You can draw your shapes and lines and type your text anywhere on the page and then place them within the space they'll occupy in the final design, or you can place them precisely from the start. If you set up guides ahead of time, and assuming each of your page elements is on its own layer, you can easily position everything exactly as you need it with just a few mouse clicks and drags.

Moving Shapes and Lines to Specific Locations

To move a shape on its own layer, right-click the layer and select it by name from the resulting shortcut menu (see Figure 9.16), or activate the Move tool

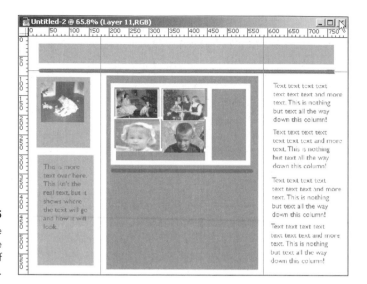

Figure 9.15

When it comes to images, use the real thing, but use sample text to indicate the placement of text on the page.

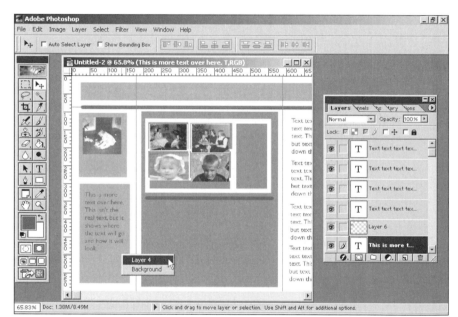

Figure 9.16

Select the exact layer you want by right-clicking it and selecting it from the list of adjacent or overlapping layers' content.

and click on items on the page. The latter approach works most of the time, but if the layer content has reduced opacity or is very close to another item on the page, it might be hard to actually grab it with your mouse.

After selecting a shape, line, or even some text, you can move it by dragging it with your mouse (as shown in Figure 9.17) or by nudging it into place with the arrow keys. It's much easier to use these tools to move something if you have your ruler displayed; otherwise, you're hard-pressed to leave the object in the desired location on the page.

If you chain two or more layers, you can use the Align and Distribute tools to arrange them relative to each other. For example, as shown in Figure 9.18, if

Figure 9.17
For less precise repositioning, use your mouse to move an item.

Figure 9.18
Align boxes, lines, and/or text layers by their sides, tops, or bottoms.

you want to make sure your array of boxes really look like a tidy table structure, you need to align them in rows.

Snapping to Guides

So you drew all the layers, carefully placing them so as to set up an overall layout for your prototype. Now what? To use the layers, you can drag shapes, lines, and text to them, placing the items alongside, above, or below the guide lines. You can make this process easier by turning on the Snap To Guides option (View|Snap To|Guides), as shown in Figure 9.19. When this feature is on, you'll feel your items pulled to nearby guides as you drag them around on the page, as though there's some magnetic quality to the guides, drawing the shapes, lines, and text to them.

Chain, Chain, Chain... Chain of Layers

Remember that to link your layers, you must activate one of the layers in the intended group, and then click the checkbox to the immediate left of the other layers you want to link together. A Chain icon appears in the box. When your group is complete, click the Move tool to display the alignment tools on the options bar.

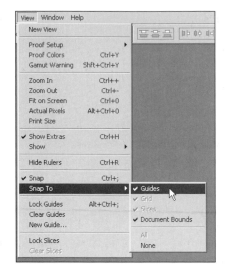

Figure 9.19
Use the guides you placed on
the page to help position your
shapes, lines, and text.

Nudging Items into Position

Using your arrow keys to move layers is a faster technique than you might think, and in many ways, it's more effective than dragging things into place with the mouse, even if you're using guides and are set to snap to them. How can this be? Imagine that you have two items that are currently positioned properly from a horizontal perspective, but you wish they were higher (vertically) on the page. If you drag them with your mouse (one at a time or after chaining them), you will invariably move them to the left or right as well as up. It's not that you're uncoordinated or not really good with your mouse—it's just that as a human, you're not capable of the level of precision required to reliably move anything in just one direction with your mouse.

If in this same scenario you used your arrow keys (the up arrow, specifically) to move the item(s) up on the page, you know you're not changing horizontal position as well. The arrow keys can move things only one direction at a time, and you can control how much they move by counting the number of times you press the key. If you want to move two items (or two separate groups of linked items) the same amount, you can use a single arrow key on each one, and if you press the key the same number of times for each item or group, they'll both be moved the same amount.

Keeping HTML Reality in Mind

When you design your page prototype, be careful not to get carried away with what looks good and is possible within the Photoshop environment and forget what you can actually accomplish in a Web page. It's easy to forget the limitations of actual Web page layouts and content (not to mention Web browsers), so don't feel bad if your first prototype attempt is difficult, if not impossible, to actually create in HTML or through a WYSIWYG design tool like Dreamweaver or GoLive. The key is to make sure your layout is achievable and that your design doesn't require technology that's not supported by all browsers in at least two versions. You don't want to design a page that excludes all but the users of the latest browser versions, and you don't want to leave out entire groups of users by designing something that works only in Internet Explorer or that only Netscape Navigator can display properly.

Posting Your Design Online

You can print your prototype and show it to people on paper, or you can send them the file (saved as a JPEG or GIF so that they can't tinker with original layers or text content too easily) and allow them to view the prototype on their own computers. If you have a notebook computer, you can visit your client, open Photoshop on your computer, and display the prototype image file on screen. These are all perfectly acceptable ways of sharing your design ideas with those who want or need to have input in the process, or with the person or persons who will make the final decision about the Web page design you're proposing.

A better way to share your prototype with people is to put it online. If you have your own Web site, or if you have FTP access to the client's Web server, create a staging folder (call it "Staging" or "Prototype") and create a Web page (call it prototype.htm or something similar) and place the prototype image (in JPEG or GIF format) on that page. Then upload the page to that new folder on the server, and inform those who need to see the prototype that they can view it at www.*domain*.com/**prototype.htm** (substitute the appropriate address). You can send the link to that page via email to all parties concerned and ask that they email their comments to you, simply by typing the address in the body of your email—most email applications (Outlook, Outlook Express, Netscape's email software) will turn any string of text that begins with "www." into a link. You can even place an email link (**mailto:*youraddress*@*yourisp*.com**) on the prototype page so that they can compose an email response while they're viewing the page online.

Build a Page Prototype

In this project, you'll build a prototype image for an 800×600 page. You'll include shapes to indicate structural tables and layers, graphics, and text.

Set Up a New Image

Create a new Photoshop file that's 800 pixels wide by 600 pixels tall. Make sure the image is in RGB mode, at 72 pixels per inch, with a white background.

Insert Layers

Create layers for each element of the image. Figure 9.20 shows a prototype in its final form. Each shape and line should be on its own layer, and of course, the text layers will be created automatically when you type the text.

Create the Prototype Content

Build content into each of your layers. You can follow the image found in Figure 9.20, or you can be inventive and create your own version of this prototype. The only requirement is that your prototype include some level of structural representation—rectangles indicating a table or layers, for example—and that you position them in a way that's actually possible on a real Web page.

Printed Pitfalls

When you print your prototype, be aware that the color printer you use may skew the colors a bit, and you might not get exact (or even very close) representations of the colors you used in your prototype. I found this out the hard way with a client who specifically asked for her Web page to use a cranberry color, a mossy green, and a slate blue. When she printed the prototype on her printer, the cranberry color looked purple, and she was convinced that I had used purple instead of cranberry. Had I put the file online (posting it as a graphic on a Web page), she would have seen the page as her future viewers would see it.

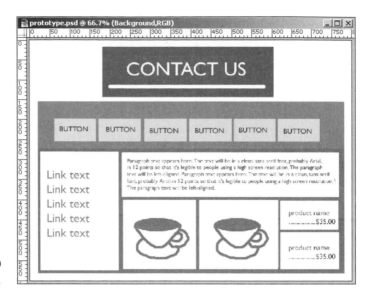

Figure 9.20
A page prototype to inspire you.

Add Shapes

Draw shapes that represent layers, tables, frames, or any combination thereof. If you're following the image in Figure 9.20, you need to draw several rectangles and use guides and/or the alignment tools to position them realistically.

Insert Graphics

You can use the image found in the Chapter 9 Project folder to represent the graphics found in the prototype. The file is called teacup.gif, so you should have no trouble identifying it.

Type Page Text

You can type any sample sentence and repeat it (copy and paste it over and over to create a paragraph or series of paragraph). There's no need for the prototype text to be anything other than representational.

Format Page Text

Even though your text is only representational, you need it to be in the size, color, and font in which it will appear in the actual Web page.

Save in Photoshop Format

Save the file as prototype.psd. You want to keep a PSD version of the file so that you can move things around (the items on individual layers) as feedback comes in suggesting moving this here, nudging that a bit in that direction, changing the color of this or that, and so forth.

Save for the Web

If you intend to put the image on a Web page and post that page to the Web for people to access for review, you need to save the image in JPEG or GIF format. Choose a format that supports the nature of the graphics and colors in the image. A complex and detailed layout with photographs, shading, embossing, and so forth should probably be saved in JPEG format, while a simple graphic with solid-colored shapes and no special effects applied could be saved in the GIF format.

Moving On

Now that you've explored Photoshop's tools for creating static images, it's time to check out ImageReady. You'll find that Photoshop and ImageReady are virtually identical in terms of the workspace—the tools, palettes, and menus are pretty much the same. Where they differ is in the Rollover and Animation windows, which you use to create mouse-over effects and simple movies for use on the Web. Chapter 10 will introduce you to the ImageReady interface, and Chapter 11 will have you building your own rollovers and animations.

The Name's the Same

It's always a good idea to give the PSD and GIF/JPEG files the same name (the file extension will differentiate them). This helps you pair them up later, and it makes updating both versions, as changes are made, much easier. If you saved your PSD version of the file as directed, the Web-safe version should be called prototype.jpg or prototype.gif.

Chapter 10

Touring the ImageReady Interface

When you open the ImageReady application, you might think you've opened Photoshop because the two interfaces are so similar. An integral difference exists, however, in the form of the Animation, Rollover, and Image Map palettes. In this chapter, you'll learn how they work.

What ImageReady Does

ImageReady makes graphics move, change, and connect to files, Web pages, and Web sites. It also enables you to slice images into pieces for easier handling and faster loading, but Photoshop does that, too (you'll find out more about slicing in Chapter 12). The focus of this chapter and the one that follows, however, is how you can use ImageReady to create animated GIF files (graphics that move), rollover effects (graphics that change in response to the movement of your mouse in proximity to them), and image maps.

Animated GIF Files

So how does a graphic move? Rather than storing information about the way the image looks in one static position, an animated GIF image contains information about the image in a series of frames, each one containing different parts of a single image. The GIF itself contains all the parts of the image, but each frame has some of the image layers visible and others hidden (see Figure 10.1). When the image is displayed, the frames "play," one at a time. The order in which the frames play, the duration that each one is displayed before moving on to the next, and the number of times the entire series of frames plays (looping forever or just once) are all stored as part of the file so that when the file appears in a Web browser window, the animation occurs.

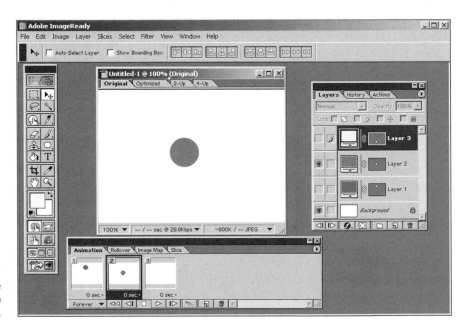

Figure 10.1

The image consists of three circles, but only one is visible in each frame.

Rollover Images

Rollovers created in ImageReady are really multiple images that are swapped as the Web page visitor's mouse moves over a graphic. You can set up rollovers through such programs as Dreamweaver or GoLive. You just select two distinct graphics and set one up as the image that appears when the visitor's mouse is nowhere near the image. Then you set up the other graphic as the image that appears in place of the first one as soon as the visitor moves the mouse over the image. ImageReady rollovers go a step further, allowing you to create an HTML file that stores a single image in several states: Normal, where the mouse isn't near the image; Over, where the mouse is on the image; and other states, such as Click, which requires that the visitor click the image to make a third change to it. The Rollover HTML file stores the image and its states and plays in a Web browser window. See the various states in a rollover image-in-progress in Figure 10.2.

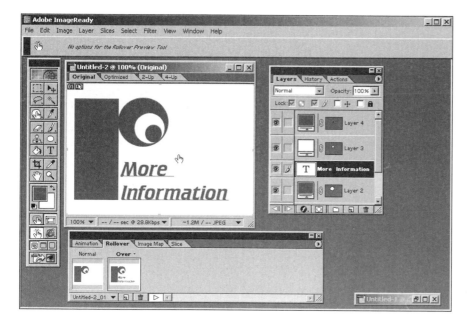

Figure 10.2
Choose the visitor mouse actions that will cause a change in the image, and turn layers on and off to dictate what happens to the image in each state.

Image Maps

The third focus of our coverage of ImageReady is the ability to map sections of an image and turn each of the mapped sections into a different hyperlink. This ability comes in handy when you're creating images containing graphic text; you can select individual words, phrases, or sentences and associate them with specific URLs or files. You can also map sections of a large picture, making it possible to click on parts of the photo and go to relevant pages. Figure 10.3 shows a picture with mapped areas, each associated with a different Web page.

Understanding the Role of Animated Effects in Web Design

My cousin once referred to a Web site he'd visited as an "all singing and dancing" Web site. I thought his description really summed up that site in particular, and other sites like it, where there's something moving or making noise on every page. This can be a good thing, if the site is aimed at kids or pertains to

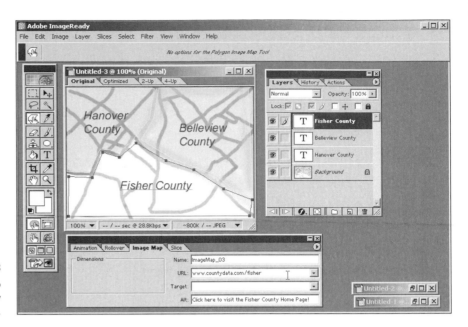

Figure 10.3

Make a single image link to several pages in your Web site by mapping sections of the picture.

something fun or silly. On the other hand, a lot of animation—elements that move on their own, or things that move in response to the visitor's mouse—can be distracting and lend a frivolous tone to your site.

So should you not use animated GIFs or rollovers at all? Of course you should. A rollover can be useful because it draws attention to a graphic (or graphic text) that a visitor might not have realized was a link or might not have stopped to look at or read otherwise. Animated GIFs can encourage visitors to linger on a page or to notice a portion of the page that might not be terribly eye-catching on its own. Another reason to use some level of animation is that so many sites, even professionally designed business sites, are using Flash movies and similar animated content, and for many visitors, any site that "just sits there" can be written off as dull. Certainly no one expects singing and dancing at a medical research site or a site devoted to financial-planning information. However, using some animation to make a point or to just add some visual excitement won't hurt even those sites that pertain to very sober topics.

ImageReady makes it possible to create a lot of animation or very subtle animated effects. An animated GIF can perform its actions very quickly and then remain as a static image on screen, or it can be looped, playing over and over so that the image is never still while the page is viewed. Rollovers can swap two entirely different images so that the results of the visitor's mouse movements are rather drastic. Or your rollover can simply add to or take something out of an image, making a very slight change in the graphic content when the visitor moves the mouse. The degree and type of animation is up to you—ImageReady is poised to help you achieve your goals, no matter what they are.

Working with the ImageReady Tools

The ImageReady application window is very similar to the Photoshop application window—in fact, you might not even be able to tell them apart without looking at the title bar, where the application name appears. As shown in Figure 10.4, the ImageReady toolbox, menus, palettes, and even the Image window closely resemble those that appear in Photoshop.

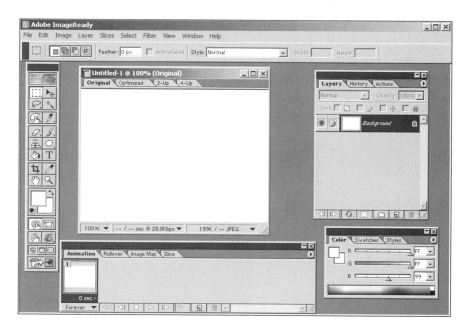

Low Equals Slow

If your computer doesn't have a lot of memory (less than 128MB), you might find that you can't run both ImageReady and Photoshop at the same time without some noticeable slowness in the operation of one or both of the applications. If this occurs, make sure any other nonessential applications are closed. If the slowness continues, consider closing the application that's not essential to the image creation or editing that you're doing at that exact moment.

Figure 10.4

The similarity between Photoshop and ImageReady can work to your advantage—you can take what you know about one and use it in the other.

Starting the ImageReady Application

You can open ImageReady from the Start menu's Programs list (probably in an Adobe submenu) or from within the Photoshop application. At the foot of the Photoshop toolbox, click the Jump To ImageReady button, as shown in Figure 10.5.

When you open the application through either method, the next step is to open an existing image (virtually any graphic file type is acceptable, as shown in Figure 10.6), or you can start a new one. Figure 10.7 shows the New Document dialog box, where you designate the size of the new image and the color of the Background layer. It's called the "First Layer," but it appears as "Background" on the Layers palette, just as it would in a new Photoshop file.

Once the new or existing image is open in its own window, you can begin using the toolbox, menus, and palettes to operate on the image, adding, changing, and removing content. You'll find that what you already know about Photoshop can be put to instant use in ImageReady; many of the tools are the same in appearance and function, and the differences are rather subtle. If you're new to ImageReady, the best way to learn it is to dive in and just start creating something—an animation, a rollover, or map areas on an existing image.

Figure 10.5

Working in Photoshop and want to make a quick leap to ImageReady? Click the Jump To ImageReady button.

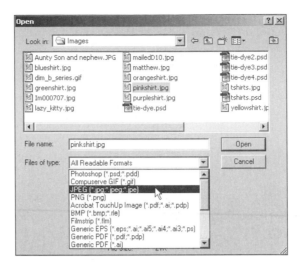

Figure 10.6
Open any existing image—PSD files from Photoshop, JPG or GIF files already saved for the Web, or any other bitmap or vector file.

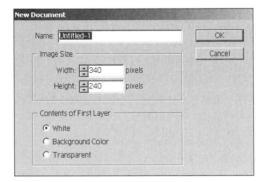

Figure 10.7
ImageReady images are measured in pixels by default.

Take It Apart

If you open a PSD file, you can use the layers from the image as you saved it in Photoshop. ImageReady makes extensive use of the Layers palette, where you decide which layers are visible in specific animation frames or rollover states.

Photoshop vs. ImageReady Tools: What's the Difference?

The major differences between Photoshop and ImageReady are slight. You'll find these differences in the toolbox and when you're in the Animation/Rollover/Image Map window. You'll probably notice this extra window first, but upon even casual inspection, you'll spot the differences in the toolbox, as shown in Figure 10.8.

The lack of the tiny triangle in the corner of several of the toolbox buttons is an immediate indicator that some of the tools common to both applications are different in that they can't be switched to a related alternate button. The Paint Bucket is the only fill tool you have (although you can use the Paintbrush to paint any sort of fill you want); the Gradient tool is gone. The Air Brush tool appears to be gone, but you'll find it among the Paintbrush alternate tools (along with the Pencil).

The Eraser tool is missing an alternate—the Background Eraser is gone. You still have the Magic Eraser and the basic Eraser tools, though. Other changes and omissions:

- The Dodge, Burn, Sharpen, Blur, and Sponge tools are now alternates to the default Clone Stamp tool (see Figure 10.9).

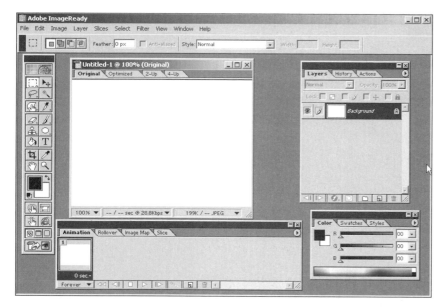

Figure 10.8

From "missing" tools to new tools, to tools that are different, the ImageReady toolbox holds some changes in store for you.

- You can't create a Text mask with the Text tool, and there is no Quick Mask mode.

- The History and Art History brushes are gone.

- There is no Notes tool for annotating your images.

You might be thinking that these changes—and certainly the omissions—in the toolbox will limit your ability to create great images in ImageReady. Not so! Remember that you can build any image you like in Photoshop, save it in PSD format, and then open it in ImageReady, making it possible to animate the image, turn the image into a rollover, or map areas of the image and assign links. The tools available for image editing and creation in ImageReady are aimed at simpler images, the sort of images that lend themselves to the GIF format. This doesn't mean you can't use photographic content, shadows, and/or embossing effects (not to mention some of the artistic patterns that you can apply through Photoshop). If you use a complex image for an animated GIF, however, you might see some reduction in clarity or color representation in the GIF version of the file. This isn't usually a problem, though, especially if the image remains in motion; people won't see the less-than-crisp edges or notice any color problems if the image is moving.

Figure 10.9

These tools aren't "missing"; they're just accessed through a single tool.

Save Me!

When you save a file in ImageReady, you use the Save command to create a PSD version of the file, and you use the Save Optimized command to save a Web-safe version of the file appropriate to the type of image you're creating. If you're working with an animation, the Save Optimized command automatically saves the file in GIF format. If you're saving a rollover, it is automatically saved as an HTML (HTM) format. Using the Image Map tools doesn't impose a particular format—you can choose JPEG, GIF, or PNG as the format for the image.

Working with the Animation Window

You display the Animation window by clicking the Animation tab on the multitabbed palette shown in Figure 10.10. The window consists of a single frame as well as tools for creating and deleting frames and for playing your animation to test it. You should begin drawing your animation's elements right away, using the Image window, and you'll see whatever you draw in the first frame.

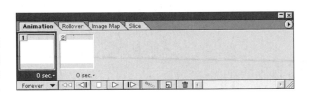

Figure 10.10

Insert, rearrange, remove, and play the frames of your animation from this window.

In addition to the obvious tools, you can access menus from within the Animation window. Click the timing display at the bottom of any frame (see Figure 10.11) to display a list of timing alternatives. By default, frames are displayed for less than half a second (shown as zero seconds), but normally, you'll want to tinker with the timing of one or more of your frames to control the speed at which the animation plays.

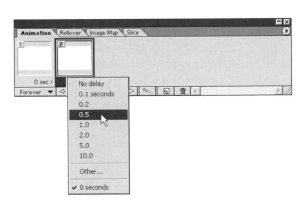

Figure 10.11

Click 0 Sec. and choose how long your frame will display before the next frame plays.

Frame See, Frame Do

Once you've adjusted a frame's timing, if that frame is the selected frame when you click the Duplicates Current Frame button, the timing (along with any content) is applied to the new frame.

To choose from a more varied list of commands, click the triangle button on the far right of the Animation window. A menu appears, offering such commands as New Frame (unlike the Duplicates Current Frame button at the bottom of the window), Copy Frame, Delete Frame, and Select All. Figure 10.12 shows the menu, which contains many of the same commands found in the Animation window, plus a few that are found nowhere else.

Inserting Frames

Your new animation starts with a single frame, but obviously, you'll need at least one more in order for animation to occur. To insert a frame, you can click the Duplicates Current Frame button at the bottom of the Animation palette, or you can click the Animation Options menu triangle on the right side of the palette and choose New Frame or Copy Frame. The latter command is the

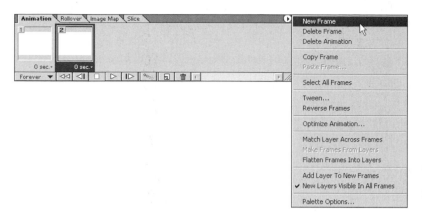

Figure 10.12
Additional commands for building and customizing your animation are found in the Animation menu.

same as clicking the Duplicates Current Frame button, because it creates a new frame that's identical to the selected frame already in your animation.

Once a frame is inserted, you can begin deciding which content in your image should appear in that frame and where it should appear within the Image window. The best approach to creating an animation in ImageReady is to create a new or open an existing image, and make sure that it's complete—the content for every frame of your animation is part of the image, and the image looks the way it will look online when the animation is complete or completes one repetition. Figure 10.13 demonstrates this goal: The image of a completed logo shows how it will look when the animation finishes. All of the shapes, each on its own layer, will have moved to their desired locations in the center of the Image window. Each frame of the animation displays and then moves the shapes, one at a time, into place as they're seen in the Image window.

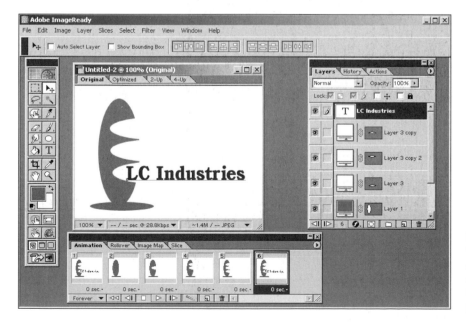

Figure 10.13
The complete logo, intact, with all the pieces in the right place, is drawn before the individual frames and their content and positions are set up.

After you create your image (or open an existing image, preferably a PSD file with layers for each element of the image), you can start adding frames and choosing which parts of the final image should appear in each frame. For example, in the logo example, each ellipse is on its own layer, and each frame includes the shape from the previous frame, along with a new shape. Only Frame 1 has a single shape in it. Figure 10.14 shows the frames for the image. Each frame is a step in the process of building the final image, and the appearance of each logo shape is the goal of the animation itself.

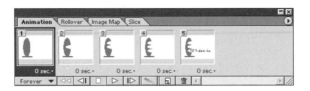

Figure 10.14
Each frame adds a new shape and moves it into position.

Controlling Frame Content

To choose what will appear in each frame, click on the frame you want to set up, and then go to the Layers palette and use the Layer Visibility checkbox to turn some layers on and others off. The layers that are off won't be seen while that frame plays, while the layers that are on will be seen. You can also use the Image window to move visible elements around, and wherever they're located while the current frame is selected is where they'll appear when that frame is played.

Go through each of your frames and choose what will be seen and where the content will be. When all of your frames are set up, click the Play button, as shown in Figure 10.15. The animation will play in the Image window.

Figure 10.15
Click Play to test your animation.

Rearranging Frames

After you set up all of your frames and test the animation by playing it, you might decide that the frames are all fine but that they're appearing in the wrong order. Using our logo example, say you decide that a particular shape should appear before another shape appears. To change the order of your frames, simply drag them to the left and right with your mouse, as shown in Figure 10.16. As you drag them, your mouse pointer changes from an arrow to a closed fist, indicating that you've grabbed and are pulling the frame into a new location in the series of frames.

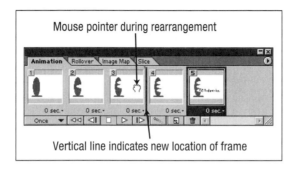

Figure 10.16
Drag your frames to the left or right to rearrange them.

Deleting Frames

If you have an extra frame, you can get rid of it in one of two ways:

- Select the unwanted frame and drag it to the Garbage Pail button at the bottom of the Animation palette. As I explain later, you can select more than one frame at a time.

- With the unwanted frame(s) selected, click the Animation Options menu triangle and choose Delete Frame from the menu. If you've selected multiple frames, the command changes to Delete Frames.

Once you've deleted the frame(s), you can undo the deletion if necessary by pressing Ctrl+Z or choosing Edit|Undo.

If you want to do anything to multiple frames, you need to select them before the action is taken—before deleting unwanted frames, inserting multiple frames, copying multiple frames, or setting the frame speed for multiple frames. To select two or more frames, try these methods:

- Click once on any one of the frames you want to select and then press the Ctrl key. Hold the key down as you click on the other frames you want to copy or delete, or for which a new frame speed is desired. When selected, frames turn blue, as shown in Figure 10.17.

Figure 10.17
You can tell which frames are selected by their color—dark blue.

- Press and hold the Shift key as you click the first frame in a series and then click the last frame in a series. The entire series, including the first and last frames you clicked, will become selected. This is a good technique if you want to select frames 3 through 7, for example, but not good if you want frames 2, 5, 8, and 9. If you want nonconsecutive frames, use the Ctrl key method.

Customizing Frame Speed

By default, all frames play at 0 seconds per frame. That sounds as if they don't play at all, but what it means is that they play for just a tiny fraction of a second, a portion too small to quantify. For most animations, that's way too fast, so you'll want to decrease the frame speed of one or more of your frames.

Give Me Everything

If you want to select all of the frames in your animation, click any one of them and then click the Animation Options Menu triangle. From the resulting menu, choose Select All Frames.

To change the speed at which one frame plays, click the triangle next to 0 Sec. at the bottom of the frame in question. You'll see a drop-down list, as shown in Figure 10.18. Choose a speed from the list and the list disappears, leaving the new speed displayed at the bottom of the frame. The Other option in the menu simply allows you to enter a timing other than those in the list—3 seconds, .75 seconds, 6 seconds, 20 seconds—any number of seconds you want. To apply a speed to more than one frame, select the frames you want to change, and then use the 0 Sec. triangle on any one of them to access the list and choose a speed.

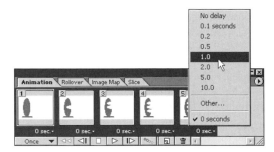

Figure 10.18

From a tenth of a second to 10 seconds, choose the time that the current frame will display before the next frame is played.

Tweening Frames

You can build animations one frame at a time, turning layers on and off and moving content around in each frame, or you can create two frames—a before frame and an after frame—and then ask ImageReady to create the intervening frames for you. The process is called *tweening*, and it's a term that's not exclusive to ImageReady; you can create tweens in any animation application, including Adobe's LiveMotion and Macromedia's Flash. Figure 10.19 shows the two frames that will have intervening frames added be*tween* them, and Figure 10.20 shows the frames created by the Tween command.

Figure 10.19

The first frame shows the image as it should begin, and the second shows how it should end up.

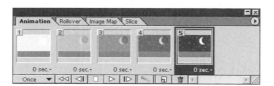

Figure 10.20
The size, color, and position of items in the first frame is gradually changed to match the size, color, and position of items in the second frame, achieved in as many intervening frames as you want.

Choose the Tween command from the Animation Options menu, and the dialog box shown in Figure 10.21 opens. In this dialog box, you can control the direction of the tween—backward (to the appearance of the Previous frame) or forward (to the appearance of the Next frame). You can also control the number of frames created by the tween and what items in the image are tweened. By default, these options are selected:

- *Position*—The location of elements in the frame.

- *Opacity*—The color of the elements. If you leave Opacity on, items that are added in the tweening process will slowly appear, faded at first, full color in the end.

- *Effects*—Any layer styles that were applied—shadows, embossing, highlights—to the elements.

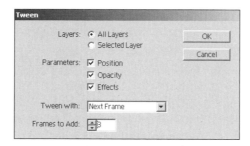

Figure 10.21
Set up the tweening process to achieve the results you want.

Of course, you can combine techniques, creating individual frames by hand and using the Tween command to create other frames automatically. You can also perform multiple tweens in the same animation. All you have to do is tell ImageReady whether to tween with the frame before or after the selected frame, and how many frames to use to create the tween effect. The more frames you allow to be created by the tweening, the more subtle and smooth the animation will be, but it will also take longer to occur, and it will be a larger file when saved in GIF format.

Previewing Your Animation

Of course, when you click the Play button in the Animation palette, the animation plays in the Image window. The animation you see there is virtually the same as it would appear in a browser window, but if you want to see it exactly how it will appear online, click the Preview In Default Browser button shown in Figure 10.22. The browser that is considered the default is the one that your computer sees as the default for HTML files—if you're a Windows user, you can change this through the Windows Explorer's Tools menu.

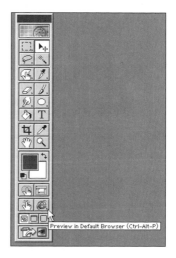

Figure 10.22
Click the Preview In Default Browser button (shown here) to see your animation online.

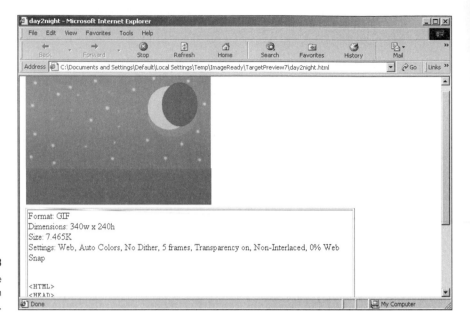

Figure 10.23

See the animation as well as the code involved in displaying it on a Web page.

The resulting browser window will do more than preview your animation—you also see the HTML code involved in playing the animation, as shown in Figure 10.23. If you want to add the animation to your Web page, you can use the following code:

```
<!-- ImageReady Slices (day2night.psd) -->
<IMG SRC="day2night.gif" WIDTH=340 HEIGHT=240>
<!-- End ImageReady Slices -->
```

You'll want to place the code within your **<BODY> </BODY>** tags, and of course, if the animation should appear at a certain point within existing page content, place it accordingly. If you're working with a WYSIWYG application such as Adobe GoLive or Macromedia Dreamweaver, you can use the Select|Image Source command and select the image from the resulting dialog box (Dreamweaver's Insert Image dialog box is shown in Figure 10.24).

Working with the Rollover Window

Much of the rollover-creation process is the same as the animation-creation process. You work in a series of *states* rather than frames, but you use the Layers palette to turn layers on and off in each state, and you move things around in the Image window to dictate how they'll look and where they'll appear in the graphic for each state. So what do I mean by *state*? The states you have to choose from are Over, Down, Up, Click, Out, and None. These are the relationships between a graphic and a site visitor's mouse: The visitor's mouse is nowhere near the graphic (None), on top of it (Over), pressing the

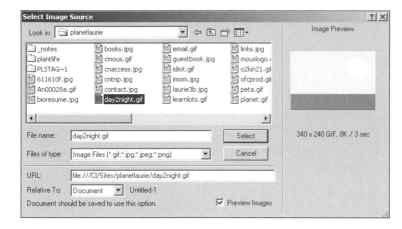

Figure 10.24
Select the image by name and double-click it to add it to your Web page at the cursor's current location.

mouse button and holding it (Down), releasing the mouse button (Up), clicking the graphic (Click), or moving, away from the image (Out). The way you want the graphic to look when any of these mouse actions occurs is dictated by how the individual states look in the Rollover window. Figure 10.25 shows a series of states and the logo we've used throughout this chapter as it appears in each state.

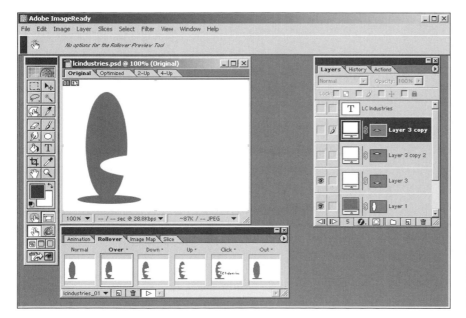

Figure 10.25
When the visitor points to the graphic, the image changes, and it changes again when the mouse moves up or down and away from the image.

Most rollovers consist of two states: None and Over. This creates a smaller file, and a simpler experience for the visitor. A common and useful rollover effect is one that adds text (instructional or descriptive words or a paragraph) when the visitor mouses over the graphic. If the graphic is a link, visitors then know what to expect when they click it, as shown in Figure 10.26.

Figure 10.26

First it's a shape, then it's a shape with instructions, beckoning the visitor to click and move to another page.

Adding and Changing Rollover States

To add a state, click the Creates New Rollover State button. A state is added to the left of the selected state. If you add states starting with the Normal state that appears by default, they appear in the order shown in Figure 10.27. You can also change the state of an existing state. Just click the State name at the top of the state and choose a new state from the drop-down list (see Figure 10.28), or you can drag states to the left or right with your mouse.

Figure 10.27

Five states, including Normal, appear in an order representing a visitor's most likely mouse activities relative to the graphic in question.

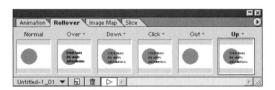

Figure 10.28

If you want your states in a different order, you can drag them around with your mouse, or you can change the state of an existing state in the Rollover palette.

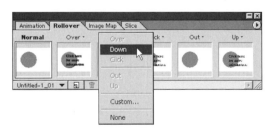

Testing Your Rollover

Once your rollover states are created and your image is set up as you want it to appear in each state, you can test your rollover by clicking the Preview Behavior button shown in Figure 10.29. After you invoke this Preview mode, you can test the rollover by pointing to the image in the Image window. The None graphic state is swapped for the Over state, and if you have additional states, as you move up, down, or click the image, the states for each one of those mouse actions appears.

Figure 10.29
Click here to turn your Image window into a testing ground for your rollover.

You can also test your rollover in a browser window by clicking the Preview In Default Browser button on the toolbox. Your system's default browser (Internet Explorer for me, as shown in Figure 10.30) opens, and the rollover graphic appears in its None state. If you point to, move up, down, or click on the image, your rollover states appear one at a time.

Less Is More

If you decide you want to get rid of a state altogether (as opposed to changing it to another state), drag the state to the garbage pail in the Rollover palette.

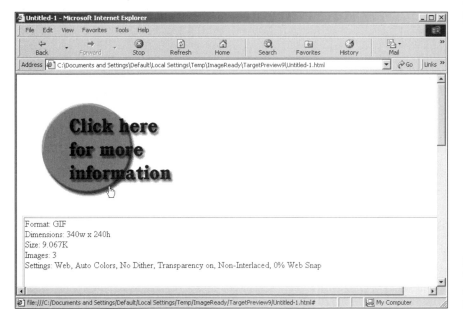

Figure 10.30
To see your rollover as it will appear online, click the Preview In Default Browser button.

Using the Image Map Tools

The Image Map palette gives you tools for drawing shapes on the surface of an image and designating those areas as links to Web pages, files, or multimedia—sound or movies—and for making these mapped regions part of the file so that when the image is inserted into a document, the mapped areas and their associated links come with them. You can also designate Alt text (the text that appears in a ScreenTip when a visitor mouses over the link, as the image loads, or should the image be missing or the visitor have chosen not to display graphics) and how the linked page or file will appear—in a new window, replacing the current page, or in a page within the existing page. As shown in Figure 10.31, the palette provides simple text boxes and drop-down lists for you to set up your mapped links.

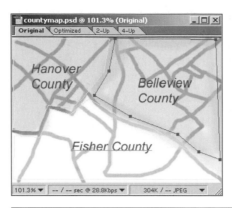

Figure 10.31

Type the URL and any Alt text if
you want a simple Web page link.

If the image you're mapping will be inside a Web page frame, or if you want to
make sure that a new page opens for the linked page (so that your current
page isn't replaced by the linked page), you can use the Target drop-down list.
Your options are:

- *Blank*—This option opens the linked page in a new window so that the
  original window (containing the mapped image) is left open in its own
  window.

- *Self (the default)*—The window containing the mapped image replaces the
  current page with the linked page. If your page has frames, the linked
  page appears in the same frame as the original page.

- *Parent*—Use this option only if your page has frames. This option is useful
  if your HTML file has frames and the frame containing the mapped image is a child (a frame inside a frame). The linked page appears inside
  the parent frame if this option is chosen.

- *Top*—This is a frames-only option that enables you to replace all current
  frames with a single window for the page to which the mapped image (or
  a section thereof) is linked.

To create a mapped area on an image, click the Rectangle Image Map tool.
This is the version of the tool that appears by default. If you want to map a
circular or polygonal shape, click the tiny triangle in the Rectangle Image
Map tool and choose Circle Image Map or Polygon Image Map from the resulting palette (see Figure 10.32).

Figure 10.32

Choose the shape you want to
draw on your image, designating
an area of the image for a link to
a Web page or file.

After selecting to tool for the shape you want to draw, move your mouse out to
the image. If you're using the Rectangle or Circle Image Map tool, click and
drag to create the shape. If you're using the Polygon Image Map tool, click
and then move your mouse to draw the sides of the shape, clicking at each
corner. When you come back to the starting point, click again, and a closed

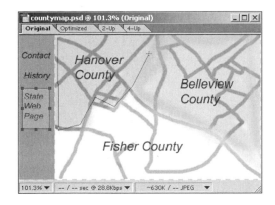

Figure 10.33
You can map out simple geometric shapes or freeform ones, depending on the Image Map tool you use.

shape is created. Figure 10.33 shows a rectangular map that was drawn with the Rectangle Image Map tool, and a polygon shape in progress.

Once a shape is drawn, the Image Map palette tools become available and you can enter a name for the mapped area, type the URL to which the link will point (this can be a file or a Web page), choose your target option if your image is in a frame, and type the Alt text if you want some instructions or explanation to appear when a visitor mouses over the mapped area of the image. If your image contains more than one map, you can switch to the Image Map Select tool to select areas you've mapped, enabling you to view and edit the map settings you created. Figure 10.34 shows the Image Map Select tool in action.

Polygonal Dimensions?

You may notice that the Dimensions area of the Image Map palette is blank when a polygonal mapped area is selected. This is because it would be virtually impossible to display the width and height of a freeform polygon shape in the dialog box. The dimensions appear for rectangular, rounded-corner rectangular, and circular shapes.

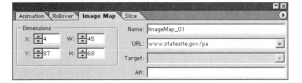

Figure 10.34
A light blue line appears around mapped areas. The selected mapped area has handles around it.

Using the Other ImageReady Palettes

The ImageReady application's palettes are very similar to Photoshop's—you have a Layers palette, a History palette, and Swatches, Color, and Styles palettes that appear by default when you open the application for the first time (see Figure 10.35). They continue to appear when the application is opened if

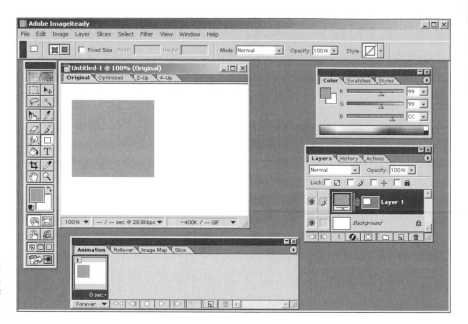

Figure 10.35
You'll recognize these basic
palettes from your use of
Photoshop.

you don't close them before exiting. To display any of ImageReady's palettes, choose the palette you want from the Window menu. Those appearing by name with the word *Show* in front of them are not currently displayed. If the word *Hide* appears in front of the palette name, the palette is already on screen.

Applying Layer Styles

The Layers palette is extremely important in Photoshop, and even more important in ImageReady. Without it, you wouldn't be able to designate which layers and their content show in different animation frames and rollover states, making it impossible to create images that move and change. Beyond this increased level of importance with regard to the use of the software, the Layers palette works very much the way it does in Photoshop: You can rearrange layers by dragging them up or down in the list of layers, you can rename layers by right-clicking them and choosing Layer Options from the shortcut menu, and you can delete layers by dragging them to the Garbage Pail icon at the foot of the palette.

There is one difference between the way the Layers palette operates in Photoshop and how it operates in ImageReady, and that's the way you apply Layer styles— shadows, embossing, highlights, and patterns. Rather than double-clicking the layer to open the Layer Styles dialog box, you right-click the layer and choose Layer Style, which spawns a submenu (see Figure 10.36) from which you can select the style you want to apply.

Once you apply a style, you can customize the way it looks by double-clicking it in the Layers palette, which opens an untitled palette with tools for adjusting the style you double-clicked. Figure 10.37 shows the Drop Shadow options for a layer to which only that style was applied.

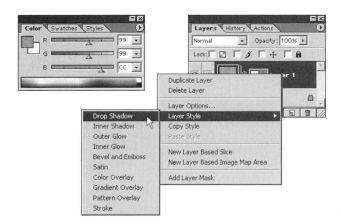

Figure 10.36

Rather than using a big dialog box, simply pick the style you want from a handy submenu.

Figure 10.37

Need to adjust that shadow, color, highlight, or pattern? Double-click the style and use this palette.

Viewing and Changing Optimization Settings

Another palette that's unique in ImageReady is the Optimize palette, shown in Figure 10.38. Through this palette (which you display by choosing Window|Show Optimize), you can access many of the settings you have in the Save For Web dialog box in Photoshop. For example, you can pick the type of Web-safe file you'll be using for the image you're working on, set the quality for the chosen format, and choose whether or not the image will be a progressive or interlaced one (an image that appears slowly as it loads rather than not appearing at all until it's fully loaded). The palette's options vary depending on the format you choose—Figure 10.39 shows the JPEG version of the Optimize palette.

Figure 10.38

If you're saving your file in the GIF format (a must if you're creating an animation), customize the quality of GIF you create with the Save Optimized command.

Moving On

Now that you know the lay of the ImageReady land, you're ready to build animations and rollovers. In the next chapter, you'll discover how to build an animated logo and create rollovers that draw attention to important links. Through the chapter's projects, you'll acquire hands-on experience with both of these valuable Web-design features.

Figure 10.39

If your image is a JPEG with mapped areas, choose the quality of the image, and make it Progressive if it's a big file that will take a while to load.

Chapter 11

Working with Animations and Rollovers

Moving elements can make your Web pages more effective, whether the movement draws attention to a graphic link or simply provides eye candy for your site's visitors. In this chapter, you'll learn to use ImageReady to create animations and rollover effects.

Creating Animations

Web page animations are often the product of applications such as Adobe's LiveMotion or Macromedia's Flash—they're actual movies that run, frame by frame, as dictated by their designers. The sort of animations you can create in ImageReady aren't really movies, though they have distinct frames—which means they load much more quickly than Flash or LiveMotion movies do, and they're simpler to create. The animations we'll be creating in this chapter are animated GIF files, and you add them to a Web page just as you'd insert any static graphic—through an **<img src=images/movingpicture.gif>** tag and attribute if you're working in HTML, or by using the Insert|Image command in a WYSIWYG application like Dreamweaver.

Creating animations in ImageReady is very simple, and we showed you the basics in Chapter 10. You learned how to use the Animation palette, and you learned about the frames that make up an animation. In this chapter, you'll discover some inspiring (I hope) techniques for creating a really dynamic animation that makes any Web page much more memorable for its visitors.

Building Image Elements

When you open a new Image window in ImageReady, after setting the size and background color, you're faced with a blank slate in terms of image content and a single starting frame for the animation-to-be. Before you add new frames, it's a good idea to build your entire image as it will appear when the animation is complete. Each element of that image should be on an individual layer. That way, you can more easily edit parts of the image and control the order in which the elements appear and disappear, as well as how they all fall together within the completed picture.

Building Image Layers

The only layers you have to build manually are those that will contain Marquee and Lasso-created shapes, lines, and selections that you plan to fill with colors or patterns, or those that will contain a freeform painting or drawing that will be part of the image. Figure 11.1 shows a completed image that consists of several shapes, each on its own layer; some text; and some drawing performed with the Paintbrush tool.

Before you start a new animation, it's a good idea to sketch the animation on paper, a process known as *storyboarding*. The storyboarding process can be very informal, as shown in Figure 11.2, or it can be more elaborate, as Figure 11.3 illustrates. The informal route can include simple boxes drawn on paper, like a cartoon, showing each frame of the animation, or it can be a serious undertaking performed in Photoshop or an actual illustration application (like Adobe Illustrator or CorelDRAW) that shows each frame of the image. I prefer the informal approach, because drawing each frame as a picture in a program like Illustrator is too much like the process of building the image in ImageReady—you're really duplicating your efforts if you do more than sketch the basic animation on paper.

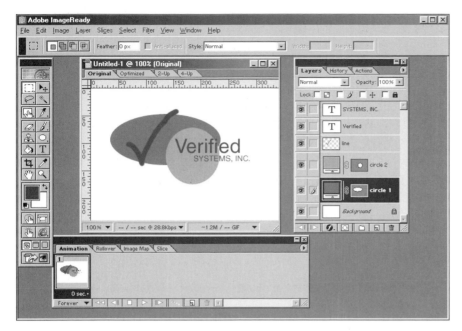

Figure 11.1
Think of your layers like building blocks—whether they appear automatically when a shape is drawn or text is typed, or if you create them manually to house a specific image element.

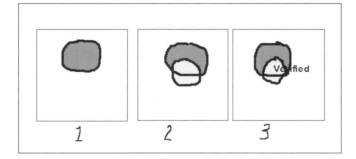

Figure 11.2
Draw simple boxes with stick figures and very elementary shapes to indicate what should appear in each frame. Use a pencil so you can erase!

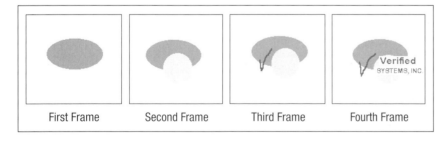

First Frame   Second Frame   Third Frame   Fourth Frame

Figure 11.3
If you just love to plan or have to submit your ideas to someone else for approval, you may prefer to use an illustration program to draw each frame's content in individual boxes.

After storyboarding your animation, you can begin creating the individual layers for your image, and then add content to the layers.

Creating Content

When you're building your image, be sure to select the layer on which the content you're about to create will reside. It's very easy to forget that each image element should be on its own layer, and to end up including two or more elements on a single layer (see Figure 11.4). Always keep an eye on the Layers palette, and make sure you're on the right layer before you begin drawing shapes or lines, or using the Paintbrush, Pencil, or Pen tools.

Figure 11.4
Layer 1 contains both a circle and a freehand-drawn checkmark. With these two objects on the same layer, you can't introduce them individually in the animation.

You can build your image in Photoshop if you prefer and then open it in ImageReady to perform the process of animating it. Although ImageReady has virtually all the same tools you have in Photoshop, you might already have an image that you built in Photoshop, or you might simply like the Photoshop environment better. Whatever the case, if you built your image in Photoshop, you can open the .PSD file in ImageReady and then animate it.

Formatting Layer Content

Remember that animation files you build in ImageReady are animated GIF files. That means the image will be saved in GIF format, a format that's best suited to line art—simple graphics with solid colors, not a lot of shading, and very little, if any, photographic content. That doesn't mean your animations have to look like rudimentary cartoons, but you should steer clear of applying a lot of drop shadows, highlights or glows, and embossed effects. Avoid using any photographic content, unless the clarity or crispness of the image isn't integral to its role in the image. Figure 11.5 shows an image that's well suited to the GIF format, and Figure 11.6 shows an image that isn't a good candidate for animation as a GIF file.

Figure 11.5
(Left) Your graphic needn't be boring or overly simplistic, but it shouldn't be complex in terms of color content.

Figure 11.6
(Right) This graphic has too much photographic content and shading going on to be effectively animated with ImageReady.

Making Layers After the Fact

If you've already built an image in Photoshop and you want to animate it but can't do so easily because each element of the image isn't on its own layer, you can move things to new layers with the help of Photoshop's selection tools. Use the Magic Wand to select solid-colored shapes and lines that need to be moved off to its own layers, and use the Marquee tool to select other areas of existing layers that need to be on new layers. If things overlap or are inextricably connected on a single layer, consider re-creating those parts, each on their own layer, and then throwing out the layer that has them together. In short, if you didn't put all the parts on their own layers, all is not lost—you can split things up with the selection tools and the Insert|Layer|New Layer command.

What should you do if you need to animate an image that's not suited to the GIF format? Use another animation tool, such as LiveMotion or Flash. These applications provide a greater range of output options, so you're not restricted to content that doesn't go beyond the capabilities of the GIF format. To find out more about using your Photoshop images in LiveMotion and Flash, check out Chapters 13 and 14, respectively.

Of course, if your animation is still in the development phase, you can make use of all of Photoshop's and ImageReady's tools for enhancing an image. For example, you can apply drop shadows, glows, beveled and embossed effects, and even colorful styles and pattern fills. There's no limit to what you can do to an image that you intend to animate, but you should be aware that your changes might affect the visual quality of the image when it appears on a Web page. As shown in Figure 11.7, a rather complex image with drop shadows and embossed shapes looks a little fuzzy on the Web page during the animation.

Figure 11.7
Stray colored pixels (known as *artifacts*) can appear around colored areas when you have overlapping colors or colors on a white background.

Of course, because the image is moving, the loss of quality isn't as obvious as it would be if the image were a static one. In addition, because the animation is set to loop continuously, the image won't ever be seen in a static state. If your animation will be playing only once or a fixed number of times, ending up as a static image in the end, be sure to preview it in a Web browser (using ImageReady's Preview tool) before you upload it to the Web. You might want to simplify the image a bit if the image quality is unacceptable.

Setting Up Animation Frames

An animation must have at least two frames in order for any animation to occur. If your animation is a simple on/off affair, two frames will do. If you want something to happen slowly or if the animation requires several steps to complete, you'll want several frames so that the animation can occur at the speed and/or in the number of steps you want. You can build your own frames, or you can have ImageReady build them for you with the Tween command. In order to tween, however, you need at least one frame, and usually two—one to show the image as it should start, and one to show it as it should end up. The tweening process will create the interim frames.

Creating Frames

You can create frames by duplicating an existing frame (click the Duplicates Current Frame button) or by inserting a new frame (click the Animation Options menu triangle and choose New Frame). The key to creating frames effectively is choosing when to do it and what to include in the frames as they're created. For example, if you have all of your image layers showing in your first frame, any duplicates you create from that frame will also have all the layers showing. You'll have to go into each frame and turn things off to remove any parts that don't belong in the individual frames.

A more efficient approach has you starting with a blank slate. If you have nothing showing in the first frame (either because your image hasn't been built yet or because all the layers are hidden in that frame), you only need to turn things on in the subsequent duplicate frames. Figure 11.8 shows a complete image represented by layers in the Layers palette, but with nothing showing in the first frame. We've used the Duplicates Current Frame button to create three duplicate frames, and they too have nothing in them.

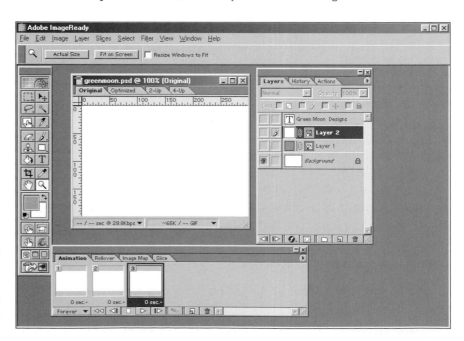

Figure 11.8

Hide your layers in the first frame so that all the duplicates are empty as well. All the layers are hidden (no eye appears in the box as on the background layer).

Hiding and Displaying Frame Layers

As shown in Figure 11.9, a successful animation requires that things be different in the individual frames—otherwise, there's nothing moving or arriving or departing as the animation occurs. The frames in this figure show an image building, one piece at a time—a flower blooming, petal-by-petal. Because each petal is on its own layer (the stem and leaves are on their own layers as well), the animation requires that each frame have a new layer added.

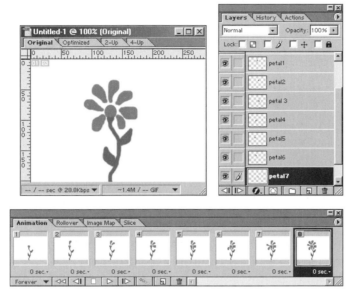

Figure 11.9
Build a flower one petal at a time. Each petal will pop into the image as each frame plays. If the animation is set to loop, the full flower will return to this first stage as the animation begins again.

Here's how the flower blooms: The first frame shows a stem with leaves but no flower. Then you see a bud, and then petals burst from the bud, one at a time. Each frame after the frame containing the bud shows one added petal until the final frame, which contains the completed flower. You can apply this approach to other animations as well. Consider these scenarios:

- A logo composes on screen, one component at a time. This works best for logos that consist of shapes and text, as shown in Figure 11.10.

- A word or sentence is "written" by the animation. Each letter of the word or sentence needs to be on its own layer (see Figure 11.11).

- Time passing can be simulated with an animation: You can have a clock face on one layer, and the hands of the clock in progressive positions on the rest of the layers (see Figure 11.12).

- You can make someone walk across a space on the Web page with an animation that consists of a person (a simple stick figure or a more elaborate drawing of a person) in different positions and moving across the width of the Image window (see Figure 11.13).

Beyond making parts of the image appear and disappear by hiding and revealing them on the Layers palette, you can affect the animation by moving different parts of the image in different frames. For example, in our walking

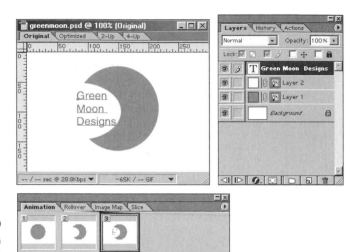

Figure 11.10
Simple construction of a multipart logo occurs in this animation.

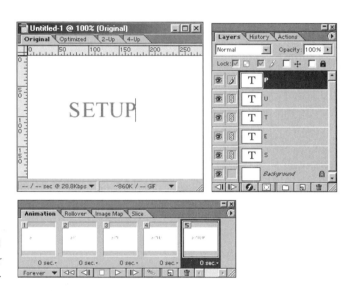

Figure 11.11
Make a word appear one letter at a time.

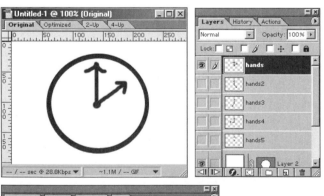

Figure 11.12
Use this graphic as a link to an employer's time sheets or to data pertaining to deadlines for a project.

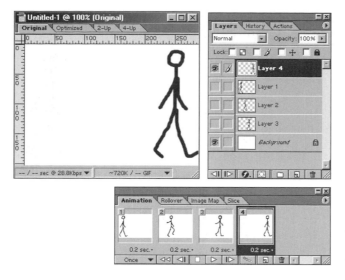

Figure 11.13
The less detailed the person's body is, the easier it is to animate the figure.

animation, the figure not only puts its left leg forward and then its right, it moves across the width of the Image window. This requires dragging the content of the layers containing the figure's body parts across the page in each frame so that as the figure walks, it moves from left to right. Otherwise, the figure would appear to be walking on a treadmill!

To demonstrate this in a simple way, consider the frames in Figure 11.14. The image contains a single circle. To look like it's rolling along the ground, the ball moves slightly from left to right in each frame, until it's all the way in the lower-right corner of the Image window. You could get fancy and add a shadow underneath the circle (in the form of a squashed darker circle that's partially overlapped by the original circle) and have the shadow move with the circle.

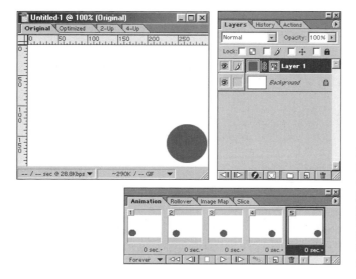

Figure 11.14
Even an image that consists of a single part can be animated—just move that element to a new position in the Image window in each frame. It will help you position the shape in each frame if you display your rulers (View|Show Rulers).

Take Baby Steps

If you're moving some parts or your entire image from one place to another through individual frames, don't duplicate the first frame where the image is at the beginning of its journey. To save yourself moving it a greater distance in each frame, duplicate the first frame for the second frame, and then after moving the content to its desired position in the second frame, duplicate that frame to make the third. In the third frame, you need only move things slightly to show movement, rather than having to move things from the starting position. Continue duplicating the last frame until the image has made its entire journey, one frame at a time.

Rearranging Frames

After you've set up all of your frames so that the right stuff appears in each one and the content of each frame is where it should be in the Image window, you might find that you want to change the order in which things occur. You can do this by changing what shows in certain frames, hiding and revealing and moving content in the frames until the right progression occurs, or you can simply drag the frames to the left or right to change their order in the animation.

You can drag frames one a time, or you can drag them in groups. Figure 11.15 shows a sentence that's formed by a series of frames, each containing a single word. Then, if you rearrange the words "now is the time", the animation plays and forms the phrase "the time is now", as shown in Figure 11.16.

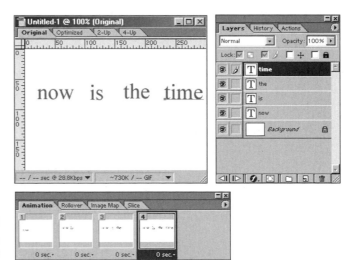

Figure 11.15

Rearrange the words in a sentence by rearranging the frames in your animation.

Deleting Frames

Of course, in your zeal to have a lot of frames and a lot of animation options, you might create more frames than you need. As shown in Figure 11.17, one frame appears too many times. To remove a frame, simply select it and drag it to the garbage pail, or click once on the frame and then click the Animation Options menu triangle and choose Delete Frame.

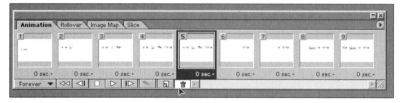

Figure 11.16
The more frames you have, the more animation options you create.

Figure 11.17
Too many frames? Throw the extras away.

Tweening Animation Frames

Although many animations can be built manually, frame by frame, some really require tweening. As you discovered in Chapter 10, tweening is the result of issuing the Tween command, whereby ImageReady creates frames for you and builds their content based on the frames that exist at the time. You can, for example, move a shape across the width of the Image window without building your own frames; just tell ImageReady to tween the first frame (where the circle is on the left side of the Image window) with the second frame (where the circle is on the right side of the Image window). ImageReady creates the interim frames, where the circle appears in stages across the width of the window, and the circle is moved at regular intervals. You dictate the number of intervals when you issue the Tween command.

I described the tweening process in Chapter 10, but here's some additional coverage from a design perspective:

- You can invoke the tweening process by selecting the starting or ending frame that will dictate the tweened frames' content, and then either click the Tweens Animation Frames button or click the Animation Options menu triangle and choose Tween. The Tween dialog box appears, as shown in Figure 11.18. Here, you can choose the number of tweened frames to create, with which frame the tweens will work (the one prior to or after the selected frame), and which things to tween—all layers or just the selected layers (you'd select them ahead of time, using the Layers palette).

Oops!

If you didn't mean to delete a frame or you deleted the wrong one, you can Undo your frame deletion by choosing Edit|Undo, or you can press Ctrl+Z.

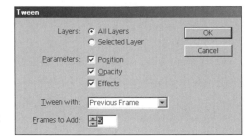

Figure 11.18
Make your content fade in or out by leaving the Opacity option on.

Location, Location, Location

If you want ImageReady to honor the positions you've specified for content that should move as the animation progresses, leave the Position option checked in the Tween dialog box. The Effects option refers to shadows and other styles you have applied to layers that are included in the tweened animation.

- As you become more comfortable with the tweening process, you might find that a good number of the animations you built manually could have been created with tweens. The blossoming flower example that was used earlier in this chapter is a great example of this. Rather than building each frame where a new petal appears, you could create the before frame (just a stem and some leaves) and an after frame (where the entire flower appears, with all of its petals) and tween the flower to create the interim frames where each petal appears. Of course, the animation result will be slightly different—rather than having each petal suddenly appear, the entire circle of petals will slowly appear, starting out faded and increasing in color intensity until it is completely displayed. Figure 11.19 shows the tween-created frames that create a six-petal flower, along with the "before" and "after" frames that showed ImageReady where the image begins and how it should end up.

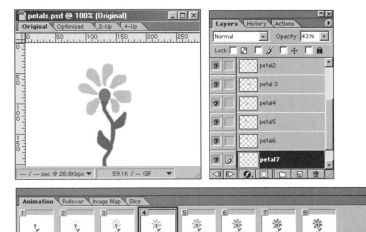

Figure 11.19
A flower goes from bud to blossom with six tweened frames. The petals slowly darken over the course of the tweened frames.

- You can set up multiple tweens in a single animation, each one representing a stage in the animation as a whole. Continuing with the blossoming flower example, a tween can take the stem from a short sprout to a tall stem, and then a second tweening process can take it from bud to full bloom. Figure 11.20 shows this two-stage tweening in the Animations panel, a total of 10 frames.

Over and Over Again

If your animation shows something building or growing, you may want it to run only once—otherwise, it will build or grow and then disappear, and then build and grow again, over and over. If you want the animation to run continuously, consider creating a disintegration process in the animation—such as the flower wilting (to continue with that example) and losing its petals, only to grow from sprout to stem with bud, and blossom again. The complete cycle of growth and wilting (or building and then tearing down, if you're building something other than a flower) is much more realistic for a continuous animation.

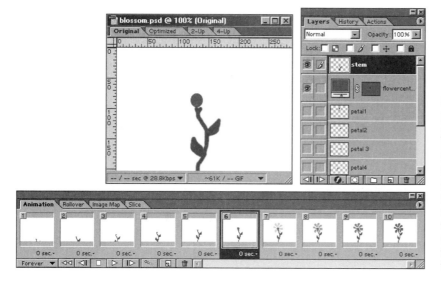

Figure 11.20

Let ImageReady create frames in just seconds that would take you hours to build manually. The first frame shows the sprout emerging from the ground. The fifth frame shows the stem at full height. The frames between one and five were created by tweening. Frames six through nine were created by tweening the fifth and sixth (now the tenth) frames.

Customizing the Animation

Whether you've built your animation frames manually or let ImageReady do it for you with the Tween command, you will want to adjust attributes like the speed at which the animation plays and how many times it plays at that speed. The Animation palette provides all the tools you need to control these features, as shown in Figure 11.21.

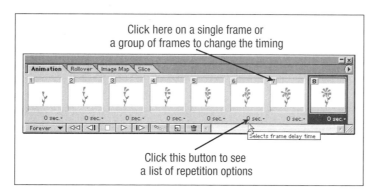

Figure 11.21

Right at your fingertips, the tools for setting up the duration of each frame and the looping options are represented by buttons on the Animation palette.

Establishing Animation Speed

By default, each frame is displayed for "0 Sec", which is technically zero seconds but really means an un-measurable fraction of a second. For many animations, especially quick, two-frame animations, this is just fine. For more elaborate animations, and certainly for animations that occur in several stages, you'll probably need to adjust the timing of one or more of your frames.

To change the timing of an individual frame, click that frame to select it, and then click the "0 Sec" timing displayed at the bottom of the frame. A list of potential timings appears, as shown in Figure 11.22. If you choose Other, a Set Frame Delay dialog box opens (see Figure 11.23), which lets you enter a specific number of seconds.

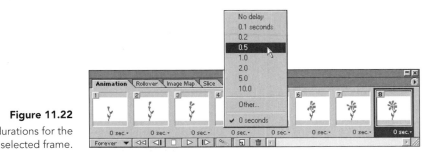

Figure 11.22
Pick some likely durations for the selected frame.

Figure 11.23
If the timing you want isn't in the list, enter it here.

Grouping Frames

To group a series of frames, click the first one in the series, press the Shift key, and then with the key still held down, click the last frame in the series you want to group. All of the frames turn blue, indicating they're selected as a group. If your desired group is not made up of contiguous frames, substitute the Ctrl key for the Shift key, and click the individual frames you want to include in the group.

Setting Your Loop Options

Some animations need to occur only once. Imagine a company logo, built one element at a time, at the top of a Web page. After it forms, the logo should stand, intact and motionless, as the visitor views the rest of the Web page. On the other hand, if your animation shows someone digging or hammering (a standard "under construction" animation for a page in progress), you probably want that activity to go on indefinitely.

By default, all ImageReady animations are set to run Forever, which means looping over and over until the page is closed or a link is clicked, taking the visitor to a new page in the same window. You can change this setting easily by clicking the Forever button and choosing Once or Other from the resulting drop-down list (see Figure 11.24). If you choose Other, a dialog box appears where you can enter the number of repetitions you want for the animation. If you enter "4", for example, after the fourth repetition of the animation the image stops moving and holds in whatever condition it's in for your final frame.

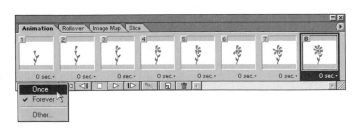

Figure 11.24
Once and for all, or Forever and ever—or, some Other number of repetitions.

Testing the Animation

Always test your animation by clicking the Play button at the bottom of the Animation palette. This will make the animation run right in the Image window with your current timings and repetition settings. If you want to see how the animation will look online, click the Preview In Default Browser button near the bottom of the toolbox. If you press and hold the button, the two most commonly used browsers, Internet Explorer and Netscape Navigator, appear in a submenu (see Figure 11.25).

Saving an Animation

When you save your animation, it's a good idea to save it in the Photoshop format (PSD) so that your layers are preserved. This enables you to edit the image and the animation easily in the future. Just choose File|Save or File|Save As. You can also press Ctrl+S to open the Save As dialog box.

After you've named and saved your image in PSD format, it's time to save it for the Web as an animated GIF. Choose File|Save Optimized, and note (as shown in Figure 11.26) that the default format is GIF. You can keep the name you gave the file when saving it in PSD format and simply click the Save button in the dialog box.

Figure 11.25
Pick your browser and view your image as it will appear on screen.

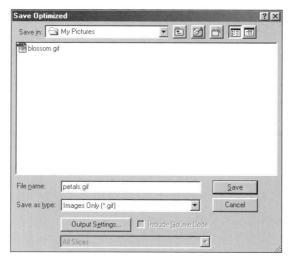

Figure 11.26
Animations are saved in GIF format by default.

Your Mileage May Vary

If your visitors are using a dial-up connection to the Internet, the first time they run the animation through a Web page, it may run very slowly. In subsequent viewings of the same page, the visitor will see the animation running more quickly, because the animation information is now in the visitor's cache (with regard to the Web, this refers to the computer's memory of which pages it's been to before). If visitors are connecting to the Web via a company network, DSL, or a reliable cable modem, the animation will run more quickly the first and all subsequent times it's viewed.

Once you save the image, you can insert it onto a Web page, using the same technique you'd use to insert any other image. The animation information—its frames and their content and timing, the overall settings for the animation's play—are stored with the file. When the image is viewed live on a Web page, the image file loads and the animation begins.

PROJECT Create an Animated GIF Image

In this project, you'll create an animated GIF for a construction company's Web site. The animation will build a house—beginning with a foundation, the construction of walls, and the appearance of a roof on the top. You'll adjust the timing and repetition of the animation so that it happens rather slowly and occurs just once.

Start a New ImageReady File

Using the File|New command, start an image that's 300 pixels wide by 300 pixels tall. The Background color should be White.

Create the Image Layers

When complete, the image will contain a floor, four walls, and a roof. The front wall will have two windows and a door, and the side walls will have a window each. There will also be a roof. In order for each of these elements to be "built" through the playing of the animation, you need to place each one on a separate layer. Create and name the following layers in preparation for drawing the shapes that will appear on them:

- Floor

- Front Wall

- Left Wall

- Right Wall

- Back Wall

- Roof

- Door

- Front Window Left

- Front Window Right

- Right Side Window

- Left Side Window

Draw Shapes on Each Layer

As shown in Figures 11.27 through 11.31, draw a rectangle for the floor, rectangles for the walls, and a roof. The figures that show the walls include the rectangles that will appear on individual layers for windows and doors. You can use the Transform submenu commands to skew and reshape the rectangles, providing the illusion of perspective.

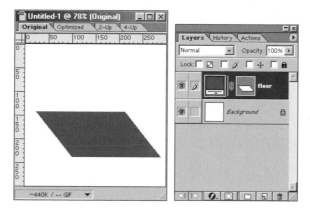

Figure 11.27
The floor is a skewed rectangle that appears to be lying on the ground.

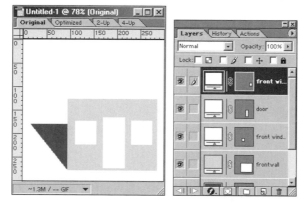

Figure 11.28
The front wall is a rectangle, with a door and two windows (each on their own layer).

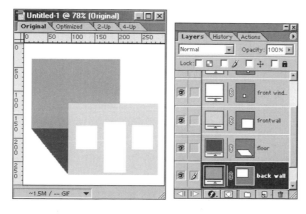

Figure 11.29
The back wall is a solid rectangle.

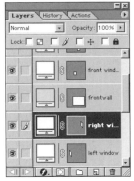

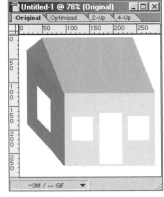

Figure 11.30
The two side walls each have a window, and are skewed so that they are parallel to each other and stand up along the sides of the floor.

Figure 11.31
This roof consists of two skewed rectangles and a triangle.

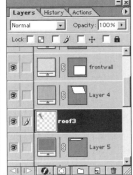

Insert Frames

For this particular animation to occur, each step of the building process must appear in a frame. Insert a frame for each layer in your image so that each component of the house—floor, walls, door, windows, roof—can appear individually as the house is built.

Adjust Visibility of Layer Content on Each Frame

Using the checkbox for visibility on each layer of the image, set up the frames as shown in Figure 11.32. The floor should appear in the first frame, followed by the front wall, the front door, front wall windows, then the back wall, then the side walls and their windows, and finally the roof. In the final frame, the house should be completely built.

Figure 11.32
One step at a time, the house is built.

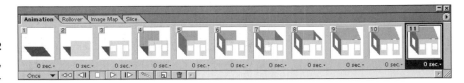

Test the Animation

Use the Play button at the bottom of the Animation palette to play the animation in the Image window. You can also use the Preview In Default Browser button to view the animation in your default Web browser's window. Figure 11.33 shows the animation in progress in an Internet Explorer window.

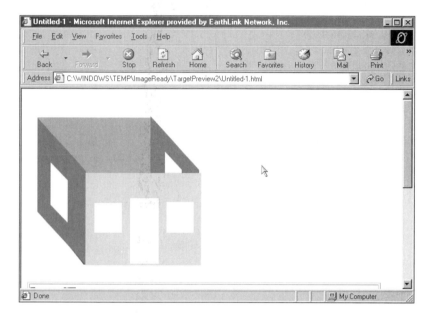

Figure 11.33
This is the house that you built!

Set the Timing of Each Frame

So that the animation doesn't occur too quickly, set each frame's timing to at least a full second. You can adjust the timing of individual frames to suit your needs.

Set the Animation to Occur Once

This animation will occur once, as the page on which it resides loads in the visitor's browser window. Change the repetition to Once as opposed to the default, which is Forever.

Save the File

Use the File|Save Optimized command to save this animation as a GIF file. You should also save it in PSD format so that you can make changes to it later, should the need arise. Name the file BUILD. GIF.

Creating a Rollover

I like to use rollovers whenever there's a chance of someone not realizing that one of my graphics is a link, or when I find myself wishing that I could whisper something to site visitors when they happen to look at one of my graphics.

Sometimes both situations exist, and I want to draw attention to the fact that a graphic is also serving as a link as well as provide additional information for the visitor. Rollovers help me with both situations because the rollover response tells people that there's something special about a given graphic, and a rollover can add text or additional/different graphic content in response to a visitor's mouse actions. Figure 11.34 shows a graphic that acquires some illuminating text when visitors point to it with their mouse—the added text tells them that the graphic is indeed a link and lets them know what to expect if they click it.

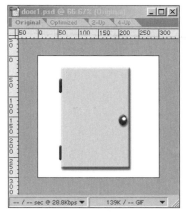

Figure 11.34

Rollovers can both entertain and edify. The image before someone points to it (left) and the image after someone points to it (right).

Rollovers can also serve much simpler goals. As shown in Figure 11.35, the rollover effect can be something silly and cartoonish or just a funny swap of images for comedy's sake. If your Web page has room for some humor, a rollover can be a subtle touch—the humor isn't always there; it appears only when someone points to a particular image.

Figure 11.35

Alleviate stress by making light of it. When no one points to the image (left), it's simply a stressed-out looking guy. When you point to him (right), he relaxes.

In the end, whatever the goal of your rollover—to edify or entertain—be sure that you don't use too many rollovers and animations on a single page. More than one or two moving images can cause sensory overload for your visitors, and no single rollover or animation will have the impact it would have had there not been so much visual competition.

Building Rollover Elements

Just like an animation, rollovers require some planning, even if it's just in your head. An animation can be more complicated, and therefore more elaborate planning, perhaps even storyboarding, can be necessary. Rollovers tend to be much simpler, however, so the planning stage might simply involve mentally picturing how your graphic will change in response to visitors' mouse movements.

Creating Image Layers

You can use the process of building your rollover's layers as part of the planning process. The act of creating and naming layers can help you sort out how your image will be constructed, and you can begin to think about which parts should be visible in one state and not in another as the rollover itself is made. Of course, if your rollover is simply an image without text that acquires text when someone points to it with a mouse, a lot of planning isn't necessary. On the other hand, keeping all the parts of the image on separate layers is still worthwhile because doing so makes it much easier to edit the image later.

As shown in Figure 11.36, an image can consist of a few shapes and lines plus a type layer, all of which should be on separate layers. That way, if you want to change the fill color of a shape or manipulate a line in some way, you can do so without affecting other parts of the image. Type is automatically on its own layer, so editing and formatting text later is no problem.

Figure 11.36

Even though this two-state rollover is very simple, it still pays to put all the parts of the image on separate layers.

Building layers for a rollover is no different than building them for any other kind of image: Use the Layer|New|Layer command. In the resulting New Layer dialog box, give your layer a name, preferably one that indicates the content of the layer or the role that content will play (see Figure 11.37). It's important to name the layers well because in the Layers palette, you can't really see what's on a particular layer (see Figure 11.38), and without selecting a layer and moving its content, you might find it hard to figure out which content is on which layer. The "Layer *N*" (where *N* is the number assigned automatic) names that are applied by default don't really serve you well as the image-creation process continues.

Figure 11.37
Give your layer a relevant name.

Figure 11.38
Can you tell what's on Layer 2?
Layer 3? Layers 1 and 3 look
the same here in the Layers
palette. Better layer names
would eliminate the mystery.

Creating Layer Content

After building your layers, you can add content to them—drawing shapes and lines, painting and drawing freeform elements—being careful to activate a specific layer before creating its content. It's easy to forget to click on a layer before drawing new content, so be prepared to use the Undo command to remove content you've inadvertently drawn on the wrong layer and start over on the right layer. Of course, shapes and type will create their own layers when you activate the Shape and Type tools and create that content. One exception: If you've chosen the Create Filled Region option on the Shape tool's options bar (see Figure 11.39), the shape you draw will become part of whichever layer is active at the time.

Figure 11.39
Click the Creates New Shape
Layer button if you want the
shape you're about to draw to
create its own new layer. If you
click the Create Filled Region
button, the shape you draw will
become part of the active layer.

You Can't Draw That Here

If the active layer is a shape layer, you won't be able to draw or type anything else on it. This is actually a good thing, though it can seem inconvenient if you want to erase or in some other way manipulate a shape you've drawn. Because you can't draw on a shape layer, you're forced to build a new layer for whatever you want to draw next.

Applying Layer Effects

Like animations, rollovers are saved as GIF files and the rollover instructions in an HTML file. This means that you must adhere to the same restrictions I mentioned earlier regarding the effects you can apply to items in your rollover. You can apply drop shadows, glows, styles, or patterns, even photographic content. Just keep in mind that the image quality might be reduced when you view the image (in its various states) online.

To apply effects to any layer in your rollover, right-click the layer in question (using the Layers palette), and then use the resulting Layer Styles menu to apply your effects and styles. Figure 11.40 shows 3-D effects (shadows, beveling) applied to a shape. After you apply the style, a palette of options for that

---

Don't Forget Filters

You can use ImageReady's Filter menu and all the filters within it to alter the appearance of your images, just as you would in Photoshop. Some of the subtleties may be lost because the files are saved in GIF format, but most of the filters will be effective in animations and rollovers. Feel free to experiment—try applying a motion blur to content in the Click or Over state, so that the content that was motionless in the Normal state literally appears to move when the visitor points to or clicks it.

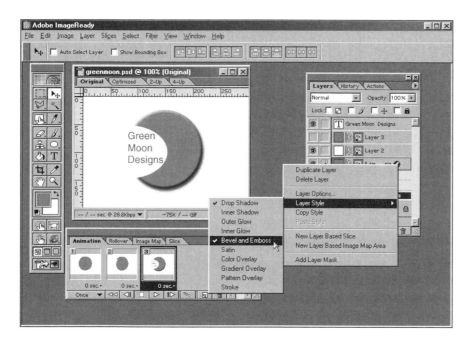

Figure 11.40
Make some or all of your rollover's elements stand out.

style will appear. You can close it or use the options to customize the way your shadows, glows, and beveled effects are applied.

Working with Rollover States

A rollover doesn't roll without states. States are the conditions under which a graphic will change in response to a page visitor's mouse movements. There are six states, as described in detail in Chapter 10:

- Normal (no one is pointing to the image)

- Over (the visitor is pointing to the image)

- Down (the visitor has pressed the mouse button on the image)

- Up (the visitor has released the mouse button)

- Click (the visitor has clicked on the image)

- Out (the visitor's mouse has moved away from the image)

Each rollover state can have a different appearance, or you can purposely make two or more states look the same so that you control the way the image looks no matter what visitors are doing with their mouse. Figure 11.41 shows a rollover with three states—Normal, Over, and Click. The Click state looks just

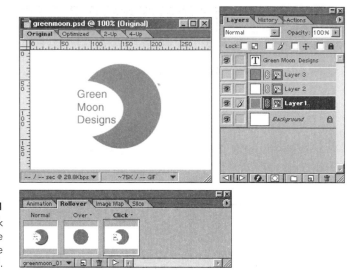

Figure 11.41
By making the Click state look like the Normal state, you ensure that the image appears to toggle on and off when clicked.

like the Normal state, so that when a visitor clicks a graphic, it changes. Without this change, because the visitor's mouse is in the same place it was when the Over state was triggered, there would be no sign that the click had been registered. If you make the Click state match the Normal state, the image reacts obviously to the visitor's click.

Inserting States

Inserting a state is very simple—just click the Creates New Rollover State button in the Rollover palette. A new state is inserted to the right of the active state. If you're adding states to a new rollover (which starts out with a Normal state already in place), the next new state will be Over, then Down, then Click, then Out, then Up. You can change states by clicking the state name at the top of each state box (see Figure 11.42). Just pick a different state from the list.

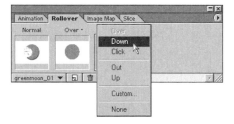

Figure 11.42
Pick a different state from the list.

Rearranging States

The order in which your states appear in the Rollover palette has no effect on the way the rollover works on a Web page—it's the visitor's mouse actions that trigger the different rollover states to play. Therefore, you don't have to rearrange the rollover states in the Rollover palette except to place them in some logical order for your own use. If you do want to rearrange them, simply drag the state boxes to the left or right with your mouse—your mouse pointer turns to a small fist, showing that you've grabbed the state (see Figure 11.43).

Figure 11.43
Put your states in order to help you set up their content.

Turning Rollover Layers On and Off

Like creating layers, there's nothing special about the process of turning them on and off as you build your rollover. To determine which parts of your image display in a given state, select that state and then use the Layers palette to hide and display specific layers. As shown in Figure 11.44, when this rollover is clicked, the target's bull's-eye is replaced by a star shape. The starburst is on its own layer, and that layer is hidden in all other states of the rollover.

Figure 11.44
Turn layers on and off by clicking the Indicates Layer Visibility box for each layer.

Cropping Rollover Images

If you look at the image in Figure 11.45, it would appear that the image consists solely of some shapes and text in the middle of the Image window. If this image were to be turned into a rollover, mousing over the image would require moving your mouse onto the shapes or text, right? Wrong. Because the shapes and text are in the middle of a 340-pixel by 240-pixel window, the entire space within the Image window is considered part of the image. As you can see in the figure, the mouse is on the edge of the window and the Over state is displayed. Simply placing the mouse on the edge of the canvas is enough to trigger the Over state.

Realizing that the background is part of the image is key to setting up a rollover. If you want the rollover image to include only the actual content and not the entire background, you either have to size the image at inception so that there will be very little extraneous background after you've drawn your content, or you have to crop the background down to the essential parts, as shown in Figure 11.46.

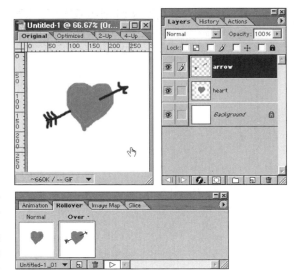

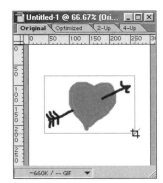

Figure 11.45

An image is made up of shapes, lines, text, and the background. The mouse pointer is on the very edge of the background (upper-left). The Over state has been triggered (the arrow appears), yet the mouse is nowhere near what you'd consider to be the image.

Figure 11.46

Crop to a rectangle that encompasses the content of your image and very little of the background.

To crop with the Marquee tool, select a rectangular area that surrounds the image closely. Then, to remove the portions of the image outside the selection, choose Image|Crop. Whether you use the Crop tool or the Marquee and Image|Crop procedure, the image is now smaller—both in terms of white space around the content and in terms of the file size, which is good when you're working with Web graphics. The smaller the file, the faster it loads.

Testing a Rollover

During the creation process, and certainly when you consider the rollover to be complete, it's a good idea to test the rollover. You can use the Play button in the Rollover palette, and then move your mouse onto the Image window to test the rollover's states. You can also click the Preview In Default Browser button to see how the image will look online. As shown in Figure 11.47, the browser preview includes the HTML code that you'll need to paste into your Web page in order to include the rollover image.

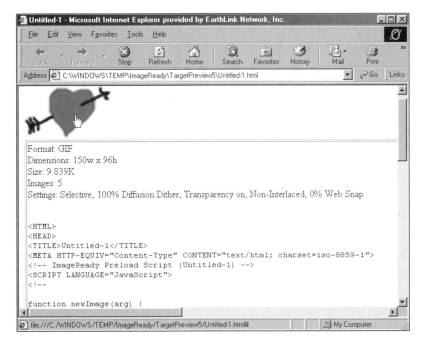

Figure 11.47
View your rollover and test its reactions to mouse movements. The image responds to the mouse pointe. This HTML code will be added to the code that makes up your Web page.

Saving the Rollover Image

Although I'm discussing the saving process toward the end of the rollover coverage in this chapter, don't wait until the end of your rollover-creation process to save your work. As you're building your rollover, you should save your image in PSD format (use the File|Save command) and then when the rollover is complete and has been tested successfully, save it in HTML (.htm) format. To save the rollover as an HTML document (including the JavaScript that makes the rollover work and the images that make up the rollover effect), choose File|Save Optimized. As shown in Figure 11.48, if you're going to be using the rollover in a Web page created in Adobe GoLive, you can click the Include GoLive Code option to add the code required to run the rollover in the GoLive environment. This won't affect the rollover's use online, beyond any browser limitations that apply to all use of rollovers.

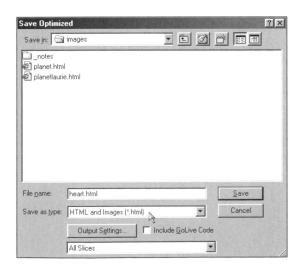

Figure 11.48
Save your rollover as an HTML document, keeping the same name as the PSD file you've saved throughout your creation process. By default, the file type is HTML and Images, meaning that both the graphic content and the rollover states are saved.

Don't Forget the Pictures!

Of course, when you upload your Web page to the Web server so that it can be viewed online, be sure to upload the GIF files that were created when you used the Save Optimized command. You should upload them to the images folder on your Web server so that the paths referenced in the HTML code for your Web page (specifically the code you copied from the rollover HTML file) match the location of the GIF files on the Web server. If you don't have an images folder on your Web server, you should make one and move your image files to it—it's much easier to maintain order and control over your Web content if your pages (the HTML files) are at the root and the images are in their own folder.

When you click the Save button in the Save Optimized dialog box, if Save As Type is set to HTML and Images, three things will happen:

- The HTML document (including the JavaScript and figure references) will be created.

- An images subfolder will be created if the current folder doesn't already include one.

- GIF files will be saved for each of the states in your rollover image.

This seems rather complex, but it's not—or at least it doesn't have to be. The name you give the HTML document is applied to the GIFs, with the state name "-over" or "-click" added to the name. So, for example, if you called your rollover "pinkcircles.htm", and the image has three states (Normal, Over, Click), three GIF files are created:

- pinkcircles.gif (for the Normal state)

- pinkcircles-over.gif

- pinkcircles-click.gif

You can customize the saving process by clicking the Output Settings button in the Save Optimized dialog box. This dialog box (shown in Figure 11.49) gives you access to tools that will control how the HTML code and JavaScript are created, and how the file names are applied to the GIF files. You don't have to tinker with these settings, but if you know HTML and JavaScript and want to make changes, the tools are there to help you.

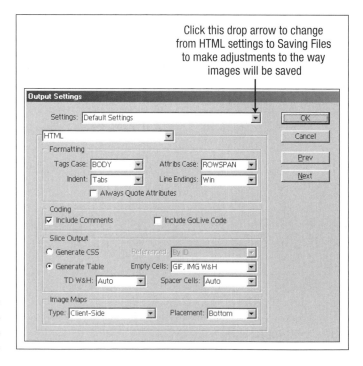

Figure 11.49
Control the output settings for your rollover in all its forms—HTML and GIF files.

Placing Your Rollover in a Web Page

To add your rollover to a Web page, you need to copy the HTML and JavaScript code that were written when you saved the image with the Save Optimized command. As shown in Figure 11.50, the code, once incorporated into your large Web document, will tell the browser which image to display and how to respond to the visitor's mouse movements.

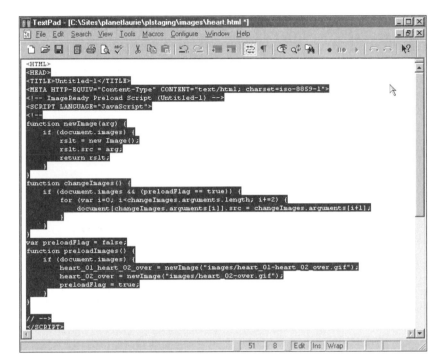

Figure 11.50
Open the HTML document and copy its content to the Clipboard.

To open the rollover file, use the File|Open command in any text editing software or your WYSIWYG Web design application (Dreamweaver, GoLive) and the file opens on screen. If you're in a WYSIWYG application, set the display to show the code as well as or instead of the graphics. Then, use your mouse to select the code and press Ctrl+C to copy it to the Clipboard.

Next, switch to your Web page (where the graphic will appear) and display its code. At the point in the page where your rollover image should appear, click to position your cursor, and press Ctrl+V to paste the code.

PROJECT Create a Rollover Image

In this project, you'll create a two-state rollover that adds text to a graphic when a visitor mouses over the original image.

Start a New ImageReady Image

Using the File|New command, create an image that's 200 pixels wide by 300 pixels tall. The background should be white.

Create an Over State

On the Rollover palette, you should already have a Normal state. Insert a new state by clicking the New Rollover State button at the bottom of the palette. By default, this state will be Over, which is what you want.

Create Layers for Each State of the Image

This image, as shown in Figures 11.51 and 11.52, will contain a graphic logo (made up of a series of geometric shapes) and some text. The text appears in the Over state. You need to create layers for each state, and if you prefer, for each component of the graphic portion of the logo—the rectangle, the oval, and the checkmark. You can also draw these elements on a single layer. The text will be on its own layer automatically.

Figure 11.51

(Left) Untouched, the image appears as a graphic logo.

Figure 11.52

(Right) When a visitor mouses over the logo, text appears.

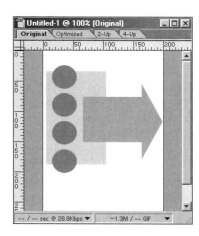
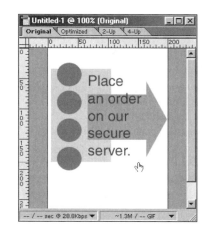

Adjust Visibility of Layers for Each State

Make sure that the text layer is visible only in the Over state and that all the graphic content is available in both the Normal and Over states, as shown in Figure 11.53.

Figure 11.53

The graphic remains in the Over state, but text is added on top of it.

Test the Rollover

You can click the Preview Behaviors button at the bottom of the Rollover palette, and then move your mouse over the graphic as it appears in the Image window. The text should appear as soon as the mouse touches the graphic content in the first state. You can also use the Preview In Default Browser button at the foot of the toolbox to test your rollover in a browser window, as shown in Figure 11.54.

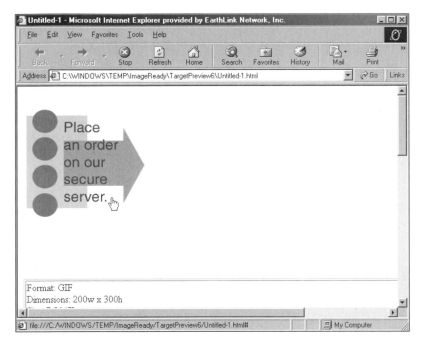

Figure 11.54
The text appears to explain where visitors will be taken if they click the link.

Save the Rollover Image

Save the rollover in both PSD and HTML formats. To save in PSD format, simply use the File|Save command, and call the file LOGOWTEXT.PSD. Then use the File|Save Optimized command, using the same file name, and ImageReady will automatically add the .htm extension.

Moving On

In the next chapter, you'll learn to slice an image into several pieces and insert the pieces into a table on a Web page. You can slice images in Photoshop and ImageReady, and you'll learn the techniques available in both applications.

Chapter 12

Slicing Images for Dynamic Effects

Whether you need a large image broken into several pieces to populate a table or you're breaking a page prototype into digestible pieces to assemble the page in HTML, Photoshop's slicing tool will save time—for you as a designer and for your page visitors.

Why Slice an Image?

If you have a very big image, in terms of dimensions and/or file size, slicing it enables you to use it as the fill for a table (one slice per table cell) or to turn the image into a Web page—one slice at a time. Figure 12.1 shows a large picture sliced into a tidy grid of rectangular slices, each one inserted into a table. Figure 12.2 shows a page prototype sliced into manageable chunks, bound for a Web page where the slices will be arranged to fill the page. The images slices can be turned into individual links.

Figure 12.1

Chop an image into small blocks and then reassemble it in a table.

Figure 12.2

Did your client love that page prototype you created in Photoshop? Slice it into pieces and then turn the slices into a Web page.

Slicing is really only used on Web-bound images, because slicing provides significant benefits to Web designers and very few, if any, benefits to designers working with print media. A large image bound for print can be as large as the paper for which it's destined, and the file size is unrestricted by concerns about upload and download time. When it comes to the Web, as I've mentioned ad nauseum in the previous chapters of this book, images need to be in pixel dimensions that fit on the page where you intend to use them, and their file sizes need to be less than 35KB so that they don't take too long to load. Slicing enables you to tuck pieces of images into table cells, layers, and frames, resulting in the appearance of a large single image with the quick loading time of several small ones. Slicing also allows you to use large, page-sized images that you've created as page prototypes as the building blocks of an actual page.

Working with the Slice Tools

It used to be that you had to fire up ImageReady if you wanted to slice an image. Not anymore! Photoshop 6 includes a slicing tool, right in the toolbox. As shown in Figure 12.3, the tool has two faces: the Slice tool itself, which enables you to create the slices, and a Slice Select tool that you can use to click on and select existing slices.

As you're building and customizing your slices, you'll find that you switch between these two versions of the tool quite often. Any time you want to tinker with settings for a slice, you need to use the Slice Select tool to select it, and when you're ready to create a new slice or subdivide an existing slice, you'll switch back to the Slice tool to make your slices.

Slicing an Image

To create slices in Photoshop, you must open an image first, and then activate the Slice tool by clicking it. The image you open can be a Photoshop (PSD) file, or an image that's already been saved in a Web-safe format—JPG, GIF, or, for pages you know will only be viewed through the latest browser versions, PNG. Once the tool is activated, your mouse pointer changes to a knife (see Figure 12.4). At this point, you can begin slicing your image into blocks of varying or uniform sizes.

Slicing your image is very much like drawing rectangles on the surface of the image—you click and drag to draw a box, as shown in Figure 12.5. The position and size of the slice, however, is very important. This means that you need to select your starting point carefully, and drag only as far out and down as necessary to create a slice the precise size that you want.

How do you know how big a slice you need? The size of the table cell into which that slice will be placed will dictate the slice size, or you can resize your table to match your slices after you insert them into the table. If you'll be making the table fit your slices, just slice away, breaking the image into as many pieces as you feel will create a fast-loading group of individual image files. For example, if your unsliced image is about 320KB (in JPG or GIF format), you want to slice it

Figure 12.3
Slice and dice your image right within Photoshop 6—no need to hop out to ImageReady for this common task.

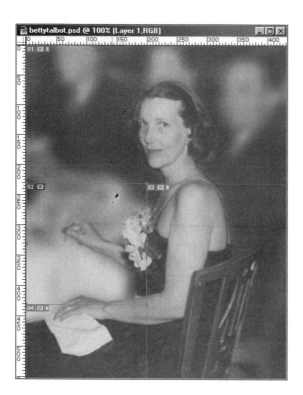

Figure 12.4
A knife is for slicing.

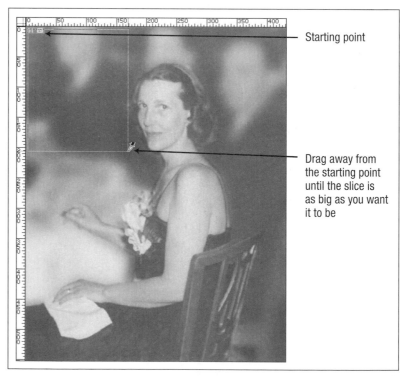

Starting point

Drag away from the starting point until the slice is as big as you want it to be

Figure 12.5
Click and drag diagonally, drawing a rectangle on the image.

into about nine pieces of 35KB each (if you're not sure how big each block should be, bring in guidelines that divide your image into nine blocks, three columns across and three down. The resulting slice images (see the slices in Figure 12.6) will be placed into nine table cells.

Figure 12.6
Slice your large image into pieces
that don't exceed the 35KB limit
for fast-loading images.

If you need slices to be the same width and height (perfect squares rather than
rectangles), you can set that control before you begin drawing. As soon as the
Slice tool is activated, the options bar changes to offer slice controls. Click the
Style drop-down list, and choose from three options:

- *Normal*—This slice style applies no constraints to your slicing at all. Slices can be
  any size you want, enabling you to slice an image into as many slices as you
  can draw within the confines of the image canvas, as shown in Figure 12.7.

Precisely!

If you want to control the size of
your slices so that they're a
certain width by a certain
height, display the rulers in your
Image window by choosing
View|Show Rulers. With the
rulers showing, you can watch
the ruler as you draw, and make
sure that the slice you're creating doesn't exceed or fall short
of the desired dimensions.

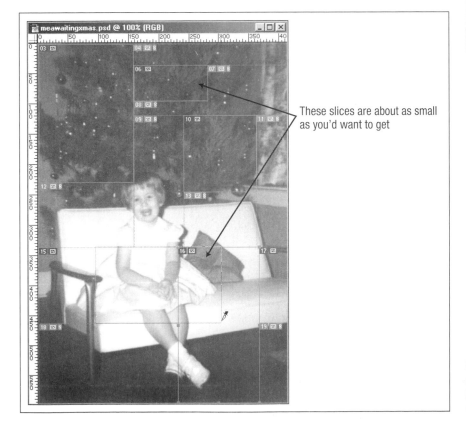

These slices are about as small
as you'd want to get

Figure 12.7
Don't go wild, of course,
but feel free to draw as many
random-sized slices as you need.

- *Constrained Aspect Ratio*—This option will prevent slices from being resized in such a way that their width and height ratio is lost. For example, if the slice starts out at 100 pixels wide by 200 pixels tall, if it's resized, the height will remain twice the width. To use this option, you can enter a ratio in the Width and Height boxes that appear as soon as the option is selected (see Figure 12.8). A 1 to 1 ratio results in slices that are the same width and height, and a 1 to 2 ratio results in a slice that's twice as tall as it is high. You can enter any ratio you choose, but 1 is the lowest number you can enter in either box.

- *Fixed Size*—Choose this option if you want to draw several slices of the exact same size. Once this option is chosen (see Figure 12.9), Width and Height options appear, and you can enter the dimensions of the fixed size slices you want to draw. You can, of course, change the dimensions after drawing some slices, so your image can be diced into two or more groups of equal-sized slices.

Figure 12.8

Choose Constrained Aspect Ratio if you want to control the relative width and height of your slices.

Figure 12.9

Chop your image into a tidy array of equal-sized blocks with the Fixed Size slice style option.

If you choose the Normal or Constrained Aspect Ratio styles for your slices, you have to drag to draw them—click a starting point and drag diagonally away from that point until the slice is the size you want. If you choose the Fixed Size style, you merely need to click on the image and move your mouse slightly, and a slice will be created automatically. You then move your mouse (don't drag) to position the pre-drawn block where it belongs. Continue clicking and moving to create all the slices you need, arranging them tightly next to one another to create a tidy grid, as shown in Figure 12.10.

Note that as you draw your slices, whether you're drawing them freehand in Normal or Constrained Aspect Ratio style or clicking to place Fixed Size slices around on the image, numbers appear in the upper-left corner of each completed slice. These numbers will become part of the slice file names, appended to the main image name. For example, if the image is already named "groupphoto.psd", the sliced images will be "groupphoto01.jpg", "groupphoto02.jpg", and so on. You don't want to name each slice something different, because this could become very confusing later as you go to position the slices in a table or directly on a page.

The numbering issue brings up another important thing to think about as you draw your images. If you want to make it easy for yourself later when you go to

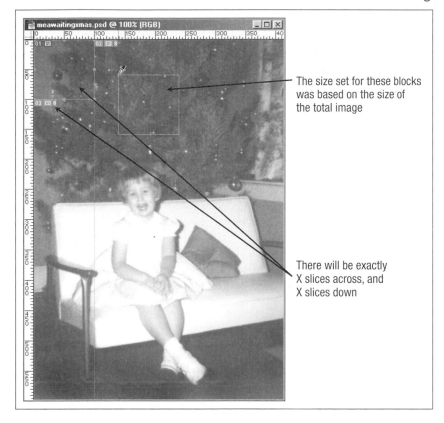

The size set for these blocks was based on the size of the total image

There will be exactly X slices across, and X slices down

Figure 12.10
Fixed Size blocks are moved into position, one at a time.

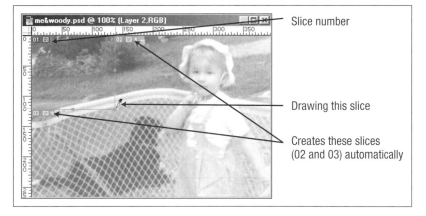

Slice number

Drawing this slice

Creates these slices (02 and 03) automatically

Figure 12.11
Use the slice numbers to your advantage by drawing your slices in order, starting in the upper-left corner of the image.

assemble your image, draw the slices in order, from left to right, top to bottom, as shown in Figure 12.11. That way, you'll know that "image01.jpg" goes in the upper-leftmost cell in the table or the upper-leftmost corner of the page.

Editing Slices

Once you've drawn a slice or sliced up your entire image, you may want to make changes—moving slices around, making some slices bigger or smaller, or removing slices entirely. You may also want to protect your slices so that once you've got them "just so" they can't be moved or changed by you or anyone else, at least not accidentally. The tools provided for editing your slices are found in a variety of dialog boxes, menus, and the options bar in its various forms.

No Grouting Required

Unlike with tiling a wall or floor, you don't want to leave space between the slices that make up your image. Why not? Because if you do, a slice is created between your slices, and:

- The numbering is then off if you're trying to draw your slices in order for easy positioning later.
- You end up with more files than you intended, some of which are too thin to fit into a table cell.

If you do manage to leave space between slices, use the Slice Select tool and drag them closer together. You'll know you've achieved a perfect placement with no space between when you see the slide numbers change—if you had a slice 03 and then drew one next to it that was numbered slice 05 (with 04 placed between it automatically to number the slice required by the too-wide spacing), when you reposition 03 or 05, slice 04 disappears and 05 is renumbered as 04.

You Deserve a Promotion

When you activate the Slice Select tool, the options bar changes to display a Promote To User Slice button. All this means is that any automatically created slices (the spacer slices that appear when you don't create your slices right up against each other or when you don't go to the edge of the image with a slice) are promoted to being slices just like those you created. User slices can be selected with the Slice Select tool, resized, moved, and deleted, unlike automatic slices, which can't be changed manually—they change size and position in response to the slices you draw.

Figure 12.12

You can tell which slice is selected by its color—a light brown border and handles appear around it, while the other slices remain bordered in blue.

Moving a Slice

If your slices aren't touching and a spacer slice was inserted automatically, you may want to move your slices so that they touch, resulting in the disappearance of the spacer slice. This is especially important if your slices are bound for a Web page table, because some of the spacer slices and the overall slice configuration they create can't be easily re-created in a table, making it hard to reassemble your image.

To move a slice, select it with the Slice Select tool, and drag it into the desired position. You can also use the arrow keys to nudge the selected slice into position. If you have guidelines displayed, slices will snap to them by default, making it easier to align your slices along a vertical or horizontal line. Figure 12.12 shows a slice being dragged into position along a vertical guideline.

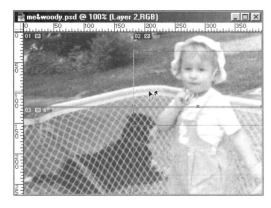

Duplicating Slices

If you've drawn a slice and want to make another one just like it, you can duplicate it by using the Alt key as you drag the existing slice into a new position. The original stays behind, and a duplicate follows you as you drag the mouse.

Of course, using the Fixed Size style for building two or more of your slices will help you make slices that are the exact same size, so if you know you want at least two slices that are the same width and height, use the options bar and choose Fixed Size from the Style drop-down list, and then enter the dimensions you want your slices to be. You can change the dimensions or switch to another style after your identical slices are drawn.

Restacking Slices

Slices can overlap, and if yours do and you want to move one up from the bottom of the stack or move one down in the stacked order, you can use the options bar to move slices up and down in the pile. To restack a slice, simply select it with the Slice Select tool and then click the buttons shown in Figure 12.13. You can move a slice from top to bottom, bottom to top, or move a slice up or down in the pile one level at a time.

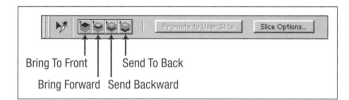

Bring To Front   Send To Back
Bring Forward   Send Backward

Figure 12.13
Change the pecking order of your overlapping slices.

Resizing Slices

If your slices are too big or too small, you can drag their handles just as you would the content on a layer while using the Transform command and tools. Simply point to a handle, and when your mouse turns to a two-headed arrow, drag—outward to increase slice size, inward to decrease the size of the slice. If you work from a corner handle, you can retain current width-height proportions, as shown in Figure 12.14.

Figure 12.14
Drag up or down as much as you drag left or right to keep the slice in proportion.

Pay attention to the surrounding slices as you resize an individual slice; overlapping part of another slice may cause a spacer slice to be inserted, and if you don't want overlapping slices, you'll have to move or resize the adjacent slice(s) to remedy the situation.

Deleting Slices

Say one of your slices is no longer needed—perhaps you drew an extra one by mistake, or you've decided to change the configuration of your slices and have to get rid of one or more of them to make the changes you need. Deleting slices is almost dangerously simple—just click the one you want to select (use the Slice Select tool, of course) and press Delete. Simple as that!

Locking and Unlocking Slices

Your slices are perfect—they're the right size, they're arranged just as you wanted them, and you don't want anything to happen to them—by accident or on purpose. If you're not the only person working on the image in question, the possibility of someone making a change is significant. To prevent any changes, choose View|Lock Slices. As soon as this command is issued, you can't select a slice or draw a new one. You can't move a slice, even if it's already selected. Figure 12.15 shows the error that appears if you try to draw a slice on an image with locked slices.

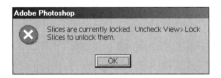

Figure 12.15

Hands off these slices! If slices are locked, you can't change them or add new ones.

If you want to unlock your slices to make changes or additions, choose View|Lock Slices again. The command appears checked when it's on, and reselecting it turns it off.

Setting Your Slice Options

The options bars that appear when the Slice and Slice Select tools are active give you the ability to dictate how slices are drawn and how they work together. On the Slice Select version of the options bar, the Slice Options button appears, and through this feature, you can do several things, from naming the slice to changing its dimensions:

- *Slice Type*—This option is set to Image by default; your alternative is No Image, which creates a blank slice into which you can type HTML code. Because we're dealing with Web images, we'll cover the Image version of the dialog box, shown in Figure 12.16.

- *Name*—As I advised earlier in this chapter, you want to keep one name for all of your slices and allow the slice number to differentiate them— "image01.jpg", "image02.jpg", and so forth. If you feel you must name your slices, however, you can do so using this option.

- *URL*—If you want a slice to act as a graphic link, type a Web address into this box. If the slice and the linked page are in the same folder (or if they will be once they're uploaded to your Web server), simply type the page file name. If the page is on another Web server or in a folder separate from your slices and other images (it should be, if your Web files are well organized), enter the complete path to the page (**http://www.domain.com/ pagename.htm**).

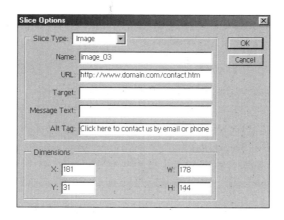

Figure 12.16
One-stop shopping for all your slice option needs.

- *Target*—If your page has frames in it, enter a frame tag into this box to tell the browser that will eventually display your page into which frame to load the slice link contents. Typical entries for this option are _blank, for a new browser window, _self, if you want the linked page to replace the frame containing the slice, or _parent, if you want the linked page to replace the frames page. The tag you enter (with the underscore preceding the word) will become available when information is entered into the URL field.

- *Message Text*—If you want text to appear at the bottom of the browser window (on the status bar, where "Done" appears when a page has completed loading) when a page visitor mouses over a particular slice, type that text in this box. This added JavaScript can be a great way to inform visitors as to the purpose of a link; for example, "Click here to visit our products page!"

- *Alt Tag*—The text you type in this box will appear as a ScreenTip when a visitor mouses over the selected slice, or instead of the slice image if the visitor's browser is set to exclude graphics. Alt text (which is actually an attribute of the img [image] tag) is a good idea if you aren't sure about the graphics capabilities and Internet connection speed of your visitors. If your visitors aren't willing to wait for a large graphic to load (or for any graphics to load if their modem is slow or they're using an older monitor with limited graphics capability), the Alt text can tell them what the picture would have communicated or advise them that the image was a link to another page.

- *Dimensions*—If you want to change the size and/or position of the selected slices, you can enter exact pixel measurements into the boxes in this section of the dialog box. The X and Y boxes allow you to enter new horizontal and vertical positions, and the W and H boxes allow you to enter a new width and height.

When your changes are complete, click OK. The changes apply to the selected slice. If you want to set options for another slice, double-click that slice with the Slice Select tool, or select the slice and then click the Slice Options button on the options bar again.

Saving Sliced Images

Like any other change you make to your image, slicing it is cause for saving the image to preserve what you've done. If you haven't saved the image pre-slicing, now's the time to save and name it in PSD format so that the image and all of the slice information is preserved for future work in Photoshop. You can use the File|Save or File|Save As command. Choosing either command opens the Save As dialog box, where you can name your file and choose a folder in which to store it.

If you've already saved the image and just want to save the slicing information along with the file, use the File|Save command to update the file. No dialog box opens, but your slices are stored as part of the file.

Saving a Sliced Image in Photoshop Format

The File|Save or File|Save As command will save your file in PSD format by default, and it's important to preserve a version of your file in this format after you've sliced it. Why? So that you can edit the image and its slices later. You don't want to save the file in a Web format, insert the slices into a Web page, and find that your slice configuration doesn't work in the Web page table or other structural device, and then have to open it in JPG or GIF format and try to tinker with it in Photoshop. Your layers will be gone, making it hard to edit parts of the image.

Saving Slices for the Web

Assuming you sliced your image so that the slices could be placed on a Web page, you want to save the image and its slices in a Web-safe format. The process is the same as for any other Web-bound image, but there's a small addition: You need to select each of your slices in the Save For Web dialog box and save them individually. Of course, you'll have chosen a format and quality level for the image and its slices—JPG for photos or complex and highly colored images, and GIF for line art and simple drawings—and then you can proceed to select individual slices for saving. Figure 12.17 shows a sliced image in Optimized view, with a single slice selected.

After selecting a slice, click the OK button to save it with your current format and quality settings. Note that instead of JPG or GIF in the Save As Type box, the default file format is HTML (see Figure 12.18). This is because the default setting for a sliced image is to save the entire image and the slice information in an HTML format so that a complete Web page can be made from the image and its slices as a whole. You'll also get a chance to save the individual slices in the Web-safe format you chose in the Save For Web dialog box, as shown in Figure 12.19.

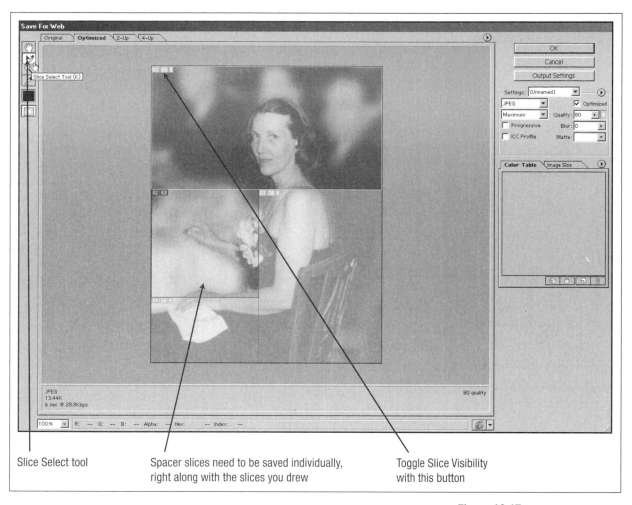

Slice Select tool

Spacer slices need to be saved individually, right along with the slices you drew

Toggle Slice Visibility with this button

Figure 12.17

The selected slice appears slightly darker than the others.

Figure 12.18

Save the image and its slices as a single HTML file—great if your image is a page prototype sliced into sections for quick loading.

Replace Files

Some of the specified files already exist in the target location. The files marked below will be replaced:

☑ bettytalbot.html
☑ bettytalbot_01.jpg
☑ bettytalbot_02.jpg
☑ bettytalbot_03.jpg
☑ bettytalbot_04.jpg

Cancel   Replace

Figure 12.19

All the slices in your image are selected for saving; their slice numbers are appended to the file names.

The slice image files are automatically inserted into the "images" folder. If an images folder already exists in the selected folder (the one you chose in the Save For Web dialog box), the slice image files will be placed in it. If no images folder exists in the selected folder, one is created automatically as soon as you save the images.

Using Image Slices in a Table

To populate a Web page table with slice images, simply click in each cell, one at a time, and use the Insert|Image command (if you're working in Dreamweaver) or drag the Image icon into the cell (if you're using GoLive, as shown in Figure 12.20). If you're working in HTML, add the appropriate tags within the tags for the table cell that should house the image:

Figure 12.20

Click in a cell and then insert an image into it.

```
<img src= "image01.jpg">
```

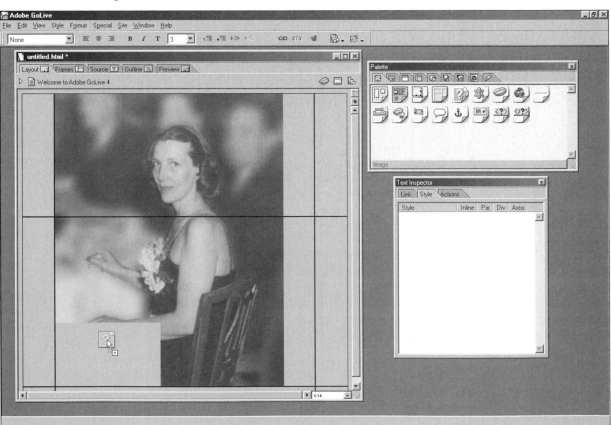

You can click in each cell of the table (working in a WYSIWYG environment) and repeat the image-insertion process, or move through your HTML code, inserting image source tags within the tags for each cell of the table. If you're reassembling a picture, you should preview the page in a Web browser to make sure the image looks the way you want it to. Figure 12.21 shows a completed image built in a table, but the slices are out of order. If you're working in HTML, this is more likely to happen, because you can't see the images you're inserting via HTML code. In a WYSIWYG environment like Dreamweaver or GoLive, you can see the images as you insert them, so you know if you aren't putting the puzzle back together properly.

The Page and Nothing But the Page

If your sliced image was a page prototype, the HTML version of the image that you saved as the first step in the Save For Web process can be uploaded to a Web server as a completed Web page unto itself. You should preview it first in a browser window, though, so that you spot any problems that might have occurred during the slicing or saving process—missing bits of the image, content changes, etc.

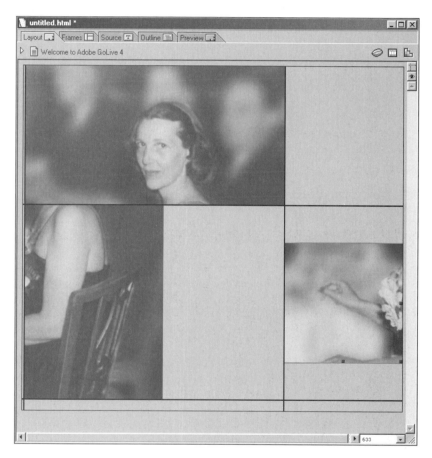

Figure 12.21

Previewing your page before uploading it to the Web server prevents sharing a snafu like this with the rest of the world.

PROJECT Slice a Large Image for Use in a Web Page Table

In this project, you'll take an existing image and slice it into four equal-sized slices for use in a Web page table. The Web page already exists, as does the table on it. Your job is to slice the image, save the slices, and then insert them into the table to reassemble the image.

Open the Image to Be Sliced

Open the image called businesscall.psd (which you'll find in the Chapter 12 folder on the CD-ROM).

Crop Away the White Edges

The image was scanned from a photograph, and the photo's white border was included. Using the Crop tool or the Marquee tool and the Image|Crop command, remove the white border. Figure 12.22 shows the image as it appears when you open it, and Figure 12.23 shows it after the white border has been cropped away.

Figure 12.22

A photo's white border was included in the scan, and thus became part of the electronic version of the picture.

Figure 12.23

Crop the white border away to eliminate an unwanted edge on the image.

Activate the Slice Tool

Click once on the Slice tool. If it is currently set to Slice Select, click the triangle in the lower-right corner of the button to display the button's alternative, and choose the Slice tool.

Create Guidelines to Assist Your Slicing

Note that the image is 400 pixels wide by 500 pixels tall (if it isn't, due to a minor variance between your cropping and mine as I write this, resize it). To slice it into four equal-sized slices, you'll either need to so some math or create guidelines to help you draw the slices freehand. Using guidelines is a better approach because you can see what you're doing and make decisions about the slice dimensions before you create them.

1. Pull down a horizontal guideline, and place it at 250 pixels (refer to the ruler).

2. Pull out a vertical guideline, and place it at 200 pixels.

This creates four equal sections on the image, each one destined to be a slice, as shown in Figure 12.24.

Figure 12.24
Guidelines are a great tool to help you plan and draw your slices.

Slice the Image into Four Equal-Sized Slices

Choose the Normal slice style if you think you have the eye-hand coordination for the task, or use the Fixed Size style and set the width and height to 200 pixels and 250 pixels, respectively. Create the slices—you should have four slices, each 200 pixels wide by 250 pixels tall. Figure 12.25 shows the image with the four slices in place.

Figure 12.25
You can edit the slices if you made a mistake drawing them—resize them by dragging their handles.

Save the Sliced Image in PSD Format

Save the image, using the File|Save As command so that you keep the original intact and create a new version. Call the new version "onthephone.psd".

Save the Slices for the Web

Using the File|Save For Web command, create your Web-safe images—four in total. Their names should be onthephone01, onthephone02, onthephone03, and onthephone04, all with a .jpg extension (of course you chose JPG as the format, because you're dealing with a photograph). Figure 12.26 shows the first slice selected in the Save For Web window, ready to be saved in JPG format.

Open an Existing HTML file in Dreamweaver, GoLive, or a Text Editing Program

Looking in the Chapter 12 folder on the CD-ROM again, find and open the file called slicetable.htm. You can open it in Dreamweaver or Adobe GoLive, or if you're HTML savvy, open it in a text editor such as Notepad or TextPad (a great text editor from Helios software—you can download an evaluation copy at **www.textpad.com**). The empty table is all set for your images—it is 400 pixels wide by 500 pixels tall, and the cells are equal in size. The table is set to be centered on the page, as shown in Figure 12.27.

Insert the Image Slices into the Existing Table

Using the Insert|Image command in Dreamweaver or GoLive, or the appropriate HTML code if you're working in a text editor, insert the images into the table. Figure 12.28 shows the table in a Dreamweaver window, with all four slices inserted.

Figure 12.26
Use the Slice Select tool to select each slice in turn, and save each one as an individual file. The chosen slice is slightly darker while selected.

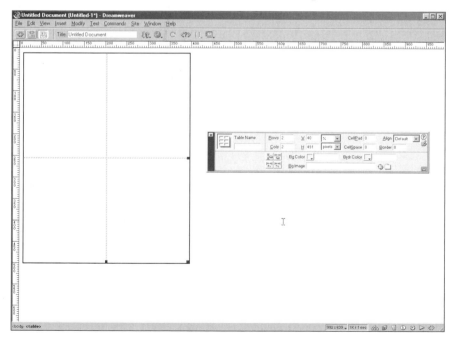

Figure 12.27
Ready and waiting for your slice images, a table is placed in the middle of a Web page.

Figure 12.28

Reassemble the picture as a set of four images, one in each cell of the table.

Save the HTML File

Use the File|Save command and resave the file to include the images.

Preview the HTML File in a Browser Window

Open the HTML document in Internet Explorer or Netscape Navigator, and see how it looks in a browser window. Any sins you committed when inserting the images or any tweaking you might have done on the table itself will show up here. Space around the images in the table cells will be the most likely problem, and you can eliminate that by making sure that table cells' dimensions match the image dimensions exactly, and that no cell padding is set in any of the cells.

Moving On

In the next chapter, you'll learn about another way to make use of your Photoshop images—adding them to a movie created in Adobe's LiveMotion. You'll save an image in a Web-safe format (of course), and then add the image to an existing LiveMotion movie. The chapter includes a tour of the LiveMotion interface, so you can hit the ground running with Adobe's latest addition to its considerable Web design arsenal.

Chapter 13

Sending Photoshop Images to LiveMotion

Adobe's Web Collection includes LiveMotion, Adobe's version of the very popular and powerful Flash from Macromedia. In this chapter, you'll enjoy a quick tour of the LiveMotion interface and find out how Photoshop images are used in LiveMotion movies.

What Does LiveMotion Do?

You can use LiveMotion to do many things, from creating rollovers and animations to designing navigation bars and button graphics. The word *Motion* in the application name tells you that the main focus is movement—creating animations that can be exported as Flash SWF (ShockWave File) and GIF files, ready for use on the Web. You can use Photoshop-created images, as well as images in JPEG, GIF, PNG, BMP, and EPS formats. These images then become part of the LiveMotion file (also known as a *composition*), and can be moved, scaled, rotated, skewed, faded, or brightened. You can set each change to occur in a separate frame in the movie and adjust the timing of individual frames so that you can control the speed at which the changes occur.

LiveMotion creations can contain a variety of elements:

- Geometric shapes (circles, ovals, rectangles, rounded-corner rectangles)

- EPS images imported from other illustration applications

- Photoshop images (PSD files, as well as images saved in Web-safe formats)

- Text (that you type in LiveMotion, using the Type tool)

- Sound objects, in the form of audio files

Just as in Photoshop and ImageReady, the elements you add to your LiveMotion file are stored on individual layers. Unlike these other two applications, however, in LiveMotion each attribute applied to the element is on its own layer as well. Layers can be offset to be embossed or filled with a gradient to achieve the illusion of three dimensions, as shown in Figure 13.1.

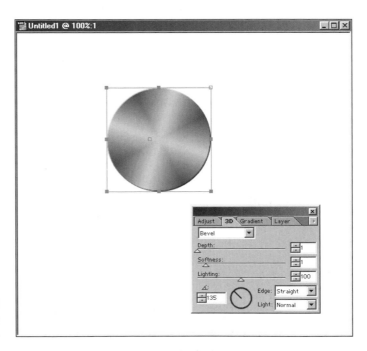

Figure 13.1

Make your image stand out by applying 3-D layer attributes.

Figure 13.2
Make your text stand out with LiveMotion's styles. Use the Color palette tab to adjust the color of the text. The Properties tab gives you access to font, size, leading, and tracking options, as well as an Align tool. The 3D and Gradient tabs can be used to apply interesting effects.

The layers can also be formatted with various styles, as shown in Figure 13.2. If you've created graphic text in Photoshop, you can insert that image, or you can type your own in LiveMotion using the Type tool. The upside of creating the text in LiveMotion is that you have more control over its appearance without having to use another application to change fonts or colors.

Touring the Basic LiveMotion Interface

The LiveMotion application window is very similar to the Photoshop and ImageReady windows. It contains a main document window, toolbox, and palettes. There are some different tools, some you'll recognize immediately, and some of the palettes are similar to those you've seen in Photoshop and ImageReady as well. Figure 13.3 shows the LiveMotion interface, with each of its main parts labeled.

The toolbox is very similar to Photoshop's and to ImageReady's, with some exceptions. The buttons are identified in Figure 13.4. Unlike Photoshop and ImageReady, the tools have but one face each—no alternative buttons appear if you press and hold your mouse button on the tools.

Displaying Windows and Palettes

To turn on additional palettes and windows, and to view variations on those already displayed, use the Window menu. As shown in Figure 13.5, the menu consists of selected and deselected items, each a tool for changing the appearance or placement of an object in the composition.

Where Did the Color Picker Go?

You'll notice that when you click on what looks like the Color Picker, no dialog box appears. You might notice that instead, the Color palette activates (if it's displayed at the time), through which you can choose any Web-safe color by entering new RGB (Red, Green, Blue) levels or by dragging the slider triangles to create the desired shade.

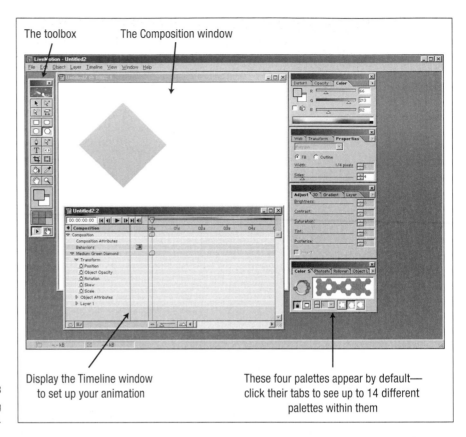

The toolbox
The Composition window

Display the Timeline window
to set up your animation

These four palettes appear by default—
click their tabs to see up to 14 different
palettes within them

Figure 13.3

Plenty of new tools, mingling
with recognized tools.

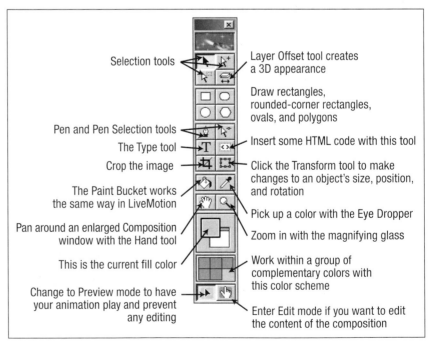

Selection tools

Layer Offset tool creates
a 3D appearance

Draw rectangles,
rounded-corner rectangles,
ovals, and polygons

Pen and Pen Selection tools

The Type tool

Insert some HTML code with this tool

Crop the image

Click the Transform tool to make
changes to an object's size, position,
and rotation

The Paint Bucket works
the same way in LiveMotion

Pick up a color with the Eye Dropper

Pan around an enlarged Composition
window with the Hand tool

Zoom in with the magnifying glass

This is the current fill color

Work within a group of
complementary colors with
this color scheme

Figure 13.4

The LiveMotion toolbox has
some familiar faces on it, with
several new ones as well.

Change to Preview mode to have
your animation play and prevent
any editing

Enter Edit mode if you want to edit
the content of the composition

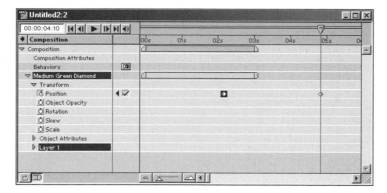

Figure 13.5
Display the Timeline window, and see the Transformation options for the animation in progress.

Once a palette is displayed, you can view its variations by clicking the tabs—just as you would in Photoshop or ImageReady. In a window, such as the Timeline window, you can click triangles to display options. As shown in Figure 13.6, if you want to see more options for part of the composition, click the right-pointing triangle, which then changes to a down-pointing triangle and offers the desired list of options. To display the Timeline window, choose Timeline|Show Timeline Window.

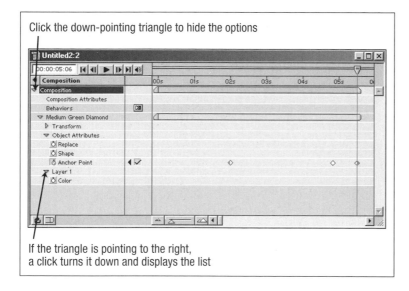

Click the down-pointing triangle to hide the options

If the triangle is pointing to the right, a click turns it down and displays the list

Figure 13.6
Known to some as *twisties*, the triangles indicate that there are more options to be seen and then allow you to see them.

Creating a LiveMotion Composition

By default, new LiveMotion compositions are 550 pixels wide by 500 pixels tall. The frames per second (the speed at which frames are displayed in succession) is 12, and the Export option is set to AutoLayout, which means that the image layout (including any slices) is maintained in the HTML page created when the composition is exported (see Figure 13.7). The other Export options are Entire Composition, which includes the entire composition as one file, and Trimmed Composition, which reduces the file to the smallest area that encompasses all the objects in the composition. If you choose AutoSlice, each element of the composition is saved in a separate image file, and an HTML page is created that references each of those files.

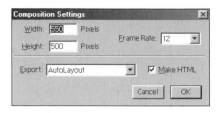

Figure 13.7
The File|New command opens
the Composition Settings dialog
box, where you can set up your
new composition.

Understanding Compositions

Think of the Composition window like you'd think of the Image window in Photoshop—it's where everything you draw or bring from other applications appears and where the animation plays. Compositions also contain information about the transformations (changes in size, color, rotation, position) that are applied to each element of the LiveMotion file, as well as the animation information that comes from your building a timeline of movements, changes in size and shape, and the introduction of new objects (see Figure 13.8). In short, everything you draw and/or insert from another graphics application is an object in the composition, and each thing you do to an item can become an event in the animation, set along the timeline.

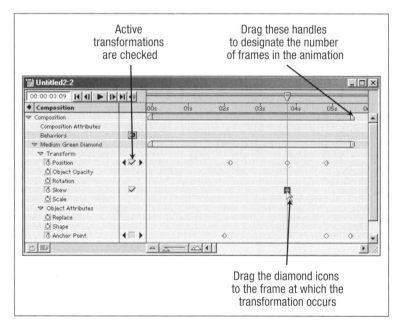

Figure 13.8
Changes occur along
the timeline.

Working with Objects, Shapes, and Layers

When you add something to the Composition window—a drawn rectangle, for example, that item becomes an object. Other objects you can add to a composition include text, images created in Photoshop, and sound files. From visual objects (anything other than a sound file) that are added to the composition, shapes are created. A shape is simply the visual boundary of any shape, text, or image added to the composition.

Drawing geometric objects is the same in LiveMotion as it is in Photoshop or ImageReady (click the tool for the shape you want to draw, and then click and drag diagonally to draw the shape), except you don't have to make a decision about creating a filled region or a shape layer. The geometric object you draw becomes part of the composition and can be transformed within the Timeline window and by using the palettes. In Figure 13.9, we're adjusting the scale of a selected rectangle by dragging the object's handles.

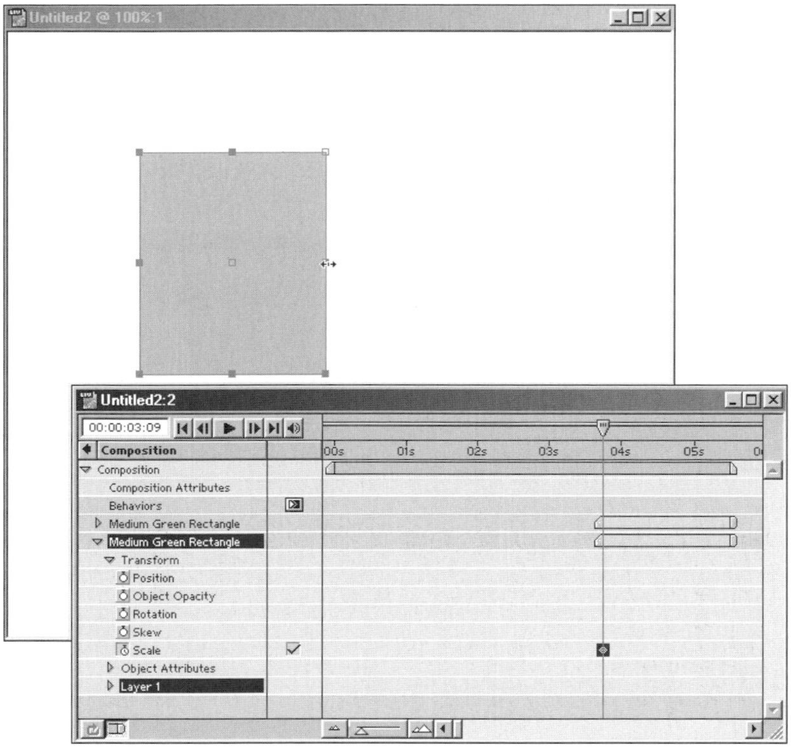

Figure 13.9
Click the triangle next to a listed object to activate that object and display handles you can use to resize and rotate it.

While a shape you've drawn is selected, you can use the Adjust, Gradient, and 3D palette tabs to apply interesting effects, rivaling many of the layer styles you can apply in Photoshop. For example, as shown in Figure 13.10, the Ripple 3D effect is similar to the effects of the Ripple filter (in the Distort category) you can apply in Photoshop. Through the 3D palette, you can change the way the ripple effect is applied, and view the adjustments you make on the shape within the Composition window.

Inserting a Photoshop Image

So you have the lay of the land—the tools, windows, and palettes that are part of the LiveMotion interface. You've seen shapes drawn in the LiveMotion Composition window and how they can be manipulated. But the simple shapes with solid color fills that can be drawn in LiveMotion do leave a bit to be desired. As a result, you'll want to bring in graphics you've created in Photoshop to jazz things up a bit, turning static graphic buttons and text into moving

When Distorted Is a Good Thing

When an object is selected, click the Distort palette tab to choose from six different distortions, such as a magnifying lens or an interesting twirl.

Double-Click Will Do the Trick

If you want to rename a layer in your composition, go to the Object palette and double-click the layer by name. A dialog box opens where you can rename the layer to something more revealing than "Layer 1".

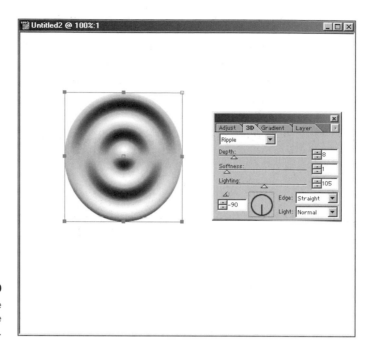

Figure 13.10

A simple shape becomes more visually interesting through the use of LiveMotion's palettes.

pictures in ways that you can't easily achieve through ImageReady's Animation and Rollover tools.

To insert a Photoshop image into a LiveMotion Composition, choose File|Place. The Place dialog box opens, as shown in Figure 13.11, and you can insert any kind of file—PSD, JPEG, GIF, PNG, or HTML. Navigate to the folder containing the file you want to insert, and double-click the file to insert it and close the dialog box simultaneously. You can also click once on the file and then click the Open button in the dialog box.

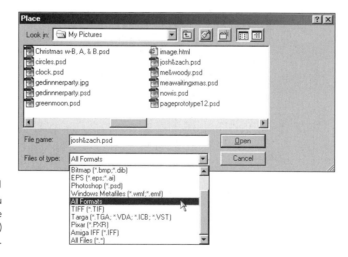

Figure 13.11

The Place dialog box allows you to choose the existing image (here from a group of PSD files) to add to your composition.

Once the image is inserted, it appears with handles around it. The image will overlap anything inserted or drawn previously, because the order in which things are drawn or placed determines their stacking order. To change the stacking order, right-click the object, choose Arrange Object from the context menu, and then choose the stacking order change from the resulting submenu (see Figure 13.12). If the Timeline window is also displayed, you can see an Object listing appear for the inserted file, and you can use that listing to access transformation options (see Figure 13.13).

Figure 13.12

Don't worry if you didn't draw and place objects in the right order—you can restack them easily.

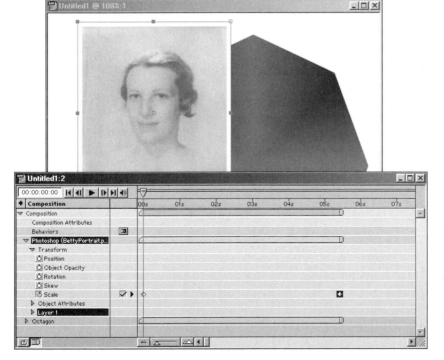

Figure 13.13

Listed as "Photoshop (*filename*.psd)" in the Timeline window, the graphic can be moved, resized, rotated, skewed, or made more or less opaque. The selected Photoshop image has handles for resizing and rotating.

276 Chapter 13

When you save the composition as an LIV file, all of the information about the things you've drawn and the Photoshop images you've placed is stored in the file. When you export to HTML or SWF (Flash) format, that detail is lost—so it's a good idea to maintain an LIV version of any file you're going to export to Flash or as an HTML file.

Animating an Image

The reason you'd consider using LiveMotion is, of course, to create animations. Whether you're going to save them as animated GIF files, similar to those you'd create in ImageReady, or export the composition to Flash so it can be turned into a movie for the Web, you need to set up the animation's steps (frames) so that you control what happens and when as the animation plays.

Of course, the Timeline window is key to the process of animating an image, and in Figure 13.14, its tools for animating and playing an animation are identified. Remember that if your Timeline window isn't displayed, you can open it by choosing Timeline|Show Timeline Window.

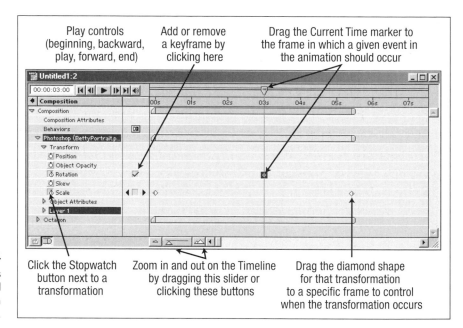

Figure 13.14

Use the Timeline window's tools for setting up and controlling the animation of composition elements.

Setting Animation Duration

When you start a new composition and display the Timeline window, a small button with an extendable handle appears in the 00s frame (see Figure 13.15). To set the total duration of the animation, drag the handle out to the frame number you feel will be the last. You can drag it past the highest frame number displayed, and the timeline will scroll with you as you drag. Figure 13.16 shows an animation set to run for eight frames.

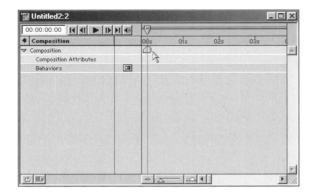

Figure 13.15
Grab this handle and drag to the right to set the duration of your animation.

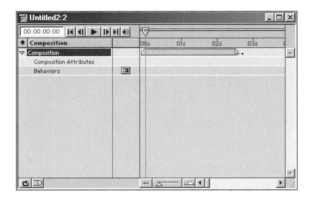

Figure 13.16
When your mouse pointer turns into a two-headed arrow, you can drag to adjust the number of frames.

Inserting Keyframes

Keyframes are frames you add to the animation when specific events will occur—when an object appears, disappears, or changes in size or shape. To insert a keyframe, select a transformation that should occur in that keyframe, and then drag the diamond icon to the point along the timeline where the keyframe should be added. Then, go back and click in the Add/Remove Keyframe checkbox to indicate that a keyframe is needed at that spot in the timeline. Figure 13.17 shows a keyframe added at frame 04, at which point the geometric object's Opacity setting will change.

Figure 13.17
It's easy to forget the order in which steps should occur; remember to choose the transformation, set the timing, and then add a keyframe.

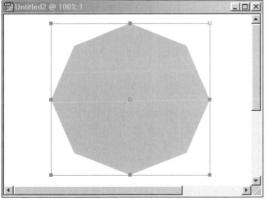
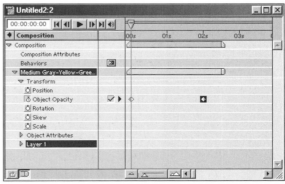

There's Always Another Way

You can choose Timeline|New Keyframe and then choose a keyframe for a series of transformations listed in the shortcut menu. To move between keyframes, choose Timeline|Next Keyframe or Previous Keyframe.

Figure 13.18

Looking a lot like controls on the front of a VCR or DVD player, these buttons allow you to rewind, fast-forward, and play your animation.

Playing the Animation

During the animation-building process, and certainly after you consider your creation complete, it's a good idea to play the animation to see how it runs. It's impossible to build an animation without playing it repeatedly as you're inserting keyframes and setting up transformations for your objects. Using the controls at the top left of the Timeline window (see Figure 13.18), you can move forward and backward through the animation, or simply play it from the beginning or the current frame. As the animation plays, the time displays in hh:mm:ss format.

To play your animation in your default browser's window, choose File|Preview In| Internet Explorer or Netscape Navigator. This extra step helps you make sure your animation will play properly in both browsers, helping you to go back and make changes as needed so that the animation runs smoothly. The Preview Mode button at the foot of the toolbox plays the animation in the Composition window, and turns off the ability to edit while the animation is ongoing and you remain in that mode.

Saving and Exporting a LiveMotion Animation

The File|Save command will save an LIV format version of the file, giving you an animation that will only play in LiveMotion. This isn't as useless as it sounds, however, because the LIV format version of your file is similar to the PSD version of a Photoshop file that you should maintain even if you save the image in JPEG, GIF, or PNG format for use on the Web. The LIV version contains all the LiveMotion-specific information about keyframes, transformations, and other object features, and you want to preserve them so that you can easily edit the animation later.

If you want to export your animation to Flash (in SWF format), choose File|Export. The Export dialog box opens (see Figure 13.19). Here you can choose where to save the file and what to call it. Once the image is saved in SWF format, you can open it in Flash and publish it there for use on the Web, a process that's covered in greater detail in Chapter 14.

Figure 13.19

Export your file in the default SWF format for use in Macromedia's Flash.

You can control your export process through the File|Export Settings command, which opens the Export dialog box (see Figure 13.20). Using this dialog box, you can choose an alternate export format, such as GIF, JPEG, PNG, or Photoshop, and set the quality and opacity resolution for the animation. If you leave the Export type set to SWF, you can also choose a Frame Rate (frames per second, from 8 fps to 40 fps, using a drop-down list). Changing to GIF, JPEG, PNG, or Photoshop results in different sets of options, one for each export format. Figure 13.21 shows the GIF format's options, which include a Frame Rate setting to be used for animated GIFs.

Figure 13.20
Set your SWF Export options.

PROJECT 13.1 Using an Existing LiveMotion File, Add a Photoshop Image to the Composition

In this project, you'll open a LIV file and insert a PSD file, providing an existing graphic for the LiveMotion animation. You'll animate the graphic, and save the file in LIV and SWF (Flash) format.

Open the LiveMotion File

On the CD, open the Chapter 13 folder and open gardenspot.liv. The composition is blank, as shown in Figure 13.22.

Figure 13.21
If you're exporting as an animated GIF (or some other format), work with settings specific to that format.

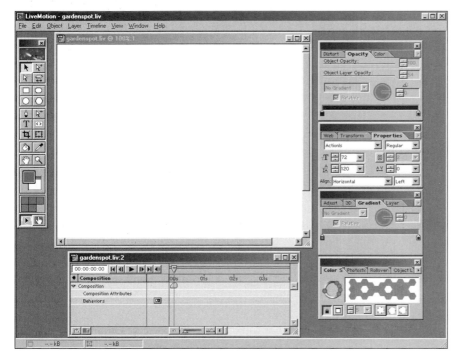

Figure 13.22
A blank canvas awaits an image for animation.

Insert a Photoshop Image

Also in the Chapter 13 folder is a graphic called flowerpot.psd. Use the Place command to insert it (see the image in place in Figure 13.23).

Figure 13.23
A simple image created in Photoshop is now ready for animation in LiveMotion.

Animate the Image

Create an animation that causes the flowerpot to move from the left side of the Composition window to the right side, at which point text (the words "Garden Spot") appear to the left of the flowerpot.

1. Create position keyframes for each step in the flowerpot's journey.

   Figure 13.24 shows the image in the last frame, where it's on the right.

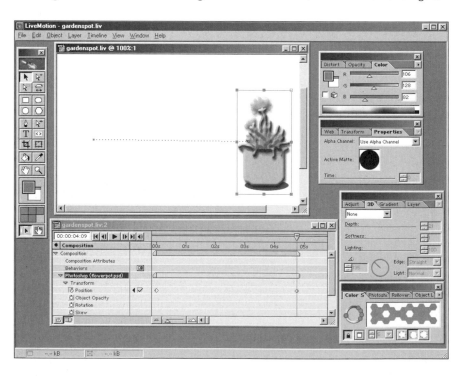

Figure 13.24
Start small and grow.

Figure 13.25
The text is in place, in the fifth frame.

2. Create a text object for the composition by typing the words "Garden Spot", using the Type tool and positioning the text as shown in Figure 13.25.

3. Make sure the text doesn't appear until the fifth frame, so that its appearance coincides with the flowerpot moving all the way to the right, as shown in Figure 13.26.

Figure 13.26
The text should not appear until the flowerpot is on the right side of the window. Use the Properties palette to set the font and size of the text.

Save the Image in LIV Format

Use the File|Save As command to save the file with a new name: newgardenspot.liv. This file will preserve all the information about your composition's objects, shapes, and layers, making it easy to edit it later. A finished version of the file, called gardenspotcomplete.liv, is on the CD in the Chapter 13 folder.

Save the Image in SWF Format for Use as a Flash Movie

Use the File|Export command to create a SWF file for use on the Web as a Flash movie. Use the same file name, and allow LiveMotion to apply the .swf extension automatically. An exported version of gardenspotcomplete.swf can be found in the Chapter 13 folder on the CD.

Moving On

With a LiveMotion tour under your belt, you're ready to move on. In the next chapter, you'll work with Macromedia's Flash, and integrate a Photoshop-created image into an existing movie. You'll also find out more about how Flash works, and get a jump-start on using the product through a tour of the interface and tools.

Chapter 14

Using Photoshop Images with Macromedia Flash

Macromedia's Flash is perhaps the most popular and powerful tool for building Web movies. Your Photoshop creations, saved in a Web-safe format, are easily added to and animated within a Flash movie. In this chapter, take a tour of Flash and see how it's done.

What Flash Does

Flash is an application that creates movies for the Web. These movies can run as objects on a Web page, or they can be a Web page unto themselves. Flash is an extremely powerful application, and in this chapter, we'll merely brush the surface of its capabilities. For a complete reference on Flash, pick up a copy of *Flash 5 In Depth* or *Flash 5 f/x & Design*, both from The Coriolis Group.

Flash movies can start out life as LiveMotion LIV files, exported to Flash for saving in Web-friendly formats, or they can be built entirely within the Flash interface, using the shapes and lines that Flash enables you to draw. You can also use photographs and original artwork created in Photoshop or any other graphics application that supports the saving of Web-safe images. Unlike LiveMotion, which lets you insert PSD files, Flash allows the insertion of JPEG, GIF, and PNG images only.

Once you insert an image, you can move and resize it as desired. You perform these changes step by step through a series of movie frames. Flash provides the ability to set up *tweens*, the steps between points A and B where an image starts out small and ends up large, or starts in one spot and ends up in an-other. You read about the concept of tweening in Chapters 10 and 11, where we covered ImageReady's animation tools.

A Quick Tour of the Flash Interface

The Flash interface is very well designed and intuitive. You might find it easier to understand and work with than the less sophisticated LiveMotion interface, perhaps because Flash has been around for a longer time and its designers have had time to develop a really useful and logical interface. Whatever the reason, your preference is just that—yours—and I don't intend to steer you one way or the other. I can simply share my experience as a Web designer and teacher of Web design and Web design applications.

The Flash interface is made up of three principle sections:

- *The Tools Box*—A vertical arrangement of buttons that allow you to select, draw, fill, and reshape original movie content. Figure 14.1 shows the Tools box.

- *The Timeline*—Gives you the ability to set up individual frames and posi-tion and scale items in those frames, and to set up the way things will progress from one frame to the next (see a movie Timeline in Figure 14.2). You can set up tweens on the Timeline, as well as build layers to keep parts of your movie separate. The function of layers in Flash is very simi-lar to Photoshop; you want to create them before you start building content, and then be sure to select a particular layer before tinkering with its drawn shapes and lines or imported graphics.

Figure 14.1

The Tools appear on the left side of the window, though they can be dragged to any useful spot in the application window.

Flash Plug-Ins

Your site visitors will be able to see Flash movies only if their computer has the Flash plug-in installed. A plug-in is a file that tells the visitor's computer how to interpret and display the Flash content of a Web page. Because so many sites have Flash content these days, it's likely that most of your visitors will already have the plug-in. You can make a Flash plug-in available from your page so that those visitors who don't have it can quickly download it and then view your movie. The latest plug-ins are available online at **www.macromedia.com**.

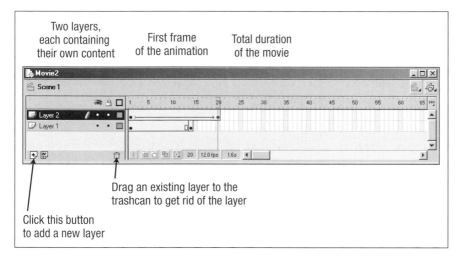

Two layers, each containing their own content

First frame of the animation

Total duration of the movie

Drag an existing layer to the trashcan to get rid of the layer

Click this button to add a new layer

Figure 14.2

The Timeline is where the items in the Work Area are set up to move, resize, or reshape as the movie plays.

- *The Work Area*—The movie canvas and scrollbars that allow you to pan from one side of the canvas to the other. As shown in Figure 14.3, the white canvas is placed on a gray background, and you can place shapes, lines, and images on that gray area if you want them to start or end beyond the area that the viewer can see.

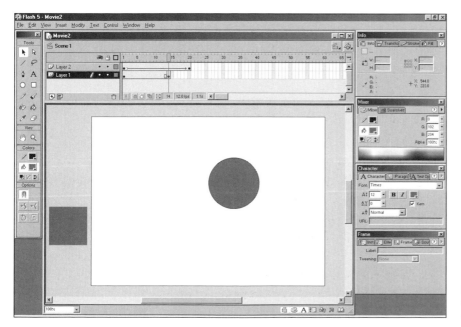

Figure 14.3

Use the movie canvas and supporting gray area to set up the starting and ending positions/sizes/shapes of movie content.

Figure 14.4
Get a quick ScreenTip and help for mouse-less activation of tools in the future.

Figure 14.5
If you're painting, you want to control the size of the strokes and the angle at which lines are painted by choosing the correct brush size and shape from the menu bar.

Shall I Give You a Hand?

The View section offers two choices: Hand and Zoom. The Hand tool allows you to pan around the image by dragging on the movie Work Area. You can use the Zoom tool first to magnify the movie and then pan around when the movie is magnified beyond the point at which the entire canvas can be seen at once.

The Flash Tools

The Tools box is broken into four main areas: tools for selecting, drawing, filling, and erasing content; tools for changing your view of the movie Work Area; tools for setting the color of objects' fill and outline; and tools for changing the shape of items you've drawn, be they geometric shapes, straight lines, or freeform items. As shown in Figure 14.4, you can mouse over any tool and see its name and the keystroke that will activate that tool. For example, to activate the Brush tool, press the letter B on your keyboard.

The Options section changes depending on which tool is active in the Tools section—for example, as shown in Figure 14.5, if you click on the Brush (or press B to activate it), the Options section offers tools for choosing the size and angle of the brush nib.

Working with the Flash Timeline

The Timeline starts out with a single layer (called Layer 1) and a series of blank frames. The animation is set to a default of 12 frames per second, which can be increased or decreased, as you desire. The Timeline also shows an estimate of your movie's running time, which you can watch for desired increases or decreases as you adjust the frames-per-second rate or add/remove content and activity within the movie itself. Figure 14.6 shows the Timeline for a movie of a bouncing ball.

The Timeline has options for turning the visibility of individual layers on and off (click the dot under the Eye icon to hide or display a layer), making it possible to work with one element of the movie without the visual interference of other content. You can also lock layers so that they cannot be changed at all; click the dot under the Lock icon for the layer you want to protect from changes.

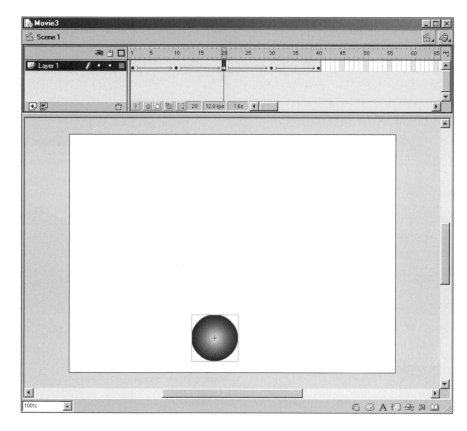

Figure 14.6
Each major milestone in the ball's progress is in a user-created keyframe, with the intermediate steps created through the Create Motion Tween command.

Flash offers *onionskins*, or transparent representations of the position and size of elements in the frames that play before and after an active frame. As shown in Figure 14.7, if you choose to see a particular layer's onionskins, you can see each position that the bouncing ball is in, between the starting point, the bounce on the ground, and the point where it bounces off the right side of the movie canvas. Onionskins are very helpful if you're manually positioning content in individual frames because you can see where the content has been, which makes it easier for you to position the content where it's going.

Understanding the Flash Work Area

The Work Area is where you build the content of your movie—drawing shapes and lines, applying fills and outline colors, inserting and positioning content of all kinds, including imported photographs and other artwork that you might have created in Photoshop. You can draw anywhere on the Work Area, and then as you insert and click on keyframes for your animation, move and resize the items you've drawn (or imported) so that they're in the location and looking as you want them to in that particular frame. Figure 14.8 shows a movie of a bouncing sphere, and we are positioning the sphere for Frame 15.

If your animation consists of two or more layers, you can turn off one or more of them on the Timeline so that they don't clutter up the Work Area as you set up animation for another layer. Figure 14.9 shows a three-layer animation (one sphere per layer), but only Layer 2 is visible. In Figure 14.10, all three layers are turned

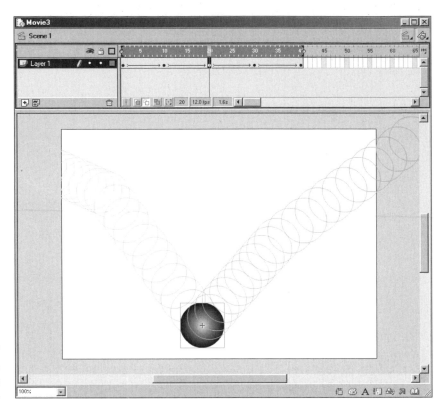

Figure 14.7

Plan your next move by displaying your animation's onionskins.

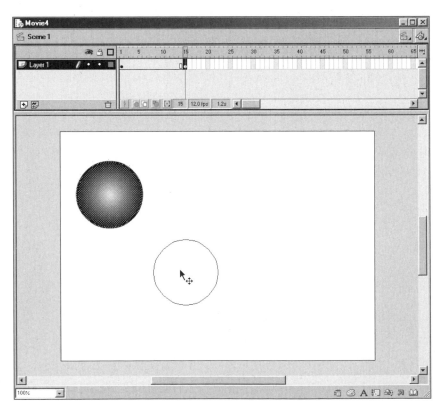

Figure 14.8

Drag the object into position so that Flash knows where it should be when a particular frame is played.

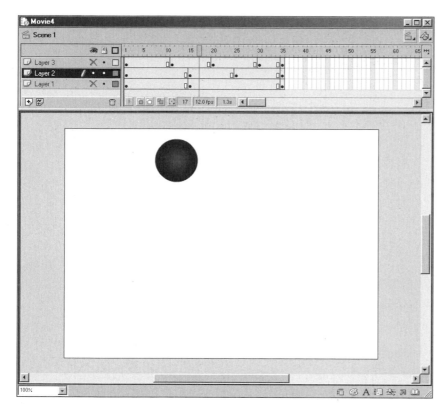

Figure 14.9
Clear the field for your per-frame placements by hiding layers.

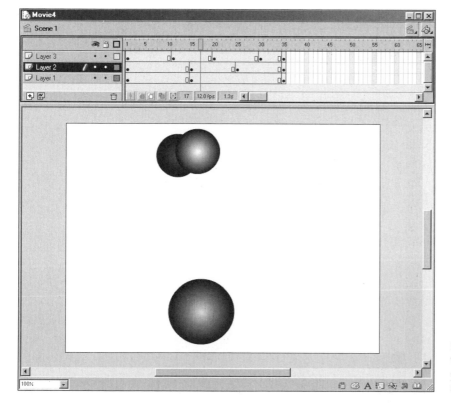

Figure 14.10
With all the spheres displayed, you can see where they all appear on a particular frame.

on, and you can see how the presence of the other spheres would have made it difficult to operate on the content of a single layer.

Inserting a Photoshop Image

To add an image that you created in Photoshop to your movie, you must first save the Photoshop image in a Web-safe format such as JPEG or GIF. Obviously, if the image is a photo or complex image, JPEG is your best bet, and simple line art is well suited to GIF. The File|Save For Web command in Photoshop will allow you to optimize your images for use on the Web. After that's been done, you can use the File|Import command in Flash to insert the image into your movie.

When you issue the File|Import command, the Import dialog box opens, as shown in Figure 14.11. To select and insert an image, simply navigate to the folder containing the image you want to use, and double-click it or click once on it and then click the Open button. If you attempt to import a file format that's not Web safe, an error prompt appears, such as the one shown in Figure 14.12.

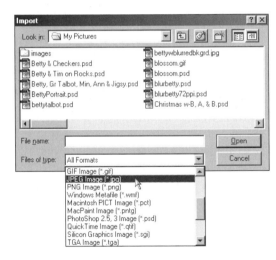

Figure 14.11

Reduce the list of available images to the format of your desired file by clicking the Files Of Type drop-down list and making a selection.

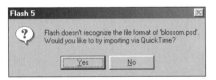

Figure 14.12

Flash will remind you that PSD files can't be imported into a movie.

Animating an Image in Flash

Once your image is inserted into the Flash movie and appears in the Work Area, you're ready to animate it. As I advised you earlier, your image should be on its own layer, making it possible to hide everything else (the content on other layers) while you animate the image. Whether your image is alone in the movie or you have other content hidden, you can begin animating it by

The Layered Look

Before you insert your image, it's a good idea to create a new layer for it with the Insert|Layer command. You can name the layer anything you want (just double-click the generic "Layer #" name it has by default and type a new one), and you can turn layers on and off in terms of visibility. If you're inserting two or more images, put each one on its own layer so you can keep them separate visually (hide the layers you're not working on), and you can easily delete one if you want to start over or inserted the wrong image to begin with.

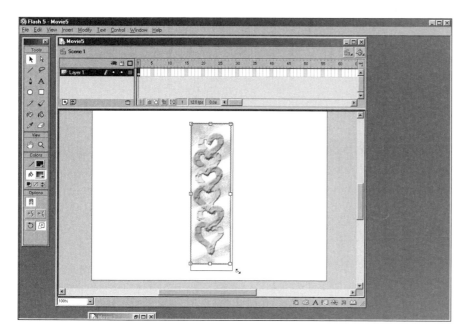

Figure 14.13
Click the Scale button to resize the object or select the image, and drag a corner handle to resize it while maintaining its current width-height ratio.

inserting keyframes to mark changes in position and size over the span of the movie. In each keyframe, you can move your image to a new spot and/or change its size, as shown in Figure 14.13. In this case, a graphic is being increased in size so that it will grow from its size in Frame 1 to a larger size in Frame 10.

Working with Frames

All this talk about frames, but what are they really? You saw frames in Chapters 10 and 11, where ImageReady's animation tools were discussed and demonstrated, and Chapter 13 on LiveMotion discussed them to an extent. In Flash, unlike ImageReady, frames can take one of three forms:

- *Keyframes*—Frames that are key to the action going on in your movie. You insert a keyframe when you're going to make something happen—a shape move or resize, a drawing swap for another one, a line lengthening or an image slide across the movie canvas. When you insert a keyframe, the contents of other frames on that layer are inserted, eliminating the need to re-import images or redraw shapes and lines.

- *Blank Keyframes*—Keyframes that don't include the content from other keyframes on the same layer. You'd insert a blank keyframe when you want to have nothing on screen for a moment, perhaps to provide a visual gap between the disappearance of one object and the appearance of another.

- *Frames*—Simply blocks of time in the movie, which you insert if you want to increase the distance between two existing frames.

Inserting any kind of frame is quite simple: You can use the aforementioned Insert|Keyframe (or Blank Keyframe or Frame) command, or you can right-click the Timeline at the spot where you want the new frame and choose the type of frame you want from the context menu. This technique is shown in Figure 14.14.

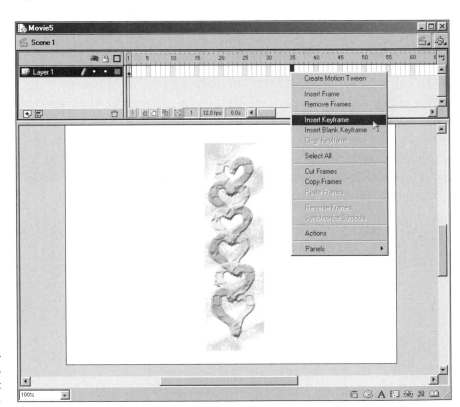

Figure 14.14

Need to make a change in the position or size of an object at Frame 35? Insert a keyframe.

Tweening Frames

So you have a shape or image in Frames 1 through 10, and in Frame 10, you want the object to move or change size. You've inserted a keyframe, made the change to the object's size or position in that frame, and now when you play the movie, you find there's a sudden leap in size or position between Frames 9 and 10—and you wanted a smooth transition. How do you make that happen?

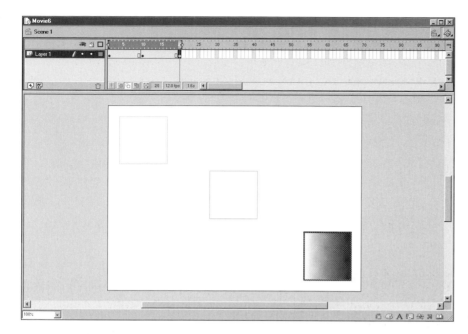

Figure 14.15

For a less-than-smooth animation, make your own baby steps from big to small or from left to right or top to bottom.

Well, you could insert several keyframes in succession and make incremental changes in the size or position of the object in each of the keyframes (see Figure 14.15). Or you could perform a *tween* that creates those steps from small to large or from left to right for you. Figure 14.16 shows a motion tween on a layer where an image makes the trip from the top of the canvas to the bottom, increasing in size as it completes the journey.

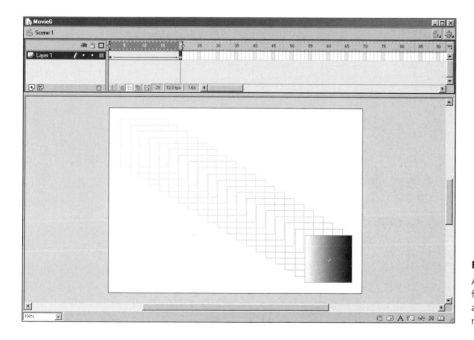

Figure 14.16

A similar action (box moves from top to bottom and grows as it goes) runs smoothly with a motion tween.

Obviously, if you build the steps from point A to point B yourself, the motion or resizing process will be rather halting; no one has the time or patience to insert keyframes at each frame in the Timeline and move or resize an object in tiny increments per keyframe and create a completely smooth transition manually. If you want the look of a choppy progression (perhaps to convey a step-by-step process or to imitate the look of stop-motion photography), creating your own intervening keyframes is the way to go.

If, on the other hand, you want a smooth progression from small to large, left to right, or any other seamless change from point A to point B, tweens are the better alternative. The tweening process creates the baby steps for you, taking as few as two keyframes and creating the steps in between them.

To tween your Photoshop-created image, you need to take one of two preparatory steps:

- Convert the image to a symbol, so it can be motion tweened.

- Use the Modify|Trace Bitmap command to convert the image to a series of shapes (you can adjust the technique applied so that there is no visual degradation of the image) so that a shape tween can be applied to the image.

If you opt to convert the image to a symbol, you can then right-click the first frame where it appears and choose Create Motion Tween from the context menu. An arrow line appears, pointing from the starting frame to the ending frame (see Figure 14.17). Press the Enter key to see the tweened action take place.

Figure 14.17

Create a motion tween that takes your image from point A to point B seamlessly, with no jerking or halting motion when the movie plays.

If you choose to use the Trace Bitmap command, you can use a shape tween to move and/or resize your image in an equally seamless fashion. The trick to using the Trace Bitmap command is to adjust the Color Threshold and Minimum Area setting for how the image is broken into areas of color. Figure 14.18 shows the Trace Bitmap dialog box and suggested settings for ending up with an

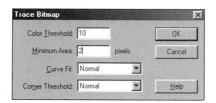

Figure 14.18
Convert your image into a series of cohesive shapes that can be tweened in a variety of ways with the Trace Bitmap command.

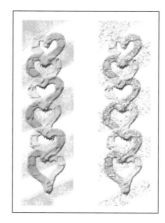

Figure 14.19
Tinker with the Trace Bitmap settings until the results are acceptable—this one's a little grainy.

image that's still sharp and clean after the Trace Bitmap is applied. Figure 14.19 shows the resulting image, with each group of like-colored pixels grouped into a shape, which is part of a larger group of shapes.

Working with Shape Tweens

You can turn an apple into a pen or a car into a dog, or a word into a person with a shape tween. Where a motion tween takes something from point A to point B in a smooth succession of automatically created frames, a shape tween will turn something into something else, creating all the interim steps between condition A and condition B. You can access the Shape Tween feature through the Frame palette, using the Frame tab, as shown in Figure 14.20.

Setting Animation Timing and Repetition

How fast and how often your movie plays are integral to its success on a Web page. If you want it to play slowly and methodically or if you want it to play really quickly, you'll need to adjust the *frame rate* or frames-per-second (fps) setting for the movie. If you want the movie to play only once, you need to insert an action that tells it to stop after the last frame. Both of these adjustments are easily made.

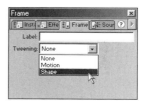

Figure 14.20
Choose Window|Panels|Frame to display this palette and select a shape tween for your shape or converted image.

Changing the Speed of Your Movie

By default, your animation will play at 12 frames per second, a frame rate that's agreeable to most computers' display capabilities. You might want to increase the frames per second, or perhaps decrease them, to speed up or slow down the movie. You can achieve a slow-motion effect with a very low frames-per-second rate, or the illusion of fast-forwarding with a high frame rate. To

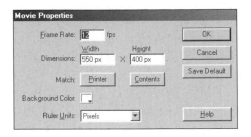

Figure 14.21

Adjust your frame rate, movie canvas size, and apply a background color (something other than white) with the Movie Properties dialog box.

change the rate, double-click the displayed 12.0 fps along the bottom of the Timeline and enter a new Frame Rate setting in the Movie Properties dialog box, as shown in Figure 14.21. You can also access this dialog box by choosing Modify|Movie.

Preventing Unwanted Looping

Another default that you might want to change is the loop settings for your movie. By default, your movie will play over and over, beginning again each time the last frame is played. If you want it to play only once, add a stop action to the end of the movie, coinciding with the last frame. You'll want to insert the action on its own layer.

To create a stop action, go to the frame on the new layer that plays at the same time as the last frame in your other layers. Figure 14.22 shows a new layer in place, and the frame that will contain the stop action selected. Next, right-click the selected frame and choose Actions from the context menu. In the resulting Frame Actions window (see Figure 14.23), double-click Basic Actions on the Frame Actions tab and double-click Stop. The stop action is added to the selected frame and the Frame Actions window closes.

Figure 14.22

Add a new layer to house the stop action that prevents your movie looping forever.

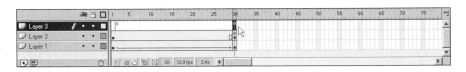

Figure 14.23

Choose Stop from the list of Basic Actions.

Testing Your Animation

Once you've set up your movie, and certainly throughout the setup process, you should test it. Run it from beginning to end several times to make sure things are happening in the right order and at the right time, and that things look and act as you want them to. To test your movie within the Work Area, press the Enter key. This will play the movie from the first frame, one time. To see the movie in a way that more closely resembles its online appearance, press Ctrl+Enter to see it play in a new window, as shown in Figure 14.24. If you've added a stop action to the movie, it will play only once in this window; otherwise, it will play over and over, stopping only when you press Esc. To resume, press Enter.

Figure 14.24
Watch your movie in a new window to see how it will look online.

Saving and Publishing an Animation

As you work on your movie, you should save it in FLA format. You should do this early in the development process, not after hours of work. The risk of losing what you've done to a power failure or system crash is too great. After you've saved your animation, you can take it a step further, preparing it for use on the Web by publishing it in one or more formats, depending on how you intend to use it online.

Saving a Flash File

To save a file as you work, choose File|Save, and on the first save, you'll be asked for a file name and location to store the file. The Save As dialog box saves the movie in Flash Movie format, with an .fla extension. The Flash movie file is viewable only within the Flash application, so if you send this type of file to someone, that person needs to have Flash installed on his or her computer in order to play the movie. Similarly, the FLA version of the movie cannot be inserted into a Web page as an object, because the browser through which the page is viewed won't know what to do with the file. Browser applications (such as Microsoft Internet Explorer or Netscape Navigator) only recognize the SWF version of the movie. (SWF stands for Shockwave File.)

If you want to save your movie to send to someone as an email attachment (for review, perhaps) or to add it to a Web page as an object on the page (rather than as the page itself), you can use the File|Export Movie command and accept the SWF format that is applied by default. This format does not require that you also send any image files for pictures you've imported into the movie, because the images are part of the file itself. The SWF file will run on any computer that has the Flash plug-in installed, but the Flash application need not be installed.

Publishing in Flash and HTML Formats

The File|Publish command creates, by default, the SWF version of your movie and an HTML document that calls for the SWF file. The SWF version can be played on any computer with the Flash plug-in, and you can add it to a Web page (the process is similar to that of inserting a static graphic or an animated GIF). If you send someone the HTML version of your movie, you must also send the SWF file, and the recipient must store these two items in the same folder in order to play the movie and see the images.

Customizing Your Publish Settings

If you want to publish your movie in more than two formats (GIF, JPEG, PNG, Windows or Macintosh Projector files, QuickTime, or RealPlayer), you need to open the Publish Settings dialog box, as shown in Figure 14.25. You access this dialog box by choosing File|Publish Settings, and of course you want to do this prior to issuing the File|Publish command.

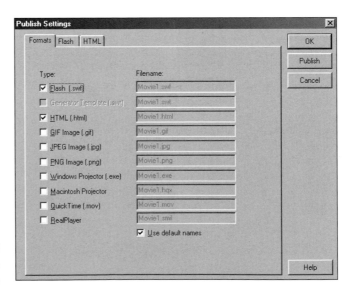

Figure 14.25
Click the Formats tab to choose other formats for your movie.

The Flash tab of this dialog box gives you options for controlling the image quality of the movie and specifying the version of Flash that recipients of the Flash file will be using. The HTML tab allows you to choose how the movie will be aligned within the Web page, if it will be scaled to fit the window, or, if the window isn't maximized, whether parts of the movie will be cut off. This dialog box tab also provides a way to set the movie to play only once; simply click to remove the checkmark next to the Loop option, as shown in Figure 14.26.

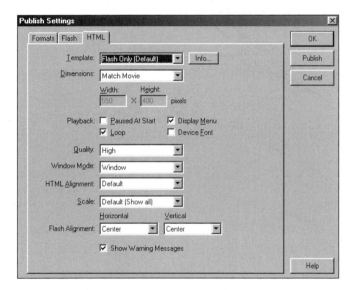

Figure 14.26

Customize the HTML document settings before you publish your movie as a Web page.

PROJECT Using an Existing Flash Movie, Add a Photoshop Image to one of the Flash Frames

In this project, you'll save two PSD files in Web-safe JPEG format and insert them into an existing Flash movie. You'll adjust their role in the animation, and then publish the Flash movie for use on the Web.

Open the PSD Files

The files are titled annleft.psd and annright.psd, and you can find them in the Chapter 14 folder on the CD. Figure 14.27 shows both images open in a Photoshop window.

Save Both files in JPEG Format, at Maximum Quality

You can keep the annleft and annright file names, and let Photoshop's Save For Web procedure apply the .jpg extension automatically.

Open the Flash Movie

Found in the Chapter 14 folder, the movie is called "flashgirl.swf". Choose File|Open in Flash, and select this file by double-clicking it.

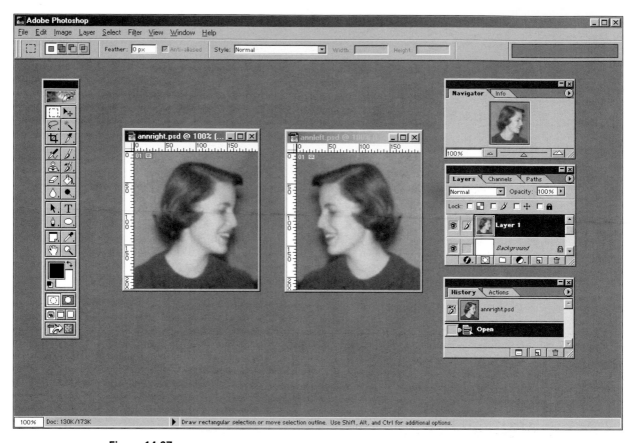

Figure 14.27

These flipped versions of the same image will become two faces in a Flash movie.

Create Two Layers

The movie starts with one layer, so adding one more, you'll end up with two. You can name them Left and Right, or leave them with the generic "Layer 1" and "Layer 2" names that Flash applies by default.

Insert the annright.jpg Image into the Right or Layer 2 Layer

Place the image on the left side of the window, as shown in Figure 14.28. Make a note of the vertical position so that you can place the other image (annleft.jpg) on the same level on the opposite side of the window.

Insert the annleft.jpg Image into the Left or Layer 1 Layer

Place the image on the right side of the window, as shown in Figure 14.29. Place it at the same vertical level that you placed annright.jpg on the left side of the window so that the images can pass one another and for a brief moment share the same vertical and horizontal space.

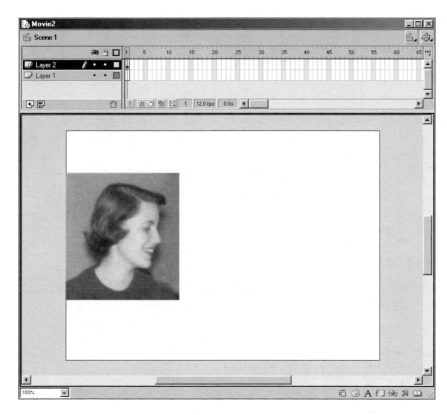

Figure 14.28
The woman looking to the right needs to start out on the left side of the window.

Figure 14.29
Now there's the same woman on the other side, looking at the middle of the page.

Create the Animation

The woman looking to the left and the one looking to the right need to start out on opposite sides of the movie canvas and pass each other in the center, ending up side by side, as shown in Figure 14.30. This requires setting up a motion tween to get annright.jpg from the left side of the window to the right, and annleft.jpg from the right side of the window to the left, stopping when they're side by side. The rest of the movie content is fine as is, although you're free to tinker with it as you see fit.

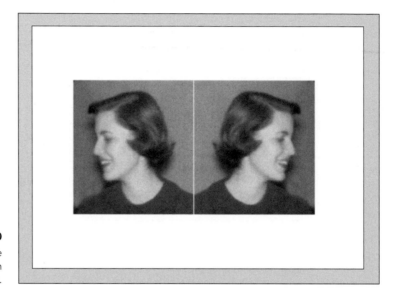

Figure 14.30
By the time the movie ends, the pictures have swapped position and are sitting side by side.

Preview the Movie as It Will Play Online

Press Ctrl+Enter to see the movie in a full-screen, browser-like window. Figure 14.31 shows the animation in progress.

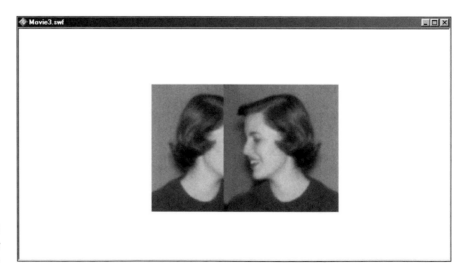

Figure 14.31
Watch your full-screen movie play out as it will appear online.

Save the Flash Movie

Using the File|Save As command, save the updated movie as flashgirl2.fla.

Publish the Movie

Using the File|Publish command, create an HTML and an SWF version of the file. Use the File|Publish Settings command to make sure that these are the only two formats in which the movie should be published.

Moving On

Animating images in LiveMotion and Flash is probably the least common way that Photoshop images are utilized. The graphic buttons, navigation bars, backgrounds, and other pictures that make Web pages interesting to look at get their start in Photoshop, are saved in a Web-safe format, and find themselves in Web pages—as window dressing and functional works of art that link visitors to new pages, sites, files, and forms. In the next chapter, you'll see Photoshop images inserted into a Web page through Macromedia Dreamweaver and Adobe GoLive, and you'll learn the basics of working with images on a Web page through a WYSIWYG page design application.

Chapter 15

WYSIWYG Web Design with Photoshop

As a Web designer, you probably use both a text editor to create HTML code and an application like Dreamweaver or GoLive for your designs. This chapter shows you how to use these popular applications to add your Photoshop creations to Web pages.

What Is a WYSIWYG Design Application?

WYSIWYG stands for What You See Is What You Get. This means that what's happening on screen—the text you're typing, the formats and colors you're applying, the images you're positioning—will look exactly as they do on screen when printed. That's the original definition of the term, back when printing was the only way to share documents. When it comes to documents that will be viewed online, the term means that what you're seeing in the design environment—the workspace in which you design and build your Web page—is roughly the same as what you'll see if you view the document in a browser window. When it comes to viewing pages through a browser, the way the browser interprets the Web page document can result in minor to major variations between what you're seeing in the Dreamweaver or GoLive design window and how the same page will appear to visitors on the Web.

So a WYSIWYG design application is a tool for designing Web pages in a graphical environment, enabling the designer to build the page graphically. Instead of typing HTML code, the designer uses toolbars and menu-driven commands to apply colors, type and format text, set up tables and other structural devices, and insert images. The design environment mimics the browser window through which the page will eventually be viewed. Figure 15.1 shows the Dreamweaver window with a page in progress.

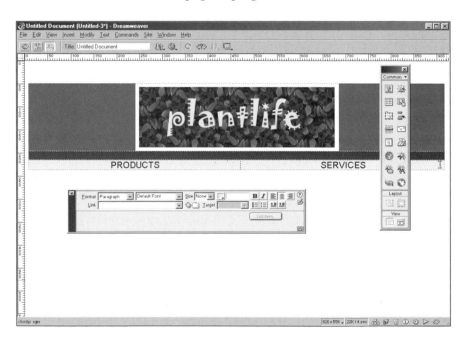

Figure 15.1

Let Dreamweaver create the HTML code for you as you build your Web page graphically.

As you're working in the WYSIWYG environment, the software is converting all of your actions—typing text, applying formats, inserting images, and setting up tables, layers, or frames—to HTML code. It's HTML that the browser software (Microsoft Internet Explorer, Netscape Navigator) interprets, enabling it to display the content of the page. Figure 15.2 shows the code window in Adobe GoLive. You're able to look at your graphically designed page and then see the resulting HTML code.

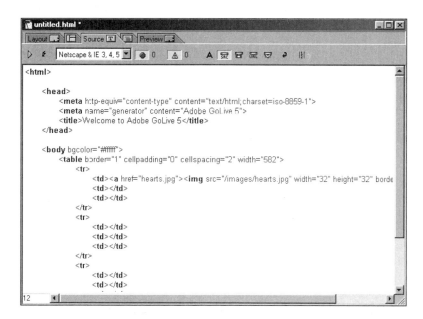

Figure 15.2
If you know any HTML code, you can edit the code that's created by the WYSIWYG software.

A Tour of a WYSIWYG Workspace

Macromedia's Dreamweaver is perhaps the most popular Web design application today—due to its logical layout, intuitive features and commands, and the fact that with just a little training or demonstration, you can be up and running, designing Web pages in very short order. Figure 15.3 shows the Dreamweaver interface with a Web page in progress. The page includes a graphic and some text, and the default Properties Inspector and Objects panel are displayed.

ScreenTips identify individual tools in the Properties Inspector and Objects panel (see Figure 15.4), and Dreamweaver's Help files are well written and organized. As shown in Figure 15.5, you can get assistance from the Reference tab of the Assets panel (choose Window|Assets).

The entire white space within the application window is available for Web page content: You can type on the page, insert images, and add structural devices, such as tables and layers, anywhere on the page. If you want to convert your page into a frames page, made up of several separate frames, you can do that easily as well, choosing from preset frame configurations or creating your own configuration from scratch. Figure 15.6 shows a table inserted on a blank page; the cursor sits in an empty table cell, awaiting content.

Click these buttons to switch between
(l-r) Code view, Code & Design view,
and Design view

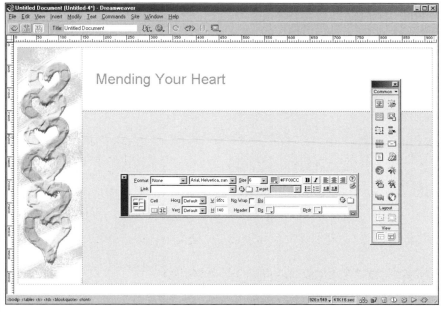

The Objects panel
comes in seven flavors,
the default being Common,
through which images, tables,
layers, frames, graphics, and
imported content can be inserted

Mending Your Heart

The Properties Inspector shows the specifics
and settings for selected text, structural devices
(tables, layers, frames), and graphics

Figure 15.3

(Above) The Dreamweaver
interface is relatively simple to
use, disguising the very powerful
application beneath it.

Figure 15.4

(Left) Click this button to insert a
table on the page.

Figure 15.5

(Right) Want to know more about
the IMG tag that's inserted when
you add an image to your page?
Check the Assets panel.

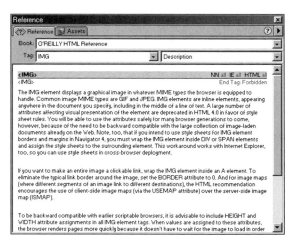

Inserting Images in a WYSIWYG Environment

It's quite easy to insert both static and interactive images on a Web page in Dreamweaver, whether you want to place the image directly on the page or within a table, layer, or frame. You can click the Insert Image button on the

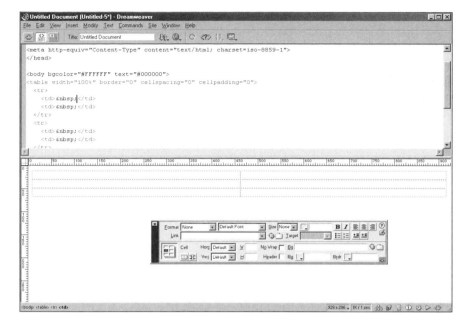

Figure 15.6

Working in Code and Design view, we can see the underlying HTML code for the table. To create a table, click the Insert Table button and specify the number of columns and rows the table should have.

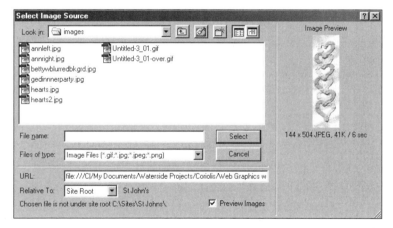

Figure 15.7

In your images folder, double-click the image to be inserted.

Objects panel, or you can choose Insert|Image. In either case, a dialog box opens, asking you to identify the image to insert. Figure 15.7 shows the Select Image Source dialog box.

By default, you can insert only images that are in appropriate Web-safe formats—JPEG, GIF, and PNG. By default, only these types are displayed in the Select Image Source dialog box. If you attempt to insert a file of another type, the image won't appear on the page.

Once the image is inserted, you can move it by dragging it with your mouse, although the image doesn't move freely. You can only drag it to another line on the page or to another cell in the table. You can resize images with your mouse, and you can turn them into hyperlinks by providing link information via the Properties Inspector.

Positioning Images on the Page

Web pages are a lot like word processing documents: You can type directly onto the page and insert graphics onto the page, and at first, they live on one line or another, not floating above the page, but anchored to one of the lines on the page. You can also build a table in a word processing document, and then insert text and pictures into that table. With that analogy in mind, look at Figure 15.8. As you can see, you can add your images to the page and see them appear among your existing page text, or you can add the images to a table, giving you much more control over their placement in relation to surrounding text.

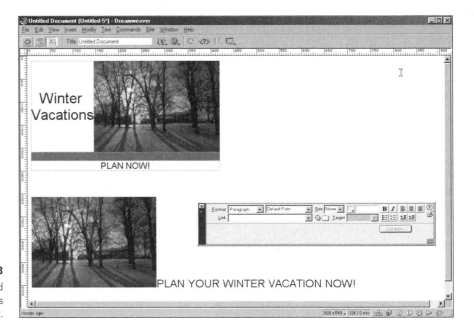

Figure 15.8

Out loose on the page or nestled in a table, images speak nearly as clearly as text.

To place an image on the page (rather than in a table or layer), click your mouse on the page and when your cursor blinks, issue the Insert|Image command or click the Insert Image button in Dreamweaver. If you're working in Adobe GoLive, drag the Image icon from the Objects palette to the page (see Figure 15.9) and release your mouse at the spot where you want the image to appear. A dialog box opens, where you can select the image to be inserted.

Inserting Images into a Table

To gain more control over the placement of images, you can tuck them into table cells. The cells of the table constrain the adjoining text, making it possible to place text and graphics next to each other without the odd stacking of tall items (an image) and short items (the text) on a single line in the document. Figure 15.10 shows text and an image on the page without the benefit of a table, and Figure 15.11 shows the same text and image in a table.

The Image icon   The Objects palette

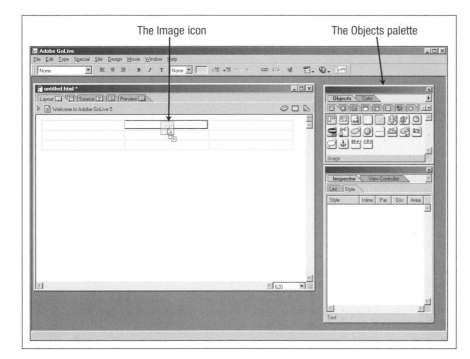

Figure 15.9
GoLive's Objects palette contains an Image icon, which can be dragged onto the page, beginning the image-insertion process.

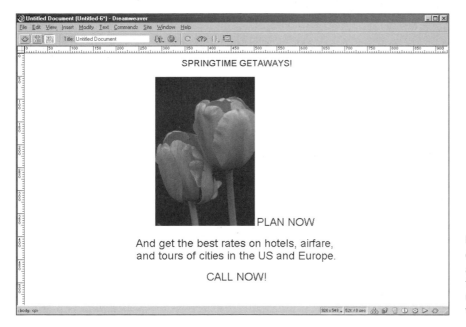

Figure 15.10
Other than stacking lines of text and images on separate lines in the document, you don't have much control over image position without using tables or layers.

If you're designing for the latest versions of popular browser software, you may be working with layers. These, too, provide control over the placement of text and images, because you can place text in one layer and then place another layer next to it or even on top of it, with the latter holding an image that relates to the text (see Figure 15.12). You can also place tables inside layers, giving you another level of control. To insert a layer, click the Insert Layer button on the Dreamweaver Objects panel, or choose Insert|Layer. If you're working in GoLive, drag the Floating Box icon from the Objects palette onto the page.

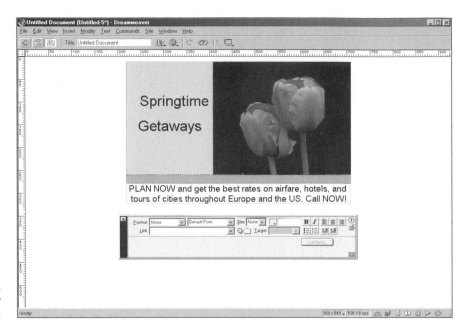

Figure 15.11

Housed in separate table cells, text and images can live together in visual harmony.

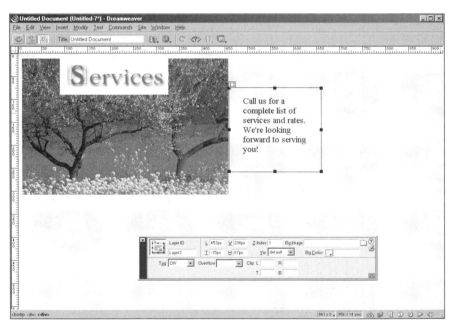

Figure 15.12

Layers work well in post-4.0 version browsers, and they provide a flexible structure for text and images.

Creating Interactive Images

In Chapters 10 and 11, you learned about rollovers and how to create them in ImageReady. If you didn't commit those chapters to memory yet, it might make you happy to know that Dreamweaver gives you the ability to turn two static images into an interactive image, creating a rollover that works by swapping one image for another when someone mouses over the first image. This mimics a two-state rollover you'd create in ImageReady and can be even more convenient because you can use two static images that might have use elsewhere in their static form, and create the illusion of automated movement.

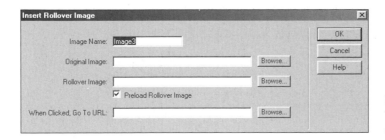

Figure 15.13
Turn two static images into a quick rollover in Dreamweaver.

To create an interactive image in Dreamweaver, choose Insert|Interactive Images|Rollover Image. In the resulting dialog box (see Figure 15.13), give the rollover a name, click the Browse button next to the Original Image and Rollover Image boxes, and choose the first and second images to use for the interaction. If the rollover is a link, type the URL (Web address) in the designated box.

Resizing Images

Once an image is inserted, you may be compelled to make it larger or smaller. It's difficult, unless you've done a lot of scrupulous planning, to know exactly how big an image needs to be to have the visual impact it should, so we often insert an image and regret its dimensions. Perhaps your image is too small and the detail isn't visible, or it's too big and it's overwhelming the page. In either case, resist the temptation to resize the image in Dreamweaver or GoLive; go back to the original image in Photoshop (you don't necessarily have to go back to the PSD version, but to the JPEG or GIF version) and resize it there. If you resize it in Dreamweaver or GoLive, the image may lose its crispness and clarity, as shown in Figure 15.14. It's easy to resize in both of these applications (drag the image handles or enter new dimensions into the appropriate palette/dialog box), but it's not a good idea.

What Are Those Leaves in the Background?

Create a very faded image in Photoshop (reduce the opacity to about 20 percent) and you can insert it as a background in Dreamweaver. Choose Modify|Page Properties, and specify the image you want to serve as the background for the page. The image will tile (repeat in stacked blocks) until it fills the page.

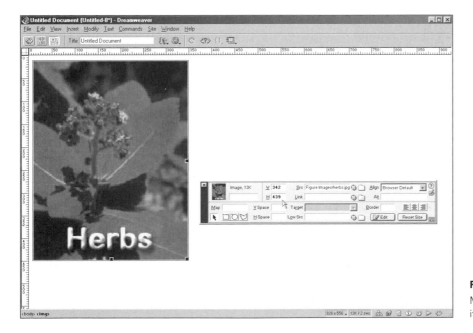

Figure 15.14
Making this image bigger made its edges choppy.

Rollover Sizes

If you're inserting an interactive image in Dreamweaver, be sure that both of the images that make up the rollover are the same exact size. If you don't, the space allocated by the browser for the first image (the original, that's loaded first) may not be the right size for the second image (the one that appears when someone mouses over the original). Some of the second image may be cut off, or if it's a smaller image than the first, it may look lost in a large block of space.

Turning Images into Links

Both Dreamweaver and GoLive make it easy to associate a graphic with a Web page and to turn the graphic into a link to that page. In Dreamweaver, typing the URL of the linked page into the Properties Inspector's Link box will do the trick, and in GoLive, there's a slightly more complex process, involving the Inspector palette and a few clicks and selections before the link is established. Figure 15.15 shows a selected image in Dreamweaver and the Properties Inspector, where a link is established. Figure 15.16 shows the GoLive environment, and an inserted image is being linked to a Web page.

Figure 15.15
Dreamweaver's Properties Inspector is key to establishing graphic or text links to Web pages and files.

Figure 15.16
Click the Chain icon to indicate that the image is a link, type the URL in the Target box, and you've created a graphic link in Adobe GoLive.

Working with Hotspots

Chapter 10 introduced you to hotspots, but ImageReady, the topic of that chapter, calls them image maps. Image maps and hotspots are areas on larger images that link to Web pages. Unlike a graphic that in its entirety is linked to a single URL or file, a graphic with hotspots on it can link to several pages or files, making it a very economical way to turn a large image into a significant navigational tool. If you've ever gone to a Web page that included a map and you could click on a particular country, state, or other defined region to go to a page pertaining to that location, you've used a hotspot.

If you didn't apply an image map to your graphic within ImageReady, you don't need to go back and do it now—Dreamweaver makes it very easy to map regions on an image and designate them as links to Web pages or files, and it's all done through the Properties Inspector, shown in Figure 15.17. The process of building a hotspot requires a little drawing (dragging to draw shapes on an image) and a little typing (the URL or file location to which the spot is linked), and the hotspot is created. Dreamweaver turns the shapes and associated links into HTML code for you, saving you a considerable amount of work.

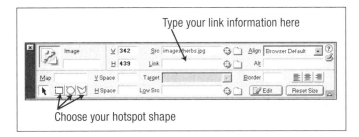

Type your link information here

Choose your hotspot shape

Figure 15.17

Rectangles, ovals, or polygons— you can map any size or shape hotspot on any image on your Dreamweaver-designed Web page.

Choosing a Hotspot Shape

The region on the image that you want to map out as a separate link dictates the shape you choose for your hotspots—rectangle, oval, or polygon. As shown in Figure 15.18, if your image is a map, you'll want to use the polygon hotspot tool so that you can outline borders of states, countries, counties, or towns. If your image is a navigation bar or similar item, you can draw rectangles around the tabs or buttons on the bar, or use the oval hotspot tool to draw an ellipse around a round shape within the image. Figure 15.19 shows a large graphic with simple round and square shapes that require hotspots to turn them into individual links.

What about Freeform Shapes?

The polygon hotspot tool can be used to create very intricate freeform shapes. You can create a polygon with an unlimited number of sides, conceivably ending up with rounded-looking shapes of any size and configuration simply by drawing a shape with many sides.

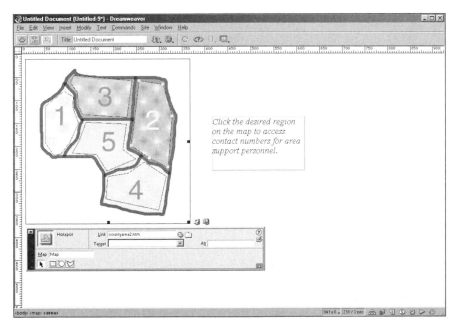

Figure 15.18

Map out a state or region of the country to help visitors go to the geographically specific information they need.

Figure 15.19

Use Photoshop to draw a large navigational graphic, and then use Dreamweaver's hotspot tools to map areas of the image as links.

Drawing Hotspots

To draw the hotspot, click on the hotspot button for the shape you want, and then click and drag to draw the shape on the surface of the image. Figure 15.20 shows a rectangular hotspot in progress.

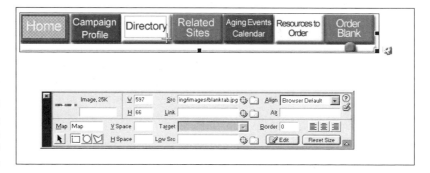

Figure 15.20

Draw a box around the area you want to turn into a link. Here, the Directory tab is being turned into a hotspot.

Polygonal hotspots can be used to draw odd shapes—like the border of a complex region on a map, or around a person or product in a group photo. When drawing any shape hotspot, make sure the spots don't overlap or come so close that a visitor could easily click the wrong area. If possible, leave a little buffer, as shown in Figure 15.21.

After your hotspot is drawn, you can grab and drag its handles to resize it as needed. If you made the shape too big or too small, you can remedy that easily. If your polygon hotspot is the wrong shape, you can resize it or click along the edges of the shape to add more handles that can be dragged to change the shape of the hotspot. Figure 15.22 shows a polygonal hotspot being reshaped by adding a handle along a previously long side of the shape.

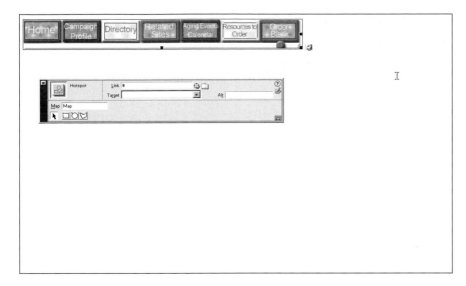

Figure 15.21

Visitors will watch for their mouse to turn to a pointing hand—use as small an area as possible when you have a tight grouping of hotspot areas.

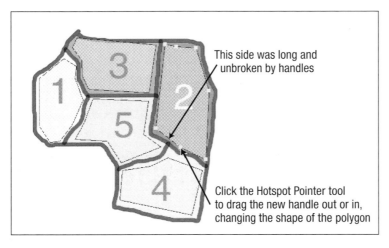

This side was long and unbroken by handles

Click the Hotspot Pointer tool to drag the new handle out or in, changing the shape of the polygon

Figure 15.22

Here we need to bump out the shape to include an area of the image previously excluded.

Entering Hotspot Link Information

Once the hotspot shape is drawn, it's time to enter the link information. As soon as you draw the shape, the Properties Inspector changes (see Figure 15.23) and offers a Link box, into which you can type the URL or file location for the link. If you want some kind of text ScreenTip to appear when someone mouses onto a hotspot, type that text in the Alt box.

Figure 15.23

You can name your hotspot in the Map box, and enter the full URL to the Web page to which the hotspot should link your site visitors.

Testing Hotspots

It's a good idea to test your hotspots before posting the page to the Web, if only to make sure that you have all the mapped areas linked to the right pages or files, and to make sure that your hotspots are user-friendly. If you find yourself accidentally clicking an adjoining hotspot because your spots are too close

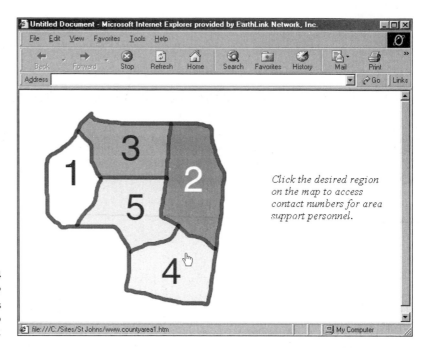

Figure 15.24
Too many? Too close? Link typo?
Find out by testing your hotspots
before uploading your page to
the Web server.

together, imagine the difficulty your visitors will have. To test your hotspots, click the Preview In Browser button on the main toolbar, or choose File|Preview In Browser. The Web page appears in a local browser window (see Figure 15.24), and you can mouse over your links and click them to make sure they work as intended.

Photoshop vs. Fireworks

Macromedia Fireworks is a Photoshop competitor, and it offers virtually all of the same tools for creating and retouching images as you'll find in Photoshop. If you learned to use Photoshop first, you might find Fireworks to be less intuitive, and you might be thrown by the fact that the default file format for images created in Fireworks is PNG, which, as of this writing, is not the most browser-friendly image format. In fact, many browsers prior to the latest versions don't recognize this format at all. Figure 15.25 shows the Fireworks workspace and identifies the major tools at your disposal.

You can open virtually any image file in Fireworks. As shown in Figure 15.26, the list of file types is long, and it includes Photoshop (PSD), Illustrator (AI), and the obvious choices, JPEG and GIF. You can also export (use the File|Export command) to save your Fireworks-created or -edited file in any graphic format, assuming you run the Export Wizard first, through which you designate the destination of your graphic—the Web, an image-editing application, a desktop-publishing application, or Dreamweaver. Figure 15.27 shows the Export Preview window that appears when you complete the Export Wizard process. In this window, you can choose a file format and quality, crop the image, zoom in on the image, play animations (for animated GIF files), and preview the estimated load time for the image on a 28.8Kbps modem.

The image window has a
transparent background
by default, and starts out
in PNG format

These palettes
(Optimize, Fill, Color Mixer)
appear by default when you
open the Fireworks application

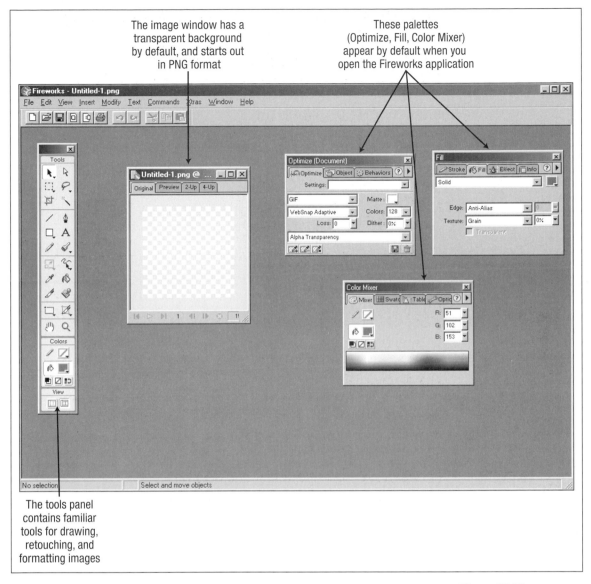

The tools panel
contains familiar
tools for drawing,
retouching, and
formatting images

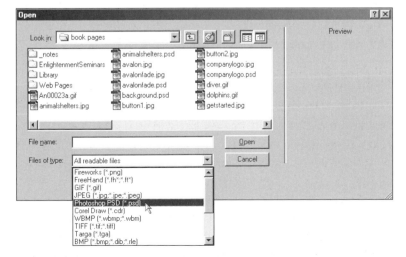

Figure 15.25

Photoshop users will be able to
figure out some of the Fireworks
tools simply by looking at button
faces and option text in dialog
boxes and palettes.

Figure 15.26

Although PNG is the default for
new Fireworks images, you can
start out with an image of just
about any type at all.

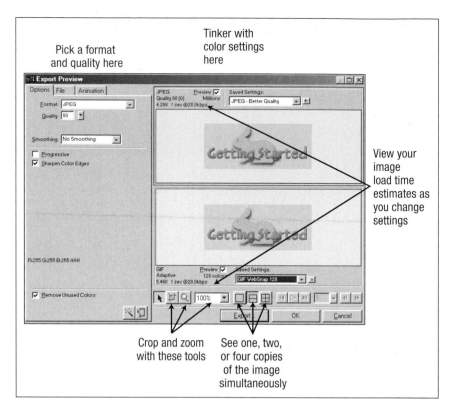

Pick a format
and quality here

Tinker with
color settings
here

View your
image
load time
estimates as
you change
settings

Crop and zoom
with these tools

See one, two,
or four copies
of the image
simultaneously

Figure 15.27
Customize the way your image
will be exported in the format
you've selected.

Insert a Photoshop Image into a Dreamweaver Page

In this project, you'll open an existing Dreamweaver document and insert a large graphic into a table. After the image is inserted, you'll use Dreamweaver's tools to create hotspots on the surface of the image, directing each one to a different Web page.

Open the Dreamweaver File

Of course, doing this requires that you have Dreamweaver on your computer, but all you need to do is use the Dreamweaver File|Open command and open mapnav.htm, which you'll find in the Chapter 15 folder on the CD. The page as it will appear when you open it is shown in Figure 15.28.

Position Your Cursor

Click inside the top cell in the table; it spans a row of three cells, each with text in them.

Insert the Image

Using the Insert Image button on the Objects panel or the Insert|Image command on the menu, select the file called local_areas.jpg, which you'll find in the Chapter 15 folder on the CD. The image should fit inside the cell with little room to spare around it, as shown in Figure 15.29.

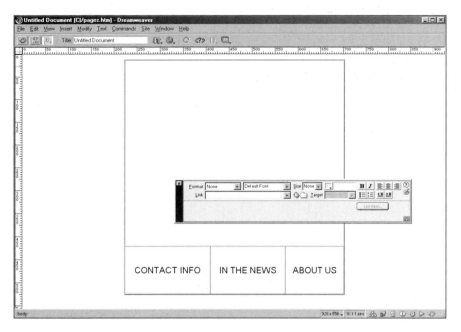

Figure 15.28
A Dreamweaver Web page, awaiting your image.

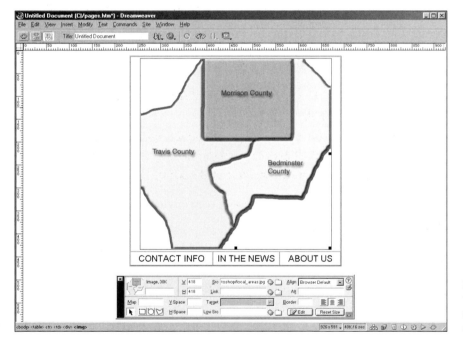

Figure 15.29
The image appears where your cursor was when the Insert|Image command was issued.

Create Hotspots

Using the Properties Inspector (choose Window|Properties if it's not currently displayed), select the polygon hotspot tool and draw shapes that encompass the odd-shaped areas on the map, and select the rectangular hotspot tool to encompass the square region on the map. Your results should look like those shown in Figure 15.30.

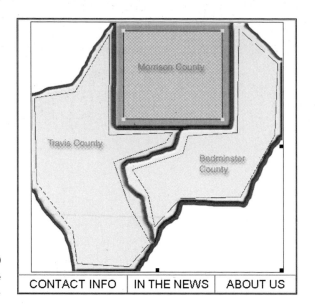

Figure 15.30
Create three hotspots for the
three colored regions of the map.

Set Up the Hotspot Links

Apply the following links:

- To the red region, create a link to **www.amazon.com**.

- To the blue region, create a link to **www.cnn.com**.

- To the green region, create a link to **www.google.com**.

Remember to leave a little buffer between regions so people using the page won't click an adjoining hotspot by mistake.

Test Your Hotspots

Use the File|Preview In Browser command to preview the page, and test your links to make sure you've assigned them correctly and that your hotspots are drawn accurately.

Moving On

This final chapter of the book shows you how to place your Photoshop creations on a Web page—the natural conclusion of the Web graphic design process. After having read the previous 14 chapters in this book, you know how to build graphics of all sorts, shapes, and sizes, and how to save them for their best look and functioning online. Now you know how to add them to Web pages, inserting them as backgrounds or freestanding graphics, and into tables and layers. Once you've mastered your own Web design application—a WYSIWYG application such as Dreamweaver or GoLive, or straight HTML coding—you can put all of your design skills in Photoshop to good use, creating beautiful and effective Web graphics.

Appendix

Joining the Online Photoshop Community

From newsgroups to chat rooms, there are plenty of ways to connect with other people who use, teach, and develop added tools for Photoshop. Search the Web yourself, or try some of these sites and groups to broaden your Photoshop horizons.

Finding the Online Photoshop Community

It all starts with a search—you can go to any search site, such as google.com, hotbot.com, yahoo.com—and the keyword "Photoshop". Your screen will fill with a list of sites that pertain to Adobe Photoshop, including these:

- **www.adobe.com/products/photoshop/main.html**—Of course, this is the Adobe Systems Photoshop page, filled with links to product information, actions for download, and advice from the people Adobe has stamped "Expert." Spend enough time here, and this could be you!

- **www.photoshopuser.com**—This is the official Web site of the National Association of Photoshop Users. Through this site, you can join the association ($99 for a "Professional" user for one year), and once you join, receive your copy of *Photoshop User*, a magazine for power-users and everyone else who wants to be one. You must be a member to access most areas of the site, and once you join the organization, passwords are sent to you to enable you to open pages and follow links within the site.

- **www.planetphotoshop.com**—This site is loaded with tips and tutorials, news, and reviews of Photoshop books and training materials. From the home page, you can download five or six new free actions, and follow a link to **actionfx.com**, where more can be downloaded for a price, though others are available for free.

- **www.photoshopcentral.com**—Touting itself as the "center of the Photoshop universe," this site provides news about Photoshop, a discussion forum, and a series of the creators' favorite Photoshop books and training materials (guides, videos, CD-ROMs) are reviewed and available for sale.

This list should get you started, and because most of the Photoshop sites on the Web contain links to other Photoshop sites, just stumbling onto a handful of sites will give you hyperlink access to potentially hundreds of sites devoted to or predominantly concerned with Photoshop.

Joining a Newsgroup

If you like the idea of receiving email every day from people who use Photoshop, you'll like joining a newsgroup. Newsgroups are membership groups where people trade questions, tips, suggestions, and news via email, and all the other members of the group receive the emails. Members can respond, and their responses are also sent to all the members of the group.

Joining a newsgroup is easy, typically a matter of sending an email to an address such as "subscribe@newsgroup.com" and responding to a reply to that email, as their way of verifying your email address. Newsgroups are free, unlike formal organizations, and you can unsubscribe at any time, usually by writing to an "unsubscribe@newsgroup.com" email address.

To find a Photoshop newsgroup, you can do a Web search for "Photoshop Newsgroups" or "Photoshop Forums" and follow the links that result. Here are some newsgroups and forums to check out:

- http://onlinedesignschool.com/cgi-bin/discus/show.cgi?9/9

- www.teamphotoshop.com/forum/index.php

- www.communityzero.com/pop

Google Groups is also a good resource for Photoshop-related groups and forums. Go to **www.groups.google.com**. After you reach that page, type "Photoshop" into the Search box, and press Enter. You'll be taken to a list of links to Usenet groups like comp.graphics.apps.photoshop and alt.graphics.photoshop, and a lot of other links, some to specific questions and answers posted by other people interested in Photoshop.

Locating Photoshop Extras

Adobe's Photoshop page (**www.adobe.com/products/photoshop/main.html**) includes links to actions you can download and links to other sites where actions are available for free and for sale. By doing a search for "Photoshop Actions" at any Web search site, you'll come up with some great sites like these (new ones pop up all the time, so don't rest on your laurels—search every few weeks and explore the new ones):

- www.actionfx.com

- www.deepspaceweb.com

- www.actionaddiction.com

- www.desktoppublishing.com/psactions.html

In addition to actions, you can download interesting third party–developed plug-ins and other "extras" for Photoshop at the following sites:

- www.adobe.com/products/plugins/photoshop/main.html

- www.beebware.com/software

- www.hallogram.com/menus/Macintosh.html

- www.boxtopsoft.com

You'll also find that a lot of people just like you have set up Web pages with actions, filters, plug-ins, tips, tricks, artwork you can use, inspirational copyrighted art—just about anything Photoshop related. As you become more confident in your Photoshop skills, especially related to designing for the Web, you may want to set up a site of your own to share your ideas and creations with the world. If you do, please let me know, and I'll be happy to add a link to your site from mine. You can write to me at laurie@planetlaurie.com. All of the artwork at my site was created in Photoshop, and I never use anything else for Web graphics.

I hope you had fun reading this book and following the projects to completion, and that you'll be getting involved in the online Photoshop community in some way—by joining a newsgroup, joining the National Association of Photoshop Professionals, or simply by sharing your own ideas with others. Have fun!

Index

What's on the CD-ROM

The *Photoshop Web Graphics fx & Design* companion CD-ROM contains elements specifically selected to enhance the usefulness of this book, including:

- Files that you'll need to complete the projects found throughout the book's chapters. These include Photoshop format files, existing Web graphics, HTML files, and Flash and LiveMotion files. Not all of the projects require existing files—some of them require you to create everything from scratch. For those projects requiring existing files, however, you'll find the file name and location on the CD listed in the project instructions.

- An HTML document that when opened in your favorite browser, displays a series of links to Web sites that will be of interest to Photoshop users of all levels–from new users to experienced professional designers. One of the links takes you to the National Association of Photoshop Professionals (NAPP), an organization that provides training, runs seminars, and offers a wide variety of resources for people who are serious about learning and developing their skills in Photoshop–it costs just $99 to join, and it's well worth it.

- A Web-safe color chart, showing the 216 colors you can use in your Web graphics. Each color swatch is accompanied by the color's hexadecimal number and RGB (Red, Green, Blue) levels. This is handy for use in matching print colors and for selecting colors to use on your web page.

- Color wheel graphics depicting primary, secondary, opposite, and complementary colors. These wheels help you see how colors are built, and help you choose colors that work well together.

System Requirements

Software

- **You can use this CD if your computer is running Microsoft Windows 98, ME, or 2000. Mac users running Mac OS/9 also can use the CD.**

- Of course it is assumed that you have Photoshop (version 6.0 for maximum compatibility with the book, although earlier versions will also be OK), and that ImageReady is installed as well.

- If you want to do the projects in Chapters 14, 15, and 16, you should have Adobe LiveMotion, Macromedia Flash, and Macromedia Dreamweaver, respectively. You can benefit from reading the chapters that pertain to these products even if you don't own them, so don't feel you must run out and buy them if you don't have them now. The Macromedia Web site offers trial versions for download if you want to give them a try – go to **www.macromedia.com**.

  Note: The following software (not included on this CD) is required to complete the exercises and tutorials (downloads available at **www.adobe.com/products/photoshop/main.html**):

- Adobe Photoshop 6.0 Demo for Mac and PC.

Hardware

- An Intel (or equivalent) Pentium 100MHz processor is the minimum platform required; an Intel (or equivalent) Pentium 133MHz processor is recommended.

- 32MB of RAM is the minimum requirement, although if you're using Microsoft Windows ME or 2000, you should have 64 MB, and will run much better on 128 MB of RAM.

- A color monitor (256 colors minimum, 32-bit True Color recommended) is assumed, as you would need one to use Photoshop in the first place.